Digging The Bronx:
Recent Archaeology in the Borough

Digging The Bronx:
Recent Archaeology in the Borough

edited by

Allan S. Gilbert
Fordham University

The Bronx County Historical Society

Printed in the United States of America.

For information, please contact
The Bronx County Historical Society
3309 Bainbridge Avenue
Bronx, New York 10467
(718) 881-8900
www.bronxhistoricalsociety.org

Library of Congress Catalogue-in-Publication Data
Gilbert, Allan S.
        Digging the Bronx: Recent Archaeology in the Borough / edited
        by Allan S. Gilbert.
        Includes bibliographical references and index.
        ISBN-10: 0-941980-75-8
        ISBN-13: 978-0-941980-75-3

CONTENTS

Preface

Ever since its *Journal* began publication in 1964, the Bronx County Historical Society has explored Bronx history through articles ranging from the colonial countryside to the continually changing mosaic of modern city neighborhoods. Narratives of past and present have sprung from documents, literature, art, photographs, and reminiscences, and no stone, it would seem, has been left unturned.

The present collection of papers turns over lots of new stones, figuratively and literally, for it offers new sources of evidence for understanding Bronx history and culture in the archaeological remains below our feet. Archaeology is no stranger to the Bronx. Excavators have sifted through the soils of the borough for over a century. Though archaeological subjects have found their way into the pages of the *Journal*, they have been only occasional visitors. Besides Valerie (DeCarlo) Hauser's description of the Riverdale Park project[1]—which is reprinted here—only Robert Apuzzo's account of ancient Native American artifacts from Pugsley Avenue[2] and my own discussion of brick research in the context of industrial archaeology[3] have appeared in recent issues.

Over the last four decades, a resurgence of archaeological exploration has taken place in New York City.[4] Beginning in the 1980s, Manhattan led the way with a series of important mitigation projects conducted in advance of major building construction, including the Stadt Huys Block (1979–80), 7 Hanover Square (1981), 175 Water Street (1981–82), the Barclays Bank site (1983–84), 60 Wall Street (1984), Broad Street Financial Center (1984), the Assay site (1984), and the two Federal building initiatives at the Five Points site and the African Burial Ground (both 1991–92). Most recently, construction at South Ferry (2005–06) of a new subway terminus unearthed sections of the British fortifications and sea wall of the colonial Battery. Paralleling these discoveries in Manhattan, new research in the Bronx has been yielding a steady stream of information that begs for more than a trickle of published reports. The papers here assembled describe some of the results produced by a number of recent projects.

This latest wave of archaeology, in the Bronx and elsewhere, has witnessed greater professional involvement. Previously, avocational diggers carried out most investigations of sites now largely swallowed up by urban expansion. Scavenging amateurs, poring through historic rubble during the late

19th and early 20th centuries, unearthed and amassed large collections of artifacts that might never have survived the city's inexorable sprawl.[5] Though many of these efforts were unscientific souvenir hunts, some combined fieldwork that was respectable for its day with eventual publication of original discoveries for all to read.[6] But times have changed, and university-trained scholars have taken an interest in urban archaeology. Scientific methods have replaced the more spontaneous enterprise of former generations, and as a result, the quality and comprehensiveness of excavation records are much improved, technical analyses are routinely being applied to finds, and artifact collections are receiving conservation treatment as well as appropriate curation in museums and repositories. More information is being recovered than ever before, and many obscure corners of historical knowledge are slowly emerging from the earth. The only task that remains is to begin telling the story so that archaeology's contribution to our understanding of the past, and the historical value of the buried sites that contain the crucial evidence, will be more widely appreciated.

The papers in this book exemplify the current practice of archaeology in the borough by describing four of the ways archaeology has been conducted in the Bronx: field schools, public archaeology, cultural resource management, and technical examination of recovered finds. An additional source of knowledge about the earliest historical periods comes from the careful pursuit of ethnohistory, which is the examination of a wide range of recorded information to document the names, geographic distribution, customs, and events associated with groups possessing little or no historic documentation themselves, such as Native American peoples encountered by the first colonial ventures.

The book is structured as follows. After an initial chapter by Michael Cohn outlining the history of archaeological research in the Bronx, the next two chapters focus on archaeological field schools, which provide practical instruction in excavation techniques to students, involving them directly in the discovery process. Hands-on training makes the point better than any lecture can that original research is constantly punctuated by pitfalls and challenges, and that the hidden riches contained within archaeological remains are really a different sort of treasure: they are not merely rare and valuable relics but lost details of the historical record, forgotten by those alive today and therefore unavailable in any book.

In chapter two, Arthur Bankoff, Frederick Winter, and Christopher Ricciardi provide an account of the Brooklyn College Summer Archaeological Field School's excavations at the Van Cortlandt House, a historic museum in Van Cortlandt Park. The Brooklyn team shows how archaeology can be used to explore a structure that is still standing through small, strategically-placed excavations that address specific questions about the house and its surroundings.

They further illustrate the legendary serendipity of archaeology by describing their discovery of one of New York's largest assemblages of historic china and other domestic objects, all recovered within a deposit of household goods used by the wealthy and prominent Van Cortlandt family and discarded as trash over 125 years ago.

Roger Wines and I follow with a discussion of the nearly two-decades-long investigation at Fordham University's Rose Hill Manor, a project that is co-sponsored by the Bronx County Historical Society. With its manor house demolished over a century ago, Rose Hill conforms to traditional notions of an archaeological site. Foundations and destruction debris slumber peacefully beneath the college lawn, and extensive exposure is required to gain a picture of the former structure and the people who occupied it. Readers will notice how dramatically the yield of information increases when a campaign of excavations lasts for an extended period. Rose Hill was actively explored continuously for 17 years, and thus the most salient accomplishments reviewed within a lengthy chapter cannot touch upon all the discoveries. Archaeological sites are like three-dimensional puzzles—with most of the pieces missing—so understanding the remains and their meaning often requires complex problem solving. The chapter was therefore written like a detective story to give the reader a sense of the logical process involved in assembling the slowly emerging evidence into historical narrative. Readers will also see how excavations can uncover the most mundane aspects of past lives. Though some might find this kind of revelation banal and tiresome, such intimate details of personal effects and the former character of grounds and buildings are often the most valuable of archaeology's contributions to the historical record. They convey a palpable authenticity that written sources rarely duplicate.

Neighborhoods can also become involved in archaeology on a volunteer basis. Public archaeology is another way in which research can be conducted, and in the fourth chapter, Valerie Hauser writes about the projects initiated by Wave Hill in the late 1980s in Riverdale Park. While describing the fragmentary clues indicating human use of the park during earlier ages, she demonstrates that volunteerism is not just for digging. Support must also cover the material costs of fieldwork, preservation of finds, and site restoration. Despite the generous donations of time and labor by enthusiastic participants, local archaeology cannot be fully effective without sufficient funding from private and institutional sponsors, as well as governmental encouragement of the public programs that coordinate the effort.

Environmental protection legislation often mandates that professional archaeologists become involved in development projects when construction threatens to damage archaeological sites. In the fifth chapter, Betsy Kearns and Cece Saunders of the cultural resource management firm Historical Perspectives,

Inc., explain the business of archaeology as they have practiced it within the Bronx. Although the law provides for the protection of significant sites under certain conditions, and it authorizes professionals to apply their expertise—contractually at developer's expense—to the salvage of remains doomed to destruction, it does not require funding of non-essential recovery or extended laboratory analyses, whether or not such exercises lead to a better understanding of history. Contract archaeologists therefore have very precisely defined responsibilities. They must work quickly to recover those remains facing the greatest harm, leaving untouched other parts of the site that survive underground into the future. Because their analysis of rescued artifacts is subject to cost limitations and deadlines, they must often leave more lengthy examinations of excavated finds to other scholars working under fewer time and budget constraints.

In the sixth paper, Jeremy Tausch, Patrick Brock, and I examine in detail the glacially-deposited boulder that bears the image of a turtle carved into its surface. A Native American origin has been assumed for the rock engraving, or petroglyph, that was found within the grounds of the New York Botanical Garden and placed on indoor display to provide it with appropriate protection. Much of the evidence suggesting an ancient origin is circumstantial, however, and does not eliminate the possibility that the carving might have been done far more recently. As is the case for other problematic archaeological finds, careful scientific examination of this object can yield new clues that help to illuminate its true pedigree, which is likely to be less ancient than first thought. Despite the petroglyph's doubtful authenticity, the care with which it was conserved attests to the respect we hold for the prehistoric inhabitants of the Bronx, whose vestiges are unfortunately rare notwithstanding their thousands of years of occupancy.

In the seventh chapter, Robert Grumet reviews the documents related to Indian occupation in the colonial Bronx and evaluates the narratives of Native American history that have arisen from them. He proposes that not all statements made by eyewitnesses and recorded by chroniclers of the first centuries after contact contain accurate information. He reminds us that "primary sources are fragmentary and often confusing when taken out of context" (personal communication). Such accounts incorporate varying name transliterations and unsupported interpretations of group affiliations, territories, and social organization at a time when the cultures of aboriginal America and colonial Europe were in direct juxtaposition. Subsequently, "secondary source inattention to context often leads to fabulistic and anachronistic suppositions." He concludes that reliance on only those details supported by the best evidence provides the most secure foundation upon which to reconstruct the final phase of prehistoric Native American life.

The last three chapters differ from the preceding ones in being more forward looking. They describe three problems faced by archaeology now and into the future: (1) storage and curation of artifacts that have been excavated, (2) creating a way for better public access to the objects recovered and their historical significance, and (3) safeguarding still buried archaeological sites so that future fieldwork can eventually continue the process of learning about the past using newer technologies.

In chapter eight, Amanda Sutphin, Urban Archaeologist of the City of New York, describes the New York City Archaeological Repository and Nan A. Rothschild Research Center, a new facility in midtown Manhattan designed to store important archaeological collections belonging to the city and provide study space for ongoing investigations, all under the care of the New York City Landmarks Preservation Commission. Without appropriate storage space, it can be difficult to locate and retrieve excavated materials for re-examination when new techniques or new perspectives create good reasons for fresh analytical applications and re-evaluation of old conclusions. Without access to renewed study, archaeological knowledge stagnates, no new hypotheses can be tested, and old explanations and reconstructions remain default conclusions with no basis for challenge. Thus, keeping old excavation finds and reports under orderly curation serves the cause of continued scientific review, which leads to increasingly more accurate interpretations of evidence, both original and newly obtained.

Camille Czerkowicz discusses the problems of public access to archaeological finds and related information in chapter nine. Previously, the only ways for most people to learn about the past was through museum displays and published literature. While these pathways of communication remain important today, a new channel for the distribution of information has developed with the rise of the internet; it is already apparent that digital communication readily reaches far more people globally than can ever hope to visit distant museums or access costly publications through purchase or libraries. On line display transfers photographs, texts, and other forms of archaeological evidence in a relatively cost-effective way to a wide range of interested persons. It can also be exploited in the pursuit of continued research, such as enabling users to set up side-by-side image comparisons in seconds to juxtapose views of buildings, artifacts, and other physical objects that exist in separate, faraway locations. We are doubtless experiencing the dawn of digital age applications in archaeology, and many innovations surely await us in the near future.

The last chapter considers another problem of urban archaeology in the Bronx (and New York City in general) that presents significant challenges for the future: archaeological site conservation. In chapter ten, I offer a summary of the plight of archaeology in the modern city. The urban world often devalues the historical importance of sites and artifacts in favor of future profits and personal conveniences, but like many of the earth's natural resources, buried remains are non-renewable and endangered by over-exploitation. If people take as active a role in archaeological conservation as they have begun to do in environmental conservation, then sites that are the source of potentially important discoveries will be preserved long enough to be scientifically investigated.

As the preceding summary indicates, this book is not an archaeological history of the Bronx. Many periods and events of significance are unrepresented within its pages because they are unrepresented among the discoveries of recent years. Focusing on the latest results provides on the one hand an overview of the most up-to-date research, while on the other, it demonstrates through its inevitable omissions the piecemeal nature of archaeological exploration. A single excavation usually opens up a relatively narrow window onto the past. These few hard-won facts must then be added to the steadily growing body of knowledge that slowly takes shape as historical narrative.

For whom is this book intended? It is surely meant to be accessible to members of the Bronx County Historical Society as well as other persons with an active curiosity about the borough's past and the city's archaeological past in general. Most of the chapters, however, contain fairly detailed discussions as well as important new information, unpublished elsewhere, that will be of interest to the professional archaeologist or historian. So, a balance was struck. The text was designed to be free of technical language and written in plain English for ease of comprehension by the non-specialist public, while extended explanations and bibliographic citations were placed within chapter endnotes, a referencing system that creates the least distraction for the avocational reader yet permits the scholar—with only slight additional page turning—to obtain further particulars and view the sources consulted. In this way, it is hoped that the book will satisfy both constituencies.

With the appearance of this book in print, we mourn the passing of two contributors who could not be with us to witness its publication: Betsy Kearns and Mike Cohn. Both made significant contributions to the archaeology of the New York area, and both will be dearly missed.

The publication of this volume owes most to the efforts of its contributors, but in addition, thanks must be expressed to Dr. Gary Hermalyn and the board of the Bronx County Historical Society for supporting excavations at the Rose Hill manor site and encouraging the present book project. Appreciation is also offered to Prof. Lloyd Ultan, the Bronx Borough Historian, for his careful pre-publication review and valued comments on the text.

Our knowledge of past events, even historic ones, will always be imperfect. The undisturbed remains of long ago that lie beneath our streets are like countless unread volumes of historical research, a priceless antiquarian encyclopedia that can further illuminate old lives and forgotten times. As such, archaeological sites deserve as much respect and protection as we bestow upon our libraries with their stacks of already published wisdom. Archaeological studies, including many new Bronx initiatives not described in this book, enrich traditional history with colorful, evocative details, and on occasion, major breakthroughs in our understanding of the human experience. We will always benefit from the insights they provide into those who came before us.

Allan S. Gilbert
Fordham University, Bronx, NY

ENDNOTES

1. Valerie G. DeCarlo, "Public archaeology in Riverdale Park." *The Bronx County Historical Society Journal* 33, no. 1 (1996): 13–20.

2. Robert Apuzzo, "The Indians of Clason Point." *The Bronx County Historical Society Journal* 26, no. 1 (1989): 9–11.

3. Allan S. Gilbert, Richard B. Marrin, Jr., Roger Wines, and Garman Harbottle, "The New Netherland/New York brick archive at Fordham University." *The Bronx County Historical Society Journal* 29, no. 2 (1992): 51–67.

4. See Anne-Marie Cantwell and Diana diZ. Wall, *Unearthing Gotham: The Archaeology of New York City.* Yale University Press, New Haven, 2001.

5. The late Dr. Theodore Kazimiroff (1914–1980), founder of the Bronx County Historical Society, maintained a lifelong interest in exploring the history buried beneath New York's streets, and though he left little to document his massive accumulation of archaeological material, in the places where he arrived before mid-20th century development, his actions saved an invaluable study collection from destruction.

6. For example, Edward J. Kaeser, "The Morris Estate Club Site." *Bulletin of the New York State Archeological Association* 27 (March, 1963): 13–21; Julius Lopez, "The history and archaeology of Fort Independence on Tetard's Hill, Bronx County, N.Y." *Bulletin, New York State Archaeological Association* 73 (July, 1978): 1–28; Michael Cohn and Robert Apuzzo, "The Pugsley Avenue Site." *The Bulletin. Journal of the New York State Archeological Association* 96 (Spring 1988): 5–7.

Introduction

Archaeologists have always loved digging in cities. Initially, they dug in ancient cities such as Ur or Tikal or in the ancient parts of modern cities such as Jerusalem or Rome. More recently, however, they have been digging in the modern parts of modern cities, including those in the United States. In fact, urban archaeology has become a big field here, acquiring a popularity that is reflected in the archaeological literature. That literature includes overviews of explorations into the American urban past as well as archaeological biographies of individual cities, including volumes made up of diverse essays as well as a single narrative about that city. Occasionally, such narratives concentrate on the people who lived in the place before the city emerged there, but more frequently they focus on just the modern parts of the city. There is even one work that has regarded a modern American city as one large archaeological site, to be studied in its entirety, pre-urban and urban, joining its deeper Native past with its briefer modern past into one narrative of all the peoples who had ever lived there. The present volume, *Digging the Bronx: Recent Archaeology in the Borough*, includes both pre-Columbian and post-Columbian sites; it is a welcome and important addition to the archaeological study of modern American cities, in general, and of New York City in particular.[1]

SEEING NEW YORK CITY AS AN ARCHAEOLOGICAL SITE

The archaeological study of New York City is unusual in several ways. First, archaeologists have been investigating its past, including that of the Bronx, for well over a century. Second, until the 1970s, most (but not all) of the work that was done there was performed by avocational archaeologists, as Michael Cohn discusses here in his chapter. Third, the land that makes up the modern city has a very deep archaeological past for an American city, one that spans thirteen thousand years and includes a myriad of dramatic social and environmental changes that occurred during that long span of time. When people first arrived in the New York area about 13,000 years ago, the shoreline—which in modern times has formed one of the finest harbors on the Atlantic Rim—was from 24 to 60 miles further to the east due to the lower Ice Age sea levels. The area that was to become the city was well inland. Finds made by the avocational archaeologists Donald Sainz and Albert Anderson at the Port Mobil site on Staten Island in the 1950s document a hunting camp left by these early immigrants to the New York area.[2]

The present volume is about recent work in the Bronx, the city's northernmost borough and the only one that lies on the continental mainland. The book covers a lot of the work that has taken place there since the beginning of professionalization in the archaeological study of New York, which started in the late 1970s. Michael Cohn sets the stage by providing a history of the archaeology of the borough. H. Arthur Bankoff, Frederick A. Winter, and Christopher Ricciardi along with Allan S. Gilbert and Roger Wines examine individual sites: a plantation and a country estate/school infirmary, respectively. These papers also explore the processes of urban archaeology, that is, how such projects get organized and accomplished—be it through field schools (see Gilbert and Wines, Bankoff et al.), public archaeology (with public involvement throughout the project; see Valerie DeCarlo Hauser), cultural resource management, whereby projects are mandated by governmental regulations (see Betsy Kearns and Cece Saunders), as well as the importance of using high-tech methods of analysis to re-examine artifacts (see Gilbert, Jeremy Tausch, and Patrick Brock), and the application of the field of ethnohistory, using the many documents and oral histories, native and European, that record information about groups that did not leave written information about themselves (see Robert Grumet). These papers also stress the importance of the curation of collections, along with making collections accessible so that they can be appreciated by the public and studied by future generations of scholars to address new research questions with new insights and new techniques (see Amanda Sutphin and Camille Czerkowicz, respectively). Gilbert finishes up the book by discussing the importance of conserving archaeological sites along with the collections they have generated.

"SEEMINGLY INCONSPICUOUS FINDS"

In his final chapter, Gilbert talks about the importance of "isolated and seemingly inconspicuous finds [that] can be critical to the solution of historical problems." We certainly agree. An example of the importance of such "inconspicuous finds" happened a century ago in the Bronx. When looked at today, that discovery offers great insights beyond local history, extending not only to the Dutch colony of New Netherland, of which the Bronx was a part, but to colonialism itself and to an understanding of the profound ecological effects that can take place when different peoples meet. Colonial New Netherland was established in the early 17th century when Europeans and Africans, enslaved and free, arrived in this ancient world with its already millennia-long history. They, together with the indigenes, created a very different world, one that, for better or worse, we have all inherited.

To elaborate on this idea of "inconspicuous finds," we're going to revisit the Weir Creek site, near Schley Avenue in the Throgs Neck section of the Bronx, which was excavated over 100 years ago. Today, the area is residential, made up of houses built at different times throughout the 20th century and some that are brand new. The site was first explored by M. R. Harrington in 1900 for the American Museum of Natural History. He then revisited it in 1917 for the Museum of the American Indian, Heye Foundation, and those excavations were taken over and completed in 1918 by Alanson B. Skinner with the assistance of Amos Oneroad and C. O. Turbyfill. Oneroad, who had met Skinner at Columbia University, was a Native American, a member of the Dakota Nation and one of the first Native American archaeologists. He was also a Presbyterian minister. He and Skinner worked together on many projects for the American Museum of Natural History and the Museum of the American Indian.[3]

The site is near what was once a freshwater spring at the mouth of Weir Creek. This waterway got its name from the early colonial settlers who reportedly had seen and copied the Native American practice of building reed weirs and placing them across the mouth of the creek to catch fish borne on the outgoing tide. Much of the creek was filled in during the 1950s as part of Robert Moses's transformation of the city, and the creek and parts of the site may now underlie sections of the Throgs Neck Expressway and a nearby park.

The site itself is rich in history and was occupied on and off for six thousand years by generations of various groups of Native Americans. The period of its occupation that interests us was during the 17th century when, Skinner argues, the Munsees (the resident Native peoples in the area) came for a short time at the height of Kieft's War in the 1640s. Along with other finds, Skinner reports pig bones amidst the usual household trash. Pigs are not, of course, native to the Americas and were brought here by the Europeans.

We don't know how the bones of this particular European domesticated animal wound up mingled with other more traditional Munsee household refuse here and at other sites in the city. The meat could have been given, bought, stolen, or hunted as game, or the livestock raised by the community; there are written accounts that suggest all of these possibilities. But no matter how the meat got here, this seemingly insignificant find brings home the profound and irrevocable economic and ecological changes taking place not only here but throughout all of 17th-century coastal New York.

As the colonial settlements grew, Dutch and English farms began expanding more and more into traditional Munsee territory. The European colonists, some with the assistance of enslaved African labor, cut down forests for lumber, cleared fields, grazed European animals, and planted European crops along with those they had adopted from their Indian neighbors. The introduction of these alien species radically altered local ecosystems and destroyed the habitats of many animals that the Munsees had traditionally hunted as well as the plants on which they had depended. Compounding these changes was the tense climate of hostility brought on by the wars of the mid-17th century. Not only did the conflicts sap energies from more productive economic activities, but both Munsee and Dutch destroyed each others' crops as part of the mutually punitive nature of these confrontations. Munsee gardens were also destroyed by wandering European animals, especially pigs and dogs. Although the Dutch administration acknowledged this problem and tried to resolve it, that attempt was in vain. Crop destruction became one of the major causes of the increase in violence that wreaked havoc in the area during the 1640s and 50s.[4]

European livestock, however, did more than damage Munsee crops and provoke conflicts. These animals also posed a "direct impact on American ecosystems," and, as William Cronon has argued for neighboring New England, the effects of this impact become clear only "when they are treated as integral elements in a complex system of environmental and cultural relationships. The pig was not merely a pig but a creature bound among other things to the fence, the dandelion, and a very special definition of property." Like pigs, the other European animals altered both local native ecosystems and cultural landscapes and subordinated them to European ones. As European activities radically altered these ecosystems, native subsistence patterns were forever changed. By default, many Munsee families could no longer rely on their customary food-stuffs and became increasingly dependent on the colonists for their subsistence. They had to find new strategies to obtain food and deal with their rapidly changing natural world, a world that they were now sharing with the European colonists and the Africans.[5]

THE IMPORTANCE OF THE PAST FOR THE PRESENT AND THE FUTURE

We offer this rethinking of these "insignificant finds," pig bones found a century ago at the Weir Creek site in the Bronx, as an example of how archaeological finds can contribute, as Gilbert noted, to the solution of historical problems long after their discovery. We ourselves are currently interested in colonialism, and these finds vividly demonstrate, we believe, the dramatic changes in the economy and landscape that were taking place in New York throughout the colonial period. What Cronon writes of nearby New England also applies to coastal New York: a "distant world and its inhabitants gradually [became] part of another people's ecosystem....but in the process, the landscape...was so transformed that the Indian's earlier way of interacting with their environment became impossible." These "inconspicuous finds," excavated so long ago, can help us today by suggesting other ways of looking at colonialism in general and in the Bronx in particular.[6]

We believe the finds reported in this volume of recent archaeological explorations in the Bronx will not only help contemporary residents appreciate that history (as they did us), but will also benefit future scholars as they search for answers to new pressing research problems. We agree wholeheartedly with Gilbert in his Preface when he concludes "We will always benefit from the insights they provide into those who came before us."

Anne-Marie Cantwell
Diana diZerega Wall
New York City

ENDNOTES

1. For an overview of the archaeology of modern American cities, see Nan A. Rothschild and Diana diZerega Wall, *The Archaeology of American Cities*. University Press of Florida, Gainesville, 2014. For an example of a book that combines both the modern and ancient pasts into one narrative, see our book *Unearthing Gotham: The Archaeology of New York City*. Yale University Press, New Haven, 2001. For an example of an edited volume on an American city, see Sarah M.K.Nelson, Lynn Berry, Richard F. Carrillo, Bonnie J. Clark, Lorie Rhodes, and Dean Saitta, *Denver. An Archaeological History*. University of Pennsylvania Press, Philadelphia, 2001; and for an example of a book with a focus solely on pre-Columbian history, see Charles Markman, *Chicago Before History: The Prehistoric Archaeology of a Modern Metropolitan Area*. Illinois Historic Preservation, Springfield, Illinois, 1991. For one that discusses the recent past see Rebecca Yamin, *Digging the City of Brotherly Love*. Yale University Press, New Haven, 2008.

2. See Joseph Schuldenrein, Curtis Larsen, Michael Aiuvaslatsit, Mark A. Smith, and Susan Malin-Boyce, *Geomorphology/Archeological Borings and GIS Model of the Submerged Paleoenvironment in the New York/New Jersey Harbor and Bight in Connection with the New York and New Jersey Harbor Naviagation Project, Port of New York and New Jersey, Draft Report*. Prepared for NEA, Portland, Maine under contract to U.S. Army Corps of Engineers, New York District, under subcontract to Hunter Research, Inc., Trenton, New Jersey. Contract No. DACW 51-01-D-00184, NEA Delivery Order 0065, Hunter Research, Inc. Project 06017, 2007. For a discussion of the Port Mobil site, see Anne-Marie Cantwell and Diana diZerega Wall, *op. cit.* (note 1), pp. 36–45, as well as Anne-Marie Cantwell and Diana diZerega Wall, "New Amsterdam: The subordination of native space." In *Soldiers, Cities, and Landscapes: Papers in Honor of Charles L. Fisher*, P.B. Drooker and J. Hart, eds., *New York State Museum Bulletin* 513 (2010): 199–212.

3. See Alanson Skinner, "Exploration of Aboriginal Sites at Throg's Neck and Clason's Point, New York City; Part I: The Throgs Neck Schley Avenue Shellheap. Part II: Snakapins, a Siwanoy Site at Clason's Point." *Contributions from the Museum of the American Indian, Heye Foundation* 5, no. 4, New York, 1919; and Diana diZerega Wall and Anne-Marie Cantwell, *Touring Gotham's Archaeological Past.* Yale University Press, New Haven, 2004, pp 119–122.

4. For a further discussion of these issues and how they affected the Dutch, see, e.g., A.J.F. van Laer, translator and editor, *New York Historical Manuscripts, Dutch, Vol. 4. Council Minutes, 1638–1649,* 1974, pp. 73–74. Genealogical Publishing Company, Baltimore; and Jaap Jacobs, *New Netherland: A Dutch Colony in Seventeenth-Century America.* Brill, Leiden, 2005, pp. 223–226. For crop destruction and increase in violence, see J. Franklin Jameson, ed., *Narratives of New Netherland, 1609–1664.* Charles Scribner's Sons, New York, 1909, pp. 209, 277; Donna Merwick, "Extortion." *De Halve Maen* 78, no. 3 (2005): 43–48; and James Homer Wilson, "Great doggs and mischievous cattle: Domesticated animals and Indian-European relations in New Netherland and New York." *New York History Quarterly Journal of the New York State Historical Society* 76 (1995): 245–264.

5. William Cronon, *Changes in the Land: Indians, Colonists, and the Ecology of New England.* Hill and Wang, New York, 1983, p. 14.

6. William Cronon, *ibid.,* pp. 14–15.

List of Contributors:

Dr. H. Arthur Bankoff is Professor of Anthropology, Brooklyn College, CUNY, and co-principal investigator of the excavations at the Van Cortlandt House. He has conducted archaeological research in southeastern Europe, Israel, and in greater New York City, and he is archaeological adviser to the Chair of the New York City Landmarks Preservation Commission.

Dr. Patrick W.G. Brock is retired Associate Professor in the School of Earth and Environmental Sciences of Queens College, CUNY, and a specialist in the geology of the New York City region.

Dr. Anne-Marie Cantwell is Professor Emerita of Anthropology at Rutgers University-Newark and a Visiting Scholar at New York University. She has excavated sites in the Midwest and the Northeast, and her work focuses on colonialism, pre-Columbian trade and ritual in eastern North America, and archaeological ethics.

Michael Cohn (1924–2011) was a cultural anthropologist and archaeologist, and a founding member of the 1950s New York Archaeological Group. He retired as curator at the Brooklyn Childrens' Museum and was subsequently curator at the Yeshiva Museum.

Camille Czerkowicz managed the digitization of New York City archaeological finds as Project Manager at the Museum of the City of New York. An archaeologist and researcher with the Museum of the City of New York and formerly with the South Street Seaport Museum, she has focused on exhibitions and programs that bring the City's past to present day audiences. She has worked in museums, archaeology, and heritage management on three continents, including with UNESCO in Central Asia.

Dr. Allan S. Gilbert is Professor of Anthropology at Fordham University, Bronx, New York, and archaeological director of the Rose Hill Manor excavations (1985–2002). He is editor-in-chief of the Springer *Encyclopedia of Geoarchaeology* (2017), and his research has been conducted mostly in the eastern Mediterranean and in New York City.

Dr. Robert S. Grumet is an anthropologist whose research interests primarily focus on the ethnohistory of the Indians of the northeastern U.S. A retired National Park Service archaeologist, he is currently a Senior Research Associate at the University of Pennsylvania's McNeil Center for Early American Studies.

Valerie Hauser is Director of Native American Affairs at the Advisory Council on Historic Preservation, Washington, D.C., and former director of the Public Archaeology Program at Wave Hill, Bronx, New York.

Elizabeth W. Kearns (d. 2010) was co-founder and partner for more than 25 years in the cultural resources management firm, Historical Perspectives, Inc. of Westport, Connecticut. She also served as a Council member of the National Trust for Historic Preservation.

Dr. Christopher Ricciardi is District Support Team Manager and Project Archaeologist in the Civil Works Integration Division of the U.S. Army Corps of Engineers, North Atlantic Division, in Fort Hamilton, Brooklyn, and he is Principal Investigator in the contract archaeology firm of Chrysalis Archaeological Consultants. He was field assistant during the excavations at Van Cortlandt House.

Cece Saunders is co-founder and principal of Historical Perspectives, Inc. in Westport, Connecticut since 1982 and has served as Principal Investigator, Primary Author, or Project Manager for numerous cultural resource compliance projects in the tri-state area. She has been a governor-appointed member of the Connecticut State Historic Preservation Review Board since 1993.

Amanda Sutphin is Director of the Archaeology Department at the New York City Landmarks Preservation Commission. The Department is responsible for assessing the potential impact of some development projects on archaeological resources and overseeing any needed ensuing archaeology. Since 2014, it also manages the NYC Archaeological Repository: The Nan A. Rothschild Research Center, which curates the City's archaeological collections. Ms. Sutphin is an urban archaeologist with over 20 years of professional experience and has been involved with dozens of projects ranging from the Federal African Burial Ground to the discovery of the World Trade Center ship.

Dr. Jeremy Tausch is currently Visiting Assistant Professor at Pratt Institute, Brooklyn, and Adjunct Assistant Professor at John Jay College, CUNY. He specializes in the study of hard tissue (bone and teeth) microanatomy in early human ancestors, and has recently produced a nature film series, "Not Your Average Nature Show," pending distribution in 2018.

Dr. Diana diZerega Wall is Professor Emerita of Anthropology at City College and the Graduate Center of the City University of New York. She has excavated extensively within New York City and focuses much of her research on colonialism and on issues of gender, class, race, and ethnicity as they have affected the social fabric of the city from colonial times through the 19th century.

Dr. Roger Wines is Professor Emeritus of History, Fordham University, Bronx, New York, and historical director of the Rose Hill Manor excavations. His historical research involves New York City, Nazi Germany, and the development of modern transportation systems and technology.

Dr. Frederick A. Winter is currently associate director of the Capitol Archaeological Institute at The George Washington University and was previously professor in the departments of Classics and Anthropology & Archaeology at Brooklyn College and The CUNY Graduate Center. In addition to his excavations as co-principal investigator at the Van Cortlandt House and other sites in the U.S., he has excavated in Cyprus, Greece, Israel, Turkey, and the former Yugoslavia.

List of Illustration Credits

Chapter 4   Public archaeology in Riverdale Park........................Hauser

Chapter 5   The business of archaeology: Cultural Resource Management in the Bronx...Kearns and Saunders

Chapter 6   A turtle in the garden.................Gilbert, Tausch, and Brock

Chapter 7   Indians in the Bronx: the ethnohistoric evidence.............Grumet

Chapter 8   An overview of the New York City Archaeological Repository: the Nan A. Rothschild Research Center...Sutphin

Chapter 9 Opportunities and challenges for Bronx archaeology in the digital age...Czerkowicz

Back Cover

Students excavating at the Rose Hill Manor site; photo by Allan S. Gilbert

1   A short history of archaeology in the Bronx

For over a century, archaeologists have been exploring the sites and objects left behind by the people who lived before us in the area now known as the Borough of the Bronx in New York City. More evidence doubtless exists of the most ancient of these people, but much of what they left behind is now submerged beneath the waters that rose, here and along the entire eastern seaboard of North America, as the ice age glaciers melted. Beneath its soil, the Bronx preserves no magnificent palaces of royal or aristocratic antiquity, but it has yielded traces of the everyday lives of Native Americans, Dutch and English colonists, and the soldiers of many nations who served here.

In 1809, interest in the early settlers of New York City brought about the foundation of the New-York Historical Society, the first historical society of many that have existed in our city.[1] The publication of James Fenimore Cooper's *The Last of the Mohicans* in 1826 changed cultural perceptions about Native Americans, transforming them from blood thirsty savages into fellow human beings—in the eastern United States at least. Out west, where Indian Wars were still being fought, a far less noble perception persisted, which led to continuing carnage in step with westward expansion.

In 1839, the New York State legislature appropriated funds to send an agent to copy all documents bearing on the history of New York State that could be found in the archives of Holland, England, and France. By 1863, the activities of the state archivist, Dr. Edmund Bailey O'Callaghan, had resulted in the publication of eleven volumes of material, and by 1887, four more had been added, making a total of 15 volumes.[2] Later in the 19th century, the New-York Historical Society published volumes of diaries and accounts of Revolutionary War participants, many of whom served in the Bronx.[3] Thus, archaeologists could compare their finds with the written accounts of governors, explorers, and traders who had met with native tribesmen, soldiers who had fought in New York's wars, and administrators who had tried to bring their form of order to the new lands of America. Historical research is used by all good archaeologists, but the written records usually deal with important events and notable persons, leaving the evidence of ordinary life to be found in the excavation of camp sites, house sites, and the refuse contained in debris piles left behind (Figure 1).

---

* In memory of Michael Cohn: 10.01.1924 to 09.13.2011.

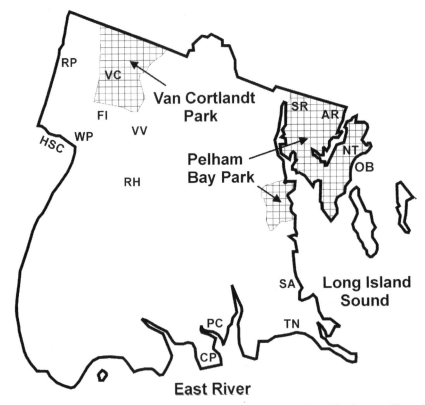

Figure 1. Map of the Bronx showing the location of sites mentioned in the text. Key: AR = Archery Range; BG = NY Botanical Garden; CP = Clason's Point; FI = Fort Independence; HSC = Harlem Ship Canal; NT = Nature Trail; OB = Orchard Beach; PC = Pugsley Creek; RH = Rose Hill Manor; RP = Riverdale Park; SA = Schley Avenue; SR = Split Rock Boulder; TG = Tibbett Garden Project; TN = Throgs Neck area (Schurz Avenue, Morris Estate); VV = Valentine-Varian House; VC = Van Cortlandt House; WP = Wading Place.

In 1900, M. R. Harrington was sent by the American Museum of Natural History to excavate the shell heaps left by various groups of native inhabitants along the shores of Throgs Neck.[4] Mark Raymond Harrington (1882–1971) was born in Ann Arbor, Michigan, the son of a university museum curator. After the family moved to Mt. Vernon, New York, and while completing his education (M.A. at Columbia in 1908), young Raymond worked with Frederick Ward Putnam at the American Museum of Natural History, conducting field explorations in the Bronx, among other places. Soon, Harrington met George Gustav Heye and became involved in the accumulation of materials for Heye's Museum of the American Indian. After 1911, Harrington's collecting and subsequent fieldwork progressively took him out west, and he eventually became director of the Southwest Museum in Los Angeles.[5]

Figure 2. Photograph of Mark Raymond Harrington at Mound 2, Ozan, Arkansas, in 1916. Courtesy of the National Museum of the American Indian, Smithsonian Institution (N03045), photograph by M. R. Harrington?

The Throgs Neck site proved to be rich in artifacts and extensive in size. Over the next hundred years, archaeologists would be working nearby along the shores of Long Island Sound at Schurz Avenue, Clason Point, Throgs Neck, and Pugsley Creek.[6] Householders and local historians would also find spear heads and stone tools along the beaches and in their gardens, some of which they donated to the American Museum of Natural History or the Museum of the American Indian. The area was also the site of an early colonial house.[7]

Another of the prominent early professionals who explored the coastal sites of the Bronx along with Harrington was Alanson B. Skinner (1885–1925).[8] Born in Buffalo, Skinner worked with the American Museum of Natural History from 1907, and like Harrington, joined the Museum of the American Indian, Heye Foundation, in 1915, from whence he began a dual career in Native American archaeology and ethnology. Resuming excavations begun by Harrington at Throgs Neck and Clason Point in 1918, Skinner uncovered

Figure 3. Portrait photograph of Alanson Skinner, date uncertain. Courtesy of the American Museum of Natural History Library, image 125304.

remains of a Late Woodland Native American settlement, possibly the village called "Snakapins" that was occupied by Munsee-speaking Indians in the early 1600s.[9] He died tragically in an automobile accident while on a collecting trip among the Sioux in North Dakota in 1925.

In 1890, construction crews leveling the land surface for the Parade Ground in Van Cortlandt Park uncovered a large number of stone and bone tools. A local resident, J. B. James, collected this material and gave it to the American Museum of Natural History, where it could be studied by later archaeologists.[10] Also uncovered at the same time were foundations thought to represent the house of Adriaen van der Donck, one of the early settlers of New Netherland and the "Jonkheer," or young lord, after which the city of Yonkers was named. Material recovered from these foundations was, unfortunately, not saved.[11] The area around the Van Cortlandt mansion also turned out to contain a vast number of valuable archaeological remains when it was excavated in the 1990s (see Bankoff *et al.*, this volume).

Figure 4. Photograph of Reginald Pelham Bolton (l.) and William Louis Calver (r.) excavating a prehistoric dog burial. Courtesy of Don Rice of the Kingsbridge Historical Society, Bronx.

The team of William Louis Calver (1859–1940) and Reginald Pelham Bolton (1856–1942) began archaeological work in 1895 and continued digging in New York City for 40 years. Indeed, it would be difficult to imagine the archaeology of northern Manhattan and the Bronx without the maps and reports produced by Bolton. A surveyor and engineer by trade and an archaeologist by avocation, Bolton dug Revolutionary War sites and Native American camps with equal enthusiasm and skill. Often, he and Calver worked just ahead of the construction crews creating new streets as the city grew northward. His field techniques were meticulous, using shovels, trowels, and sieves to recover even small finds. His clear photographs and accurate maps are still used by New York archaeologists. Bolton, like many amateur researchers, believed that the general public should be kept informed about his discoveries, which were published in a wide range of books and pamphlets,[12] and summaries of his work were reprinted as basic documents by the New-York Historical Society.[13] Bolton proceeded without official status for over 20 years, receiving recognition with Calver and others as part of the Society's "Field Exploration Committee" only in 1918.

While Calver and Bolton were trying to keep up with the discovery of new archaeological sites, professional anthropologists such as Frank Speck and Alanson Skinner deepened our understanding of Native American life in New York City by interviewing surviving members of the Mahikan and Niantic tribes, recording their tales, and photographing extant objects that would not have survived burial in the earth.[14] The U.S. Geological Survey mapped the Bronx shores as they were before the great landfills of the early 20th century reshaped the coastlines,[15] and J. R. Smith surveyed the wells and springs of the Bronx in what today would be called "non-destructive archaeology."[16]

The later 1930s and 1940s were not good times for Bronx archaeology, however. Massive public projects pushed by Mayor Fiorello La Guardia and his forceful park commissioner, Robert Moses, destroyed many sites with no attempts at archaeological mitigation. The remains of the Johnson Foundry in Kingsbridge and at least one shell heap were obliterated in the straightening of the Harlem Ship Canal in 1934 (see p. 127, Figure 2). Nearby, the Native American "Wading Place" and remains of the colonial King's Bridge, both located at the crossing point that linked the northern tip of Manhattan Island with the mainland across Spuyten Duyvil Creek, were buried under the Marble Hill Houses (1948–1952). Hunter Island disappeared under landfill that extended Rodman's Neck outward to create Orchard Beach (1935–1937), while the approaches to the Triborough/RFK (1936), Whitestone (1939), and Throgs Neck (1961) bridges destroyed many sites on the shores of the East River and Long Island Sound. Many other sites were lost during the construction of Co-Op City (1968–1971) and the high rise apartment houses in Riverdale.

New interest in New York archaeology was aroused by the publication in 1950 of Carlyle Smith's doctoral dissertation, *Archaeology of Coastal New*

York, by the American Museum of Natural History.[17] Carlyle Shreeve Smith (1915–1993) was born in Great Neck and educated at Columbia University (both undergraduate and graduate), completing his dissertation in 1949 (Figure 5).[18] Smith carefully analyzed finds in both private and public collections, and on that basis postulated a multi-level series of cultures connected to aboriginal groups beyond our immediate area. This regional chronology went far beyond the simple Algonquin-Iroquois dichotomy used by Bolton and Skinner. The new analysis was further expanded by the study of New York projectile points published by State Archaeologist, William Ritchie.[19] Smith's later research was conducted mostly in the Midwest, where he worked as curator of archaeology at the University of Kansas Museum of Natural History and taught anthropology at the University of Kansas.

Figure 5. Photograph of (l. to r.) Stanley Wisniewski, Ralph Solecki, Carlyle Smith, and Edward Kaeser at the 1978 annual meeting of the New York State Archaeological Association on the campus of the State University of New York at Stony Brook. Courtesy of Ralph S. Solecki and Edward J. Kaeser.

For a period following Smith's publication, Bronx archaeology was dominated by avocational explorers, the most prominent among whom was Bronx dentist, Dr. Theodore Kazimiroff (1914–1980). Remembered principally for his avid interest in environment and history, the indomitable "Doc" encouraged public interest in land preservation through nature walks, lectures, and campaigns against the destructive effects of development (see p. 146, Figure 1). A dynamic and enthralling speaker, he helped save the glacial Split Rock boulder from annihilation by an expansion of the New England Thruway (I-95) in 1962, and he contributed to the creation in 1967 of wildlife sanctuaries in Pelham Bay Park. In 1986–1987, a Nature Trail was established on Hunter Island in his honor and memory. Also an enthusiastic historian, Kazimiroff founded the Bronx

County Historical Society in 1955 and helped to save from demolition the historic 1758 Valentine-Varian house, which was donated to the Historical Society and moved (in 1965) out of the way of apartment building construction and across Bainbridge Avenue where it now contains the Museum of Bronx History.[20] Kazimiroff amassed a large collection of artifacts from his nearly continuous digging over many decades. Much of this archaeological material might have been irretrievably lost through the uncontrolled development ongoing in his day, but the complete lack of record-keeping on his part has meant a nearly complete lack of context for this substantial body of material. Unfortunately, the published works of Dr. Kazimiroff do not appropriately represent his experience, knowledge, and the extent of his collections.[21]

Another important figure was Julius Lopez (1918–1961), a vice-president at Seagram's and avocational archaeologist, who began a series of excavations in the Bronx and on Long Island, working for 14 years before his untimely death at the age of 43.[22] Lopez ran what amounted to an archaeological field school, of which the members assumed the title of New York Archaeological Group. A few cold days of careful troweling and sieving quickly disabused many amateur participants of any romantic notions of archaeology being glamorous and full of treasure. Lopez's emphasis on quadrangular excavation units, straight profiles, meticulous recording, and the analysis of fragments of crumbling ceramics taught much even to some of the old-timers. Lopez excavated both prehistoric and historic sites, publishing 13 papers during his life. At the same time, he helped to establish the Metropolitan Chapter of the New York State Archaeological Association, which absorbed the group he led, in order to encourage discussions of a wider range of issues. In his work, Lopez was backed by professionals such as Ralph Solecki of Columbia University, the New York State Archaeologist, William Ritchie, and Carlyle Smith of the University of Kansas, and he maintained contact with another informal group of excavators under Donald Sainz and Albert Anderson working in Staten Island.

Figure 6. Julius Lopez at Niagara Falls. Photograph courtesy of his daughter, Elizabeth J. Grieco.

In 1958, Harry Trowbridge, a long time Bronx resident and artifact collector, contacted the New York Archaeological Group to help excavate Fort Independence, a Revolutionary War site on Tetard's Hill in the West Bronx, in the short time between the demolition of the Giles Mansion and the construction of a new apartment house at the site.[23] Located between Giles Place and Cannon Place near West 238th Street, the Fort Independence project represented the first organized effort in historical archaeology carried out in New York City since the work of Bolton, and the first time a mechanical bulldozer was used to remove three feet of sterile overburden. Then, the careful scientific methods that had been used on prehistoric sites were applied to a historical one. The plan included study of botanical and faunal remains and preservation of all artifacts. Publication of the Fort Independence site[24] was accomplished after Lopez's death by Stanley Wisniewski (1918–2008), a New York Archaeological Group member with organizational skills and a keen sense for comprehensive record-keeping (Figure 5).

Another active contributor to what we know about the ancient Bronx was Edward Kaeser (1922–). Born in Manhattan and raised in the Bronx, Kaeser became an ironworker and helped erect many of the city's tallest buildings (Figure 5). In his spare time, he was a self-taught archaeologist and uncovered some of the most important evidence for Native American life during the Woodland period of prehistory. At the Morris-Schurz site near Throgs Neck, his discoveries revealed Middle Woodland (*ca.* 2000–1000 years ago) contact and exchange links between the coastal Bronx settlements and cultures of eastern Pennsylvania and the Midwest based upon recovered pottery, projectile point materials, and a cache of over 150 plates of crystalline mica.[25] At the Archery Range site in Pelham Bay Park (Figure 8), Kaeser brought to light a Late Woodland (*ca.* 1000–400 years ago) ossuary, or mass grave, containing numerous secondary burials.[26] Such ossuaries contain individuals whose remains were bundled, perhaps for transport to a communal cemetery site. Such ossuaries have been found across the mid-Atlantic and New England states. Associated with evidence of village farming, they may indicate increased sedentarization. Kaeser published his findings in clearly written papers within local archaeological journals, and he found permanent repositories for his excavated materials; thus, his work has had a lasting impact on our knowledge of the ancient Bronx while new investigations of his finds can still be conducted in the future. The Kaeser site, a shell midden on the shore of Eastchester Bay with evidence of Late Archaic through historic use, was named in his honor.[27]

In the 1960s, the city, state, and federal governments created a series of regulations for construction on sites containing archaeological remains. With these laws, it was thought, our historical heritage would be preserved. Contract archaeologists, paid for by the developers, were to investigate, and if necessary,

Figure 7. Photograph of Edward Kaeser during excavations at the Archery Range Site in Pelham Bay Park, 1957–1958. Courtesy of Edward J. Kaeser.

excavate sites before construction could take place (see the chapter by Kearns and Saunders, this volume). These laws did not work out as well as had been hoped, unfortunately, especially in the Bronx. State and federal bodies, such as the State Dormitory Authority and many others, did not consider themselves bound by the rules of the New York City Landmarks Preservation Commission. There was no provision requiring private builders to do any archaeological mitigation unless they sought a zoning variance. No method of funding was provided for publishing any results when archaeological finds were made, except for five copies of a report filed officially with the City Landmarks Commission.[28] Not a single excavation of a Bronx site was published for the public as a result of the landmark laws.

This did not mean that no field work was carried out in the borough. As described in the pages of this book, Fordham University ran a field school for 17 years, working at the Rose Hill Manor site, which lay on its Rose Hill campus in the Bronx (Gilbert and Wines, this volume). Wave Hill surveyed the archaeological resources of Riverdale Park but unfortunately lacked the financial resources to follow their survey and excavations with substantial analysis and publication (Hauser, this volume). Brooklyn College ran a summer field program that excavated around the Van Cortlandt house in 1990–1992 resulting in surprisingly rich discoveries (Bankoff *et al.*, this volume). Also, the excavation of a small Late Archaic site recovered material from the period before shellfish became the mainstay of the native diet.[29] The recent publication of *The Endless Search for the HMS Hussar* by Robert Apuzzo has revived interest in the legendary British frigate that sank off the Bronx coast in 1780.[30] At Fordham University, Allan Gilbert has also undertaken a long-term study of historic bricks, including a large collection of specimens as well as documentation about known manufacturers. While the vast bulk of the archived bricks was manufactured and recovered outside the Bronx, one of the principal goals of the project is to determine brickyard locations for old bricks based on similarities in their chemical composition.[31] Therefore, research on the collection, conducted in the Bronx, will eventually yield information of value to historical archaeologists throughout New York, New Jersey, and Connecticut.

Archaeology in New York City has recently benefitted from the reorganization of the Metropolitan Chapter, which was begun by Julius Lopez in order to give city archaeologists, professional and amateur, a chance to meet and discuss their finds. New leadership and fresh programs were initiated by Profs. Diana Wall (City College, CUNY, retired) and Anne-Marie Cantwell (Rutgers-Newark, retired). Their recent book, *Unearthing Gotham*,[32] surveyed a wide range of archaeological discoveries within New York City, including the outer boroughs, for the benefit of non-specialist readers so that they, too, could understand the challenges of urban archaeology, the principal results, and their historical significance. Career experts who are members of the Professional Archaeologists of New York City (PANYC) have raised funds and organized an annual public program every spring at the Museum of the City of New York to provide a venue for presentations of a general or thematic nature for those interested in the contributions made by archaeology to the history of the city.

With the publication of the present book, we are perhaps entering a new era of Bronx archaeology in which we will not only learn more about our past but participate in the planning and conservation of our buried cultural resources so that they, and the information about them, will remain for future generations in the Bronx.

ACKNOWLEDGMENTS

The author would like to thank the following for assistance in various ways during the preparation of this paper: Robert Apuzzo, William Asadorian, Anne-Marie Cantwell, Elizabeth Grieco, Edward Kaeser, Marie Long, Peter Ostrander, Don Rice, Nan Rothschild, Ralph Solecki, Lou Stancari, Lloyd Ultan, and Margaret Wisniewski.

ENDNOTES

1. Jan Seidler Ramirez, "A history of the New-York Historical Society." *The Magazine Antiques* (January, 2005): 138–145.

2. John Romeyn Brodhead, Berthold Fernow, and E.B. O'Callaghan, *Documents Relative to the Colonial History of the State of New-York: Procured in Holland, England, and France*, 15 vols. Weed, Parsons & Co., Albany, 1853–87.

3. Lt. John Charles Philip von Krafft, "Journal of Lieutenant John Charles Philip von Krafft, of the Regiment von Bose, 1776–1784." *Collections of the New-York Historical Society for the Year 1882, Publication Fund XV*, pp. 1–202. The New-York Historical Society, New York, 1883.

4. M.R. Harrington, "Ancient shell heaps near New York City." In *Indians of Greater New York and the Lower Hudson*, Clark Wissler, ed., pp. 167–179. Anthropological Papers of the American Museum of Natural History 3, 1909.

5. A.D. Hopkins and K.J. Evans, "Raymond of the Caves: Mark Harrington (1882–1971)." In *The First 100: Portraits of the Men and Women Who Shaped Las Vegas*. Huntington Press, Las Vegas, 1999, pp. 48–50; Marie Harrington, *On The Trail of Forgotten People: A Personal Account of the Life and Career of Mark Raymond Harrington*. Great Basin Press, Reno, 1985.

6. Alanson Skinner, "Exploration of Aboriginal Site at Throgs Neck and Clasons Point, New York City; Part I: The Throgs Neck Schley Avenue Shellheap, Part II: Snakapins, a Siwanoy Site at Clasons Point." *Contributions from the Museum of the American Indian, Heye Foundation* 5, no. 4, New York, 1919; Reginald Pelham Bolton, *Early History and Indian Remains on Throg's Neck, Borough of the Bronx, City of New York*. Bronx Society of Arts and Sciences, Document 6, 1934 (Reprinted in *Indian Notes* XI, Museum of the American Indian, Heye Foundation 1976); Julius Lopez, "Preliminary report on the Schurz Site, Throggs Neck, Bronx County, New York." *Nassau Archaeological Society Bulletin* 1, no. 1 (1955): 6–22. (Reprinted in *Long Island Archaeology and Ethnology* Vol. V, Suffolk County Archaeological Society [1982]); Michael Cohn and Robert Apuzzo, "The Pugsley Avenue Site." *The Bulletin. Journal of the New York State Archaeological Association* 96 (Spring, 1988): 5–7; Apuzzo, Robert, "The Indians of Clason Point." *The Bronx County Historical Society Journal* 26, no. 1 (1989): 9–11.

7. H. Geiger Omwake, "Kaolin pipes from the Schurz Site." *Bulletin of the Archaeological Society of Connecticut* 29 (1958): 2–13.

8. M.R. Harrington, "Alanson Skinner." *American Anthropologist* 28 N.S. (1926): 275–280.

9. Skinner, *op. cit.* (note 6). The chapter by Robert Grumet (this volume) explains the origin of the term Snakapins and the absence of reliable documentation for its use. See also Anne-Marie Cantwell and Diana diZerega,Wall, *Unearthing Gotham; the Archaeology of New York City*. Yale University Press, New Haven, 2001, p. 129.

10. Alanson Skinner, "The Indians of Manhattan Island and vicinity: a guide to the special exhibition at the American Museum of Natural History." In *Indians of Greater New York and the Lower Hudson*, Clark Wissler, ed., pp. 113–121. Anthropological Papers of the American Museum of Natural History 3, 1909; Carlyle Shreeve Smith, *The Archaeology of Coastal New York*. Anthropological Papers of the American Museum of Natural History 43, pt 2, 1950.

11. William A. Tieck, *Riverdale, Kingsbridge, Spuyten Duyvil: New York City: a Historical Epitome of the Northwest Bronx*. F.H. Revell, Old Tappan, New Jersey, 1968.

12. Reginald Pelham Bolton, "Military camp life on upper Manhattan Island and adjacent main-

land during the American Revolution: disclosed by recent archaeological excavations." *Annual Report of the American Scenic and Historic Preservation Society*, pp. 347–502. J.B. Lyon, Albany, 1915; Reginald Pelham Bolton, *Relics of the Revolution; the Story of the Discovery of the Buried Remains of Military Life in Forts and Camps on Manhattan Island*. Privately published, New York, 1916; Reginald Pelham Bolton, *New York in Indian Possession*. Indian Notes and Monographs, vol. 2, no. 7. Museum of the American Indian, Heye Foundation, New York, 1920 (reprinted 1975); Reginald Pelham Bolton, *Early History and Indian Remains on Throg's Neck, op. cit.* (note 6).

13. William Louis Calver and Reginald Pelham Bolton, *History Written with Pick and Shovel; Military Buttons, Belt-plates, Badges and Other Relics Excavated from Colonial, Revolutionary, and War of 1812 Camp Sites by the Field Exploration Committee of the New-York Historical Society*. New-York Historical Society, New York, 1950; Gary Hermalyn and Reginald Pelham Bolton, "Historical perspectives on the site of the Indian village at Throg's Neck in the Bronx." *Indian Notes, Museum of the American Indian, Heye Foundation* 11, no. 3/4 (1976): 98–127.

14. Frank G. Speck, "Notes on the Mohegan and Niantic Indians." In *Indians of Greater New York and the Lower Hudson*, Clark Wissler, ed., pp. 183–210. Anthropological Papers of the American Museum of Natural History 3, 1909: Alanson Skinner, "Notes on Mahikan Ethnology." *Bulletin of the Public Museum of the City of Milwaukee* 2, no. 3 (January 20, 1925): 87–116.

15. U.S. Geological Survey, New York–New Jersey: Harlem Quadrangle. Surveyed 1888–89 and 1897; partially revised shoreline 1924 by polyclinic projection. Washington, D.C., 1924.

16. James Reuel Smith, *Springs and Wells of Manhattan and the Bronx, New York City, at the End of the Nineteenth Century*. The New-York Historical Society, New York, 1938.

17. Smith, *The Archaeology of Coastal New York, op. cit.* (note 10).

18. Richard A. Krause, "Obituary of Carlyle Shreeve Smith, 1915–1993." *Plains Anthropologist* 39, no. 148 (1994): 221–227.

19. William A. Ritchie, *A Typology and Nomenclature for New York Projectile Points*. New York State Museum and Science Service Bulletin 384, Albany, 1961; William A. Ritchie, *Archaeology of New York State*. Natural History Press, Garden City, New York, 1965.

20. Lloyd Ultan, *Legacy of the Revolution: the Valentine-Varian House*. Bronx County Historical Society, Bronx, New York, 1983.

21. Theodore Kazimiroff, "Millstones from the Lorillard Snuff Mill." *The Garden Journal of the New York Botanical Garden* 4 (Jan.-Feb. 1954): 25–26; Theodore Kazimiroff, "A Bronx Forest 1000 B.C." *The Garden Journal of the New York Botanical Garden* (Jan.–Feb. 1955): 22–23, 26; Theodore Kazimiroff, "Explore the New York Botanical Garden." *The Garden Journal* 5, no. 2 (March–April 1955): 33–34, 58; Theodore Kazimiroff, "Nature trail." The New York Botanical Garden, Bronx, NY, 1983.

22. Stanley Wisniewski, "Julius Lopez, 1918–1961." *American Antiquity* 28, no. 1 (1962): 82.

23. Murray Schumach, "5 amateur archaeologists find Revolutionary fort in the Bronx." *The New York Times*, July 18, 1958, p. 23.

24. Julius Lopez, "History and archeology of Fort Independence on Tetard's Hill, Bronx County, N.Y." *Bulletin and Journal of the New York State Archaeological Association* 73 (July, 1978): 1–28. (Edited posthumously by Stanley Wisniewski); Julius Lopez, "Ft. Independence regimental data." *Bulletin and Journal of the New York State Archaeological Association* 87 (Summer, 1983): 40–44. (Edited posthumously by Stanley Wisniewski). See also Cantwell and Wall, *op. cit.* (note 9), pp. 274–275. See also Michael Cohn, "The fortifications of New York City during the Revolutionary War." NY Archaeological Group, 1962; later partly reprinted in the *Bulletin of the New York State Archaeological Association* 28 (July, 1963): 19–26, and 29 (November, 1963): 19–23.

25. Edward Kaeser, "The Morris Estate Club Site." *Bulletin of the New York State Archaeological Association* 27 (March, 1963): 13–21. See also Cantwell and Wall, *op. cit.* (note 9), pp. 77–82.

26. Edward Kaeser, "The Archery Range Site: A preliminary report." *Bulletin of the New York State Archaeological Association* 24 (March, 1962): 4–7 (Reprinted in *Long Island Archaeology and Ethnology*, Vol II, Suffolk County Archaeological Association); Edward Kaeser, "The Archery Range Site ossuary, Pelham Bay Park, Bronx, New York." *Pennsylvania Archaeologist* 40, no. 1–2 (1970): 9–34. See also Cantwell and Wall, *op. cit.* (note 9), pp. 100–102.

27. Nan A. Rothschild and Lucianne Lavin, "The Kaeser Site: a stratified shell midden in the Bronx, New York." *Bulletin of the New York State Archaeological Association* 70 (July, 1977): 1–27.

28. For example, see: Eugene J. Boesch and Philip Perazio, Cultural Resources Report for Chapel Farm II, Riverdale. Prepared for Robert Kahn, Hastings, NY. On file at the New York City Landmarks Preservation Commission, 1990; Eugene J. Boesch, Archaeological Evaluation and Sensitivity Assessment of the Prehistoric and Contact Period Aboriginal History of the Bronx, New York. Prepared for the New York City Landmarks Preservation Commission, July 19, 1996. On file at the New York City Landmarks Preservation Commission, 1996; and Edward J. Lenik and Nancy L. Gibbs (Sheffield Archaeological Consultants), An Evaluation of Prehistoric Cultural Resources at the Chapel Farm Estate Property, Bronx, New York. Prepared for Tim Miller Associates. On file at the New York City Landmarks Preservation Commission, 1994.

29. Cohn and Apuzzo, *op. cit.* (note 6).

30. Robert Apuzzo, *The Endless Search for the HMS Hussar*. R & L Press, New York, 2008.

31. Allan S. Gilbert, Richard B. Marrin, Jr., Roger A. Wines, and Garman Harbottle, "The New Netherland/New York brick archive at Fordham University." *The Bronx County Historical Society Journal* 29 (1992): 51–67; Allan S. Gilbert, Garman Harbottle, and Daniel deNoyelles, "A ceramic chemistry archive for New Netherland/New York." *Historical Archaeology* 27, no. 3 (1993): 17–56.

32. Cantwell and Wall, *op. cit.* (note 9).

Archaeological excavations at Van Cortlandt Park, 1990-1992

H. Arthur Bankoff, Frederick A. Winter, and Christopher Ricciardi

Nestled in the southern half of the park that bears its name, the Georgian-style house of the Van Cortlandt family gazes south towards the Spuyten Duyvil and Manhattan. Here, in three summer excavation campaigns from 1990 to 1992, 79 students under the guidance of two faculty members from Brooklyn College uncovered new information about the lives of this eminent New York family. Forty-three trenches of various sizes were opened, and over 15,000 artifacts were collected, washed, catalogued, and analyzed in at least a precursory fashion. Among the finds are over 2,500 complete or reconstructable bottles and plates, as well as a broad spectrum of other remains. The following is a short report detailing preliminary results of these excavations and the ensuing analyses, as well as a concise history of the house and its grounds.

The Van Cortlandt house was built by Frederick Van Cortlandt beginning around 1748 as the main house for the large wheat farm that was his family business. Its location on the Albany Post Road (which passed close to the house on the south and west) made it possible for the occupants to enjoy the benefits of their rural farmstead while still maintaining close ties to the city and its urban life. Despite two periods of remodeling—first in the mid 19th century and then in the early 20th century—the building appears at casual inspection to stand almost as it did two centuries ago.

The immediate impression of an unchanged and unchanging 18th century house is misleading, however. There is a world of difference between a well-kept museum (its present use) and the living nerve center of a farming and industrial complex. At one time, the house was the hub of a small community which included mills, forges, workers, animals, and a place for civic and social activities of all kinds. A primary goal of the excavations was to see what archaeology could reveal about these facets of its past.

Felicitously, the fieldwork served both the educational mission of Brooklyn College and the public mission of the New York City Department of Parks and Recreation. Students in the Brooklyn College Summer Archaeological Field School (BCSAFS) learned correct excavation techniques and gained first-hand field experience on an important historic site. The Department of Parks and Recreation obtained more information about one of the historic structures in its charge, as well as inexpensive archaeological monitoring of sensitive areas adjacent to the house where subsurface work was planned or in progress. The project was thus a cooperative venture between two New York City institutions that met both their needs at almost no cost to taxpayers. This partnership was successful at many levels and has continued over the years.[1]

BACKGROUND HISTORY

The 17th Century

As shown by excavations in the late 1890s conducted by J. B. James,[2] Native Americans used several sections of the land on which Van Cortlandt Park now stands from the late Woodland Period (*ca.* A.D. 1000) onwards. During the second half of the 17th century, large tracts in lower Westchester were acquired by the Dutch. In 1646, Adriaen van der Donck bought a 16-mile spread of land from the Wiechquaeskeck family of the Mohegan tribe of the Algonquin nation. The complete van der Donck holdings covered what would later become most of the Bronx and Yonkers, and a small part would eventually become the territory of the park.[3]

After van der Donck's death in 1655, his property underwent several subdivisions.[4] In July of 1668, George Tibbitt (or Tibbett) and William Betts bought a large portion, and by the end of the 1670s, the remaining tracts of van der Donck land were owned by Frederick Philipse.[5]

From 1638, when the Van Cortlandt family arrived in the New World, its members were prominent in the affairs of New Amsterdam/New York. Oloff Stevense Van Cortlandt was the first to settle in New Netherland. By 1674, he was the third richest man in the colony and was living on Brouwer Straat (Street).[6] In 1691, Oloff's son, Jacobus (1658–1739), returned to New York from the West Indies, where he had been managing the family's shipping business. He married Eva Philipse,[7] who over the next nine years gave birth to five children. Four years later, in 1694, Jacobus bought his first plot of land in what would later become Van Cortlandt Park.[8]

The 18th Century

In the early 18th century, Jacobus began his civic service to the city of New York. He was elected mayor for a two-year term in 1710, and again in 1719. In this, Jacobus succeeded his older brother, Stephanus Van Cortlandt, who in 1677 had become the first native-born mayor of New York.[9] Other members of the family would later also serve in civic capacities.[10] Like his father, Jacobus was a merchant. As the bulk of the family fortune was in shipping, a trade then in decline, the family began to develop farming, brewing, and farm-related work, especially milling.[11] By 1732, Jacobus had systematically purchased all the original lands of van der Donck in what is now the Bronx and parts of Westchester. Around the turn of the 18th century, a mill dam was constructed across Tibbetts Brook. The water power thus produced turned the wheels of various mills.[12] When Jacobus died in 1739, he was buried in the family plot on a hill northeast of Tibbetts Brook in present-day Van Cortlandt Park and later known as Vault Hill.[13]

Jacobus's son Frederick, who inherited his lands upon his passing, began to build "a large stone dwelling house on the plantation" on which he lived in 1748.[14] This is the house that still stands in Van Cortlandt Park, east of Broadway at about 254th Street. Frederick died in 1749, before his house was completed, and his son, James, took control of the property.[15] After James died childless in 1781, the house and lands passed to his brother Augustus (1728–1823), who moved his family there at the end of the Revolutionary War.[16]

During the War, the Van Cortlandt house played a significant role. In the battle for New York, Augustus, who was then City Clerk, was ordered to hide all the city's records from the British attackers. The records were stashed in his backyard in Manhattan until 1776, and soon thereafter they were moved to the family's burial plot on Vault Hill.[17] In 1776, Colonel Bernardus Swartwout used the family grounds to house troops. In October of that year, George Washington used the house as a headquarters prior to the Battle of White Plains.[18]

Only one battle was fought in Van Cortlandt Park. On August 31, 1778, some Stockbridge Indians (fighting with the rebel Americans) encountered combined British, Hessian, and Tory troops. The Native Americans were ambushed, and 37 were killed, including the chief, Abraham Ninham. The bodies were buried in the area of the park that would become known as Indian Field.[19]

After the fall of New York, the Van Cortlandt house became head-quarters for General Howe and remained close to or behind British lines for the duration of the War. Even with the British in control of New York, most of the Van Cortlandts still remained at the house. General Washington once again used the house on his way back to New York in 1783.[20]

The 19th Century

After Augustus's death in 1823 at the age of 95, the property came into the possession of his grandson, Augustus White, with the stipulation that, henceforth, all who inherited the house would take the Van Cortlandt name. In 1839, at the death of Augustus Van Cortlandt White, the house went to Henry, his brother, who died six months later. The estate then went to Augustus Van

Cortlandt Bibby (1825–1850), nephew of Augustus Van Cortlandt White. Under Bibby's ownership, the house was renovated, and much of the nearby land was intensively farmed.[21]

With the growth of New York, the city needed more fresh water and more efficient transport for people and goods. A new aqueduct, part of the Croton system, was opened along the northern ridge of today's Van Cortlandt Park on July 4, 1842, and, with improvements, it remained in use until 1897.[22] By 1879, the New York and Boston Railroad Company ran lines through a section of the Van Cortlandt lands just north of Van Cortlandt Lake to gain access to Albany and New England. Beset by monetary difficulties, these railways had a succession of owners and users. Although a "flag stop" station was built in the northern end of the park in 1888, the lines running through the park were, for the most part, rarely used.[23]

In 1874, the southernmost part of Westchester west of the Bronx River—which contained the Van Cortlandt land—was annexed to New York City. Fifteen years later, the remaining members of the Van Cortlandt family line deeded the house and remaining properties to the city of New York. It is possible that at least one member of the family resided in the house after the sale to the city.[24] Thus ended 140 years of Van Cortlandt life in lower Westchester.

Between 1889 and 1896, the house and grounds were used by the New York Police Department and the National Guard. At one point, a large herd of bison was kept there before being transferred to the Bronx Zoo. In 1896, the National Society of Colonial Dames in the State of New York entered into an agreement with the city to operate the Van Cortlandt house as a public museum. The house was opened to the public a year later.[25]

The 20th Century

Within the past century, extensive renovation and restoration has been accomplished in several phases at the Van Cortlandt house. The Caretaker's Cottage was added as a wing onto the north end of the original ell (thus forming the house's current C-shaped groundplan) between 1913 and 1917. At the same time, Norman Isham, a Colonial Revival architect, renovated the interior portions of the house museum. The fireplaces (reduced in the 19th century because of the addition of stoves) were enlarged to recreate their original size. Interior shutters were added to the rooms. The radiators were offset into the window niches and covered by window seats. Paneling was added to parts of the house.[26] The Caretaker's Cottage and some of the hidden infrastructure of the house were modernized in the 1960s,[27] and in 1988, the East and West Parlors were restored to their original paint colors.[28] Renovations are an ongoing necessity for old houses, and roof repairs were conducted in the mid-1990s.

Like many 18th century rural houses, the structure is a center-passage dwelling (Figure 1) containing three stories—the top two being living floors—and a basement. Brick chimney stacks with exposed backs are visible, closely resembling the architectural tradition of the Hudson Valley. The incorporation of multiple chimney stacks, an unusual feature, ensured that most of the house was heated. The fieldstone construction, with brick around the windows, is also distinctive.

Figure 1. The Van Cortlandt house viewed from the southeast showing the main south wing on the left and the servants' wing forming the northern ell on the right. Brick chimney stacks are not visible from this perspective. Photograph courtesy of the New York City Department of Parks and Recreation.

Three rooms for formal entertaining are situated on the first floor of the house, an arrangement typical of rural architecture of the time. In an urban household, rooms for entertaining would have been situated on the second floor.[29] In other details, the house built by the Van Cortlandts differed from a simple rural farmhouse. Its three full stories made it more imposing, and a service wing was added so that all labor would be removed from visitors. Although the location of the original kitchen has yet to be determined,[30] by the 19th century, it was in the basement under the main section of the first floor, similarly hidden from visitors.

THE EXCAVATIONS

Archaeological excavations at the Van Cortlandt house were conducted over three field seasons and investigated many areas of the grounds (Figure 2). Preliminary reports on the first two season's excavations have been previously distributed.[31] For clarity, the following description will combine the results of all three seasons and present the findings by area, beginning with the trenches to the east of the house.

The East Lawn

In 1990, digging began in the lawn east of the house. The first five trenches were positioned to investigate an area that had been partially disturbed by the construction of a sewer line in 1985. At that time, local newspapers carried a story reporting that the sewer installation had disturbed archaeological deposits and building foundations. The initial trenches of 1990 revealed no architectural remnants, however. Only scattered pottery fragments and other artifacts from the 18th through 20th centuries were recovered.

The *Daily News*[32] reported that one of the five trenches had come down upon a prehistoric dog burial. In fact, the dog bones found in the trench represented only a partial skeleton and were found in association with 19th century Euro-American pottery, thus precluding the possibility of the remains belonging to a pre-colonial Native American dog burial.

In 1991, two more trenches were excavated to the east of the house, considerably beyond the group of five trenches excavated in 1990. One, positioned just within the east perimeter fence of the grounds, revealed traces of a gravel pathway that would have linked the house to its pond and mill to the east.

The East Field

The East Field lies east of the current perimeter fence, between a late 19th century field house and the now abandoned railway line, beyond which is the 17th century Tibbett family burial plot and Van Cortlandt Lake. The area was investigated in 1992 with four two by two meter trenches and 36 auger tests, all excavated to sterile soil—the natural underlying base. The trenches were located so as to sample areas of differing elevation and varied ground cover. Sterile soil was reached approximately one foot below the modern ground surface. No archaeologically significant features were encountered in any trench. Evidence of prior occupation included meager amounts of flint debris (waste flakes possibly from stone tool manufacture) and sparse historic materials found as disturbed and scattered trash throughout the surface layer.

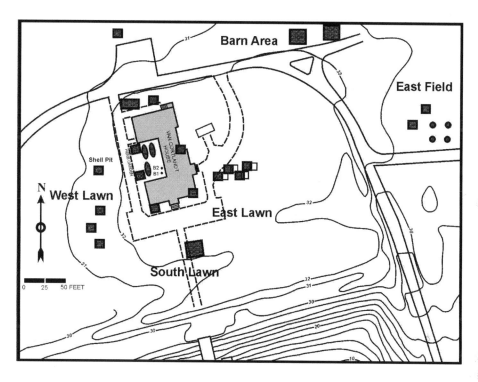

Figure 2. Map of the Van Cortlandt house grounds showing locations excavated during the 1990–92 field seasons.

The auger tests were arranged in two lines at 16 foot intervals running east to west along the southern edge of the field. A power auger was used to produce holes approximately 18 inches in diameter.[33] Only one test encountered cultural deposits. It produced darker soil and chunks of asphalt which can be interpreted as traces of an old path that might have run parallel to the rail line.

The East Field was scheduled for development as a tennis facility by the Department of Parks. The excavations and auger tests were undertaken here primarily to aid the Parks Department in making an informed judgment about a site slated for development. No remains were encountered that would preclude construction in this area.

South of the House

Excavations on the south lawn in 1990 and 1991 were conducted for research as well as more practical reasons. Not only was the ground sinking around the site of an old cesspool which would need replacement by a more modern system, but sewer construction in 1910 had exposed what was then thought to be old foundations on the very spot. Possibly, these foundations belonged to a structure predating the Van Cortlandt house, built perhaps by van der Donck or Tibbett.

The southeastern corner of an unmortared fieldstone foundation was indeed uncovered in 1990 at the bottom of a two by two meter trench, approximately seven feet below the ground surface (Figure 3). Due to the prior disturbance, however, no intact 17th or 18th century layers were found.

In 1991, a 16 by 16 foot trench was dug which incorporated the area of the 1990 trench. The foundations were again exposed, this time more extensively, revealing three dry-laid courses of fieldstones rising approximately 18 inches high and buried in a sandy fill containing only limited amounts of archaeological material. No undisturbed deposits contemporary with the foundation construction were found, and it appears likely that the 1910 sewer excavation removed most of the associated sediments from this buried structure. Artifacts found at that time were not saved for scholarly examination.

Figure 3. Dry-laid fieldstone foundation wall from the south lawn excavation in 1990.

Several small stem fragments from clay tobacco pipes were recovered, however. The diameter of the borehole in the stem has been used by archaeologists to obtain approximate dates for the pipes, since previous research has shown a progressive decrease in size from the 1600s until the early 19th century.

Borehole dating suggests that the pipestems were produced in the 17th to early 18th century.

In May 1991, an electrical resistivity survey of the area was conducted with the help of Dr. Allan S. Gilbert of Fordham University.[34] The resistivity tests suggested that the sand fill extended downward to about 13 feet, although they did not distinguish more of the foundation wall from its surrounding fill.

The House Foundations

To investigate the foundations of the Van Cortlandt house prior to the proposed installation of a new drainage system, three trenches were excavated around the perimeter of the 1748 structure. All trenches encountered late 19th to early 20th century ceramic drain pipes and other modern intrusions, some of which extended into the sterile soil below (Figure 4).

Figure 4. Corner of the house foundations with exposure of recent drainage installations.

The trenches revealed that the character of the foundation supporting the east facade differs at its northern and southern corners. The foundation protruded farther and was constructed of larger stones on the northern end. This finding may be an indication that the north wing of the house was a somewhat later addition, possibly added after Frederick Van Cortlandt's death. Other architectural details, such as the treatment of the roof, seem to argue for a unified construction program. A paint and mortar analysis of the cellar is needed to settle this point.[35]

No foundation trenches were found in the excavations, indicating that the basement walls of the house were constructed from inside the house pit and were pushed outward, flush to the dirt face of the hole. Based upon these results, it appeared that the proposed drainage project, if carefully monitored, would probably not destroy undisturbed archaeological contexts.

The Herb Garden

Between the south wing of 1748 and the modern Caretaker's Cottage to the north, an herb garden was created in the 20th century. The garden was investigated during each field season since it was originally the area behind the house where kitchen refuse might have been thrown. For at least part of the 19th century, there was a lean-to shed against the northern wall of the south wing.[36] The shed might have served as an auxiliary kitchen, and if so, archaeological finds from the garden may eventually provide some insight into the diet of earlier Van Cortlandts.

In order to minimize damage, trenches were situated within the open planting areas between the ornamental brick pathways of the herb garden layout. Household refuse from the 18th and 19th centuries was indeed recovered within one of these trenches, in addition to a stone foundation that must mark the position of the former lean-to wall—approximately 12 feet from the north wall of the south wing (Figure 5).

Herb garden deposits were substantially disturbed during the construction of the Caretaker's Cottage wing in 1917. However, two trenches at the northern end of the herb garden contained cultural deposits that continued downward to a depth of 11 feet. Artifactual material included bricks and pottery, apparently dumped into a large empty opening such as a well, large cistern, or foundation pit. The pottery was from the late 18th and early 19th centuries.

Because excavations were restricted to the planting zones only, which resulted in trenches that were less than five feet wide, safety considerations made it impossible to dig to the bottom of this deposit. Expansion of the excavation would have necessitated an unacceptable amount of damage to the herb garden walks, and therefore the nature of the buried debris remains unexplained. The trenches in the herb garden and along the road flanking it to the west indicate that this buried feature did not exceed an area of approximately 13 by 13 feet. Its overall shape and total depth are still undetermined.

The layers of sediment discovered within the herb garden trenches suggest that, at the time of initial construction in 1748, there was a considerable

Figure 5. View of the buried foundations exposed beneath the herb garden walkways; they probably belonging to a former lean-to structure built against the south wing.

slope up to the house on the north and west. The change in topography brought about by filling and leveling during the two and one-half centuries since the house's construction was confirmed by the excavation of other trenches north of the Caretaker's Cottage wing and in the baseball field. In the days of the Van Cortlandts, therefore, the house probably stood on a knoll looking out and down on the family's holdings to the north, south, and west.

West of the House

Trenches excavated in this area were intended to investigate the line of a previous roadway that ran east to west, passing directly in front of (to the south of) the 1748 south wing. This road connected the house with Broadway, approximately 800 feet to the west. Hard-packed earth and macadamized road surfaces were found along the line of the roadway, which is indicated today by flanking rows of trees.

Trenches were also placed farther west to learn something about the natural stratigraphy of the land on that side. It was not anticipated that significant archaeological remains would be discovered, but serendipitously, this location yielded a Native American shell pit (Figure 6) reminiscent of ones described in late 19th century excavations within Van Cortlandt Park.[37] The fill of the pit consisted mainly of oyster shells accompanied by a few clam shells and a very limited quantity of ash. No pottery was present, but some quartz projectile point fragments as well as flakes of rock quartz and flint from tool making were recovered. The pit appears to date to the Late Woodland period (between *ca.* A.D. 1000 to 1600).

Figure 6. Probable Late Woodland Native American shell pit from the west lawn containing mostly oyster shell debris.

North of the Caretaker's Cottage: the Parade Ground and Playing Field

The Caretaker's Cottage is a late addition that abuts onto the north wing of the original house. Excavations were conducted to the north of the cottage in the expectation that intact deposits dating to periods prior to its construction might be found. A drawing in *Harper's Weekly*[38] from autumn of 1884 indicated that there was a frame out-building approximately 32 feet north of the house. The spot is today occupied by a monumental statue. One two-by-two meter trench was positioned to the east of the statue, while a cluster of four trenches totaling 170 square feet of coverage was excavated to its west. All trenches in this area bear witness to the extensive landfilling concurrent with the construction of the Caretaker's Cottage. These fill deposits extended more than 40 inches below the modern ground surface. Remains that had lain to the north of the original house and were disturbed in the course of building the cottage were eventually dumped farther to the north. No evidence could be found of either the 1884 out-building or other features which could be dated prior to the cottage.

The area around the statue revealed two buried finds that reflect upon the later history of house renovation. To the west of the statue, a ceramic water pipe eight inches in diameter was encountered approximately four feet below the modern ground surface. This was apparently part of the early 20th century sewer system for the cottage.

About six feet farther to the west, and extending into the three neighboring trenches, a rubble paving was exposed about eight inches below the surface. The paving was a single course of rough cobbles at least 10 feet wide and may have been part of an early 20th century barn forecourt or carriage turnaround. To determine whether the cobbled paving continued under and beyond the modern road, a 13 by 3 foot trench was opened in the playing field on the opposite (northern) side of the road. No extension of the paving was found in this trench, although some 20th century construction debris appeared. Topsoil was unusually deep here, extending nearly 40 inches below the ground surface. This is another reminder of the extensive filling and leveling operations carried out on this field in the late 19th century, when the Van Cortlandt farm left private hands and was transformed into a public parade ground and park.

The Barn Area

In 1990 and 1991, excavations were conducted at a site where 19th century illustrations indicated that a large barn once stood. The location appeared to be just at the southern edge of the Van Cortlandt Park baseball field, northeast of the mansion. In 1990, elements of a fieldstone wall or foundation had been discovered there in the course of laying an electrical conduit.

Although no walls or foundations of such a barn were found, excavation did reveal two subterranean stone structures, each approximately five feet square and 10 feet deep (Figures 7 and 8). Built of dry-stone walling, possibly with wooden floors laid over a bed of sand, the stone shafts had been filled with a mixture of rock rubble and earth, including an assemblage of largely intact bottles, plates, and other artifacts. There is still no conclusive explanation of the use these stone structures served. Comparison to similar constructions at related and contemporaneous historic houses, such as Washington Irving's home at Sunnyside in Irvington, New York, suggests that they might have been root cellars. Midwestern parallels hint that they might have functioned as underground silage pits.

Artifacts retrieved from the two stone chambers included ceramic dinnerware of various types, chamber pots, crocks, unguent containers, bottles for medicine and other substances, glass syringes, the decayed remains of a number of pairs of high-heeled shoes, clay smoking pipes, cutlery, toothbrushes, and an upper plate from a set of vulcanite and porcelain false teeth. The artifacts—which, except for a few earlier pieces, date exclusively from the 19th century—appear to have been introduced into the stone shafts in a single, late 19th century dumping. The filling episode seems likely to have been associated with the house's transition from private to public ownership in 1889.

Ceramics include both Chinese porcelain and British and American earthenwares. The Chinese porcelain is found in both Nanking and Canton styles (Figure 9), and the pattern is the popular "Willow" motif.[39] Dates for such ceramics range from the 1790s to the mid-1850s.[40] Recovered shapes comprise soup bowls, dinner plates, cups, and serving platters. Although imported from China, these dishes were very popular and abundant in New York at the time.[41]

Figure 7. Openings to two subterranean stone structures exposed in the area of the former barns.

Figure 8. View into one of the subterranean stone structures after partial excavation of its contents.

Figure 9. Plate of hand-painted Chinese export porcelain in the Canton style (*ca.* 1792–1820); recovered from the stone structures.

Figure 10. Serving dish of English-made blue transfer-printed pearlware (*ca.* 1810–1840) displaying the "Willow" pattern, manufacturer unknown; recovered from the stone structures.

Five exceptional pieces of "tree style" pattern with gold leaf around the rim were also unearthed. These are some of the oldest pieces in the assemblage, dating from the early 1730s until the late 1750s.[42] A metal staple was used to repair one that had split in half, possibly attesting to either the plate's cost or its sentimental value. These plates were probably over a century old when they were discarded within the stone shafts.

Various types of British and American earthenware turned up in the assemblage. Varieties of English blue transfer-printed wares in the "Willow" style[43] were represented by flat plates, bowls, serving dishes, and pitchers (Figure 10). Again, these wares are commonly recovered on 19th century sites.[44]

Teapots and cups, a symbol of wealth and higher social rank during the 19th century,[45] are not common items on every historic site, but, as might be expected, the assemblage from the Van Cortlandt's stone boxes included three teapots and several kinds of cup (Figures 11 and 12).

Other New York sites confirm that social class plays a significant role in shaping the composition of a ceramic assemblage. In Greenwich Village, porcelain and earthenwares similar to those found at the Van Cortlandt house, including many transfer-printed wares, were uncovered from a 19th century domestic site belonging to a physician.[46] In contrast, a nearby tenement site produced an assemblage comprising common plates and other food storage vessels with little porcelain and fewer tea-related items.[47]

Examples of other ceramic items in the inventory included painted whitewares (Figure 13 and 14), a pearlware bulb pot (Figure 15), and a whiteware child's mug with maxims from Benjamin Franklin's essay "The Way

Figure 11. Whiteware teapot and cover showing a transfer-printed landscape scene in very dark blue ("Old Blue"), dated *ca.* 1825–1840; recovered from the stone structures.

Figure 12. Whiteware blue transfer-printed mug with a Chinese style water-scape, *ca.* 1815–1850; recovered from the stone structures.

Figure 13. Whiteware tea bowl with large-scale blue floral painted decoration, dated *ca.* 1815–1830; recovered from the stone structures.

Figure 14. Whiteware vessel, possibly a coffee pot with its spout broken off and large-scale blue floral painted decoration, *ca.* 1815–1830; recovered from the stone structures.

to Wealth" printed in brown on the exterior (Figure 16): "Keep thy shop and thy Shop will keep thee," and "If you would have your business done go if not send."

Wash basins and chamber pots in pearlware, creamware, and ironstone (the latter also called white granite and china white) were also recovered. There are over 15 different types of chamber pot, including chair pot types. Some are highly decorated with transfer printing and, in one instance, with thick applied bands referred to as Mocha cording.[48] Several other pieces of slipped (dipped or "dipt") ceramics included a chamber pot (Figure 17), mugs, and bowls. It is difficult to judge whether they were made in America or Britain, since this cheap everyday ware was being made on both sides of the Atlantic during the 19th century.[49] The items most likely to have been produced locally are stoneware and redware storage jars and crocks, yellowware plates, and brown slip-ware plates. These were the common types of food preparation and storage vessels in the 19th century.[50]

Figure 15. Pearlware bulb pot for forcing bulbs to flower indoors in winter, dated *ca.* 1775–1840; recovered from the stone structures.

Figure 16. Whiteware child's mug printed in brown with selected maxims from Benjamin Franklin's "The Way to Wealth," dated *ca.* 1830–1880; recovered from the stone structures.

Figure 17. White earthenware chamber pot with dipt decoration in the Common Cable motif and a green glazed rouletted band beneath the rim, dated *ca.* 1811–1850; recovered from the stone structures.

Very little stoneware emerged from the large ceramic assemblage. It would appear, therefore, that the stone structures did not contain a kitchen dump nor were they the final resting place of utensils that came from a kitchen pantry or food preparation area.

Figure 18. Dark green glass beverage bottles: (left) bottle with applied tooled "packer" style lip possibly for ale or beer, *ca.* 1825–1895; (right) wine or liquor bottle with an applied string lip, *ca.* 1780–1850. Both recovered from the stone structures.

Over three hundred complete and another six hundred reconstructable bottles (Figure 18) and glass artifacts were excavated from the stone shafts. The bottles come in many shapes, styles, and molds: free-blown and machine-made; single, double, and three piece, or "Ricketts" molds; embossed and non-embossed. The use of two- and three-piece molds dates the majority of the collection to between 1810 and 1888.[51] The wine and champagne bottles date from the late 18th to the early 19th century. Since these types are long lived, some of the free-blown wine bottles could possibly date to the late 17th or early 18th century.[52] Although it is possible that earlier wines might have been brought into the house after its construction in the mid-18th century, or that earlier bottles were retained for antiquarian interest or reuse, such an early dating seems unlikely. There are also several styles of champagne glasses and tumblers. Unlike the bottles, many of which survived intact, few of these drinking vessels were recovered whole.

Most of the bottles held either alcoholic beverages or medicinals. Alcoholic beverages are represented in the assemblage by bottles that would have contained whiskey and other liquors, ale, still wine, and champagne. At the Van Cortlandt house, medicine bottles held both prescribed medicines (dispensed by doctors) and patent medicines (bought over the counter). Some of the bottles were embossed with the names of the pharmacy, the location of the store, and the medicine.

Examination of similar material from excavations on Sullivan Street in Manhattan[53] shows a trend over time toward more "regular" medicine bottles as the century advanced, although some patent medicines were still used. There was also an apparent connection between a more rapid adoption of prescribed medicines and higher socioeconomic status. It is impossible to assess the Van

Cortlandt assemblage in the same way because the deposit was not gradually accumulated and therefore provides no means for following changes in behavior through sequential layers.

A number of artifacts that might be associated with women were found.[54] For example, there are over 20 pieces of what may have been cosmetic holders: small "checker-like" ironstone "dishes," approximately one inch in diameter, some with a gold leaf band around the rim. Ironstone and glass cold cream jars and several heels from women's shoes were also recovered. In addition, a glass syringe came to light that compares to a type associated by Howson[55] with 19th century feminine hygienic practices. It is possible that at least part of the assemblage had its origin in a woman's dressing room or bath. It may also be of interest to note that, while bone toothbrushes and hairbrushes are present, no traces are found in the assemblage of shaving brushes or razors.

This, then, is the assemblage from one specific context at the Van Cortlandt house. As noted above, this material seems to have been introduced into the subterranean stone structures during a single or several almost contemporaneous filling episodes, possibly at or slightly after the purchase of the property by the city in the late 19th century. No stratigraphic differences were determinable within these structures, and no signs of weathering or gradual infilling were observed. It is highly unlikely that these structures served as primary dump sites for day-to-day trash, but, judging from the artifacts found, the materials came originally from several discrete locations in the house. These locations probably include a dressing room or bathroom, a dining room china closet or cabinet, and a bottle storage area. Possibly, the items were left behind when the house was transferred to the city, and disposal took place shortly thereafter. Discard into the stone boxes served not only the need for disposal of abandoned articles from the Van Cortlandt household but also the removal of a possible hazard to the public represented by the empty stone-lined pits.

SUMMARY

The assemblage from the stone structures is the largest collection of informative artifactual evidence unearthed during the three field seasons. The recovered objects span the entire period of house occupation, from the mid-18th through the last quarter of the 19th century, and, as part of a secondary refuse deposit, they indicate that there was probably a diverse range of items, from older to more modern things, in the house at the same time. In contrast to the consistency of the architecture and furnishings presented by the museum restoration, the assemblage offers a microcosm of the mundane dynamics of life at the Van Cortlandt home. Chamber pots, toothbrushes, hairbrushes, and liquor bottles are rarely exhibited, but were as much a part of the family environment as the formal silver. The artifacts and the house complement each other and provide a more complete picture of everyday life.

The deep feature in the herb garden and the earlier foundations to the south may illuminate other aspects of life at the house at various times. Analysis of these and other discoveries is still in progress.

Aside from producing artifacts, the 1990–1992 excavations at the Van Cortlandt house have succeeded in the other goals set by the project. They have tested and determined the archaeological sensitivity of areas slated for possible construction and renovation. They have indicated the extent of landscape remodeling and leveling which has taken place in near unobtrusive increments around the house. They have confirmed the existence and probable date of an earlier structure to the south of the present building and have hinted at the possibility that further remains might be preserved beneath the herb garden and the area formerly occupied by the barn. The shell pit to the west of the house provides additional evidence of Native American use of the southern part of Van Cortlandt Park. The excavations have thus begun to bring us closer to a more complete picture of the Van Cortlandt house in its historic and natural context.

ENDNOTES

1. We would like to thank the New York City Department of Parks and Recreation, and especially the Historic House Trust, for the support and encouragement given to the archaeological work in Van Cortlandt Park throughout the years. We would also like to thank the National Society of Colonial Dames in the State of New York, and the Colonial Lords of Manors for their hospitality, interest, and financial backing of the project. Of the numerous people who have been indispensable to our efforts at one time or another, we must single out Mary Ellen Hearn, former director of the Historic House Trust, Linda Dockeray, Parks Administrator for the Bronx, Nancy Zeigler, Elizabeth Leckie, Julie Mursberger, and Meta Janowitz. Of course, a monumental debt is owed to the students of the Brooklyn College Summer Archaeological Field School, without whose labor and dedication none of this would have been possible.

2. Lloyd Ultan, "A History of Van Cortlandt Park–Borough of The Bronx, New York, New York," Storch Associates, New York. Typescript on file, New York City Parks Historic Houses Division, 1983, p. 2.

3. The name Yonkers comes from the term *jonkheer*, or gentleman, as it referred to young Adriaen van der Donck. Van der Donck arrived in the New World in 1641 to serve as *schout*, or administrative and judicial officer, in charge of Rensselaerswyck, the New Netherland patroonship belonging to Killaean van Rensselaer that encompassed a large area of the northern Hudson Valley surrounding Albany. In 1646, at the age of 26, van der Donck moved downriver, purchased 24,000 acres of land in southwestern Westchester and northwestern Bronx—which he called Colen Donck—and settled down with his wife, the former Mary Doughty, to raise corn and operate a saw mill. The saw mill also gave its name to the present-day parkway. His *Beschrijvinge van Nieuw Nederlant* (1655; English transl. *A Description of the New Netherlands*, 1841) remains a classic

early colonial document, penned while van der Donck was in Holland appealing to the Dutch States-General concerning the needs of the American colony and the numerous disagreements colonists had with its director, Pieter Stuyvesant.

4. J. Thomas Scharf, *History of Westchester County, New York*, Vol. I. L.E. Preston & Co., Philadelphia, 1886, pp. 258, 278; Julie Mursberger, "Van Cortlandt family history." Typescript on file, New York City Parks Historic Houses Division, 1990, p. 3.

5. Mursberger, "Van Cortlandt family history," *op. cit.* (note 4), p. 4.

6. James G. Wilson, *The Memorial History of the City of New-York from Its First Settlement to the Year 1892*, Volume I. New York History Company, New York, 1893, pp. 351–353.

7. Henry B. Hoff, "The identity of Eva (Philipse) Van Cortlandt." *The New York Genealogical and Biographical Record* 124, no. 3 (July, 1993): 153–155.

8. Pamela Herrick, "Van Cortlandt Tour Manual." Typescript on file, New York City Parks Historic Houses Division, 1992, p. 4.

9. James G. Wilson, *The Memorial History*, Vol. II, *op. cit.* (note 6), p. 144. Stephanus later moved upstate to the Van Cortlandt Manor in Croton-on-Hudson. The house still stands and has been renovated to reflect the period immediately following the Revolution. It is currently operated as a museum restoration by Historic Hudson Valley, which hosts themed tours and events, and it contains many of the original Van Cortlandt furnishings.

10. Joseph T. Butler, *Van Cortlandt Manor*. Sleepy Hollow Restorations, Tarrytown, New York, 1978, p. 14.

11. Mursberger, "Van Cortlandt family history," *op. cit.* (note 4), p. 10.

12. Mrs. Morris Patterson Ferris, *Van Cortlandt Mansion*. DeVinne Press, New York, 1897, pp. x–xi, xx; Robert Bolton, *The History of the Several Towns, Manors, and Patents of the County of Westchester, from Its First Settlement to the Present Time*, Vol. II. C.F. Roper, New York, 1881, p. 153; Ultan, *op. cit.* (note 2), p. 5.

13. Ultan, *op. cit.* (note 2), p. 5.

14. Mursberger, "Van Cortlandt family history," *op. cit.* (note 4), pp. 10–11.

15. Julie Mursberger, "Van Cortlandt House—Official Tour Manual." Typescript on file, New York City Parks Historic Houses Division, 1990, p. 11.

16. Herrick, *op. cit.* (note 8), p. 4; Mursberger, "Van Cortlandt family history," *op. cit.* (note 4), p. 8; Mursberger, "Van Cortlandt House," *op. cit.* (note 15), p. 11.

17. Herrick, *op. cit.* (note 8), p. 7.

18. Herrick, *op. cit.* (note 8), p. 7; Jacob Judd, *The Revolutionary War Memoir and Selected Correspondence of Philip Van Cortlandt*. Sleepy Hollow Restorations, Tarrytown, NY, 1976, p. 38.

19. Gary Zaboly, "The Indian Field massacre." *The Bronx County Historical Society Journal* 14, no. 2 (1977): 63–68.

20. Herrick, *op. cit.* (note 8), p. 8.

21. Mursberger, "Van Cortlandt family history," *op. cit.* (note 4), p. 7.

22. James Reuel Smith, *Spring and Wells of Manhattan and The Bronx, New York City, at the End of the Nineteenth Century.* The New-York Historical Society, New York, 1938, p. 229; Ultan, *op. cit.* (note 2), p. 22.

23. Daniel R. Gallo and Frederick A. Kramer, *The Putnam Division: New York Central's Bygone Route through Westchester County.* Quadrant Press, New York, 1981, pp. 21–22; Ultan, *op. cit.* (note 2), p. 22.

24. Elizabeth Leckie, personal communication, 1994.

25. Herrick, *op. cit.* (note 8), p. 9; Mursberger, "Van Cortlandt family history," *op. cit.* (note 4), p. 9.

26. Herrick, *op. cit.* (note 8), p. 9.

27. Bernard L. Herman, "Van Cortlandt House Museum: Architectural Inspection, February 10, 1994." Typescript on file, New York City Parks Historic Houses Division, 1994, p. 1.

28. Herrick, *op. cit.* (note 8), p. 9.

29. Herman, *op. cit.* (note 27), p. 2.

30. Herrick, *op. cit.* (note 8), p. 9.

31. H. Arthur Bankoff and Frederick A. Winter, "Van Cortlandt House Excavations." Typescript on file, Department of Anthropology, Brooklyn College, Brooklyn, New York, 1992.

32. "Dirt on Donck," *The Daily News, Bronx Edition* (Friday, June 22, 1990): 31.

33. Soil augers are tools that permit the removal of cores from the ground by screwing or pounding a casing down, then extracting the column of earth thus captured. Analysis of the recovered sediment can provide information about soil type, stratification, and the presence of buried archaeological sites. Most augers used for soil analysis and archaeological application are small (one to four inches in diameter). The unusually wide boring at Van Cortlandt Park was obtained by using a mechanical post hole digger.

34. Electrical resistivity is a form of subsurface sensing in which a low voltage current is passed through the ground in order to determine the electrical resistance of the earth. When very high resistances are encountered, it is possible that a dense or non-conducting structure, such as a wall, sand layer, or bedrock mass lies within the path of the current. Techniques permit depths to be determined, and the taking of numerous measurements across a site allows a map to be drawn up showing the areas of high and low resistance which sometimes trace out the sunken shapes of buried foundations or other remains of archaeological significance.

35. Herman, *op. cit.* (note 27), p. 5.

36. "Van Cortlandt mansion." *Harper's Weekly* XXVIII, no. 1451 (October 11, 1884), p. 665.

37. Reginald Pelham Bolton, *Indian Life of Long Ago in the City of New York*. Harmony Books, New York, 1972, pp. 136, 141.

38. "Van Cortlandt mansion," *op. cit.* (note 36), p. 666.

39. Illustrated in: David S. Howard, *New York and the China Trade*. The New-York Historical Society, New York, 1984; Jean McClure Mudge, *Chinese Export Porcelain in North America*. Clarkson N. Potter, Inc., New York, 1986, pp. 162–163. The Willow pattern emerged out of Chinese traditional motifs, but the exact design originated in the early 19th century based upon elements popularized in the late 18th century by Thomas Minton in Staffordshire, England. One of the most fashionable patterns of Victorian times, it comprised three figures crossing a three-arched bridge in the direction of a pagoda and pavilion. A willow tree overhangs the bridge, and a zig-zag fence appears in the foreground. Chinese artisans eventually copied this western invention to capitalize on its marketability and perhaps concocted a legend—of which there are several versions—to explain the scene.

40. Ivor Noël Hume, *A Guide to Artifacts of Colonial America*. Alfred A. Knopf, New York, 1969, p. 130.

41. Howard, *op. cit.* (note 39); Jean Gordon Lee, *Philadelphians and the China Trade, 1784–1844*. Philadelphia Museum of Art, Philadelphia, 1984, p. 109; Bert Salwen and Rebecca Yamin, "The Archaeology and History of Six 19th Century Lots: Sullivan Street, Greenwich Village, New York City." Typescript on file, New York City Archives, 1990, p. V-1.

42. Mudge, *op. cit.* (note 39), pp. 162–163.

43. Noël Hume, *op. cit.* (note 40), p. 130; Geoffrey A. Godden, *An Illustrated Encyclopedia of British Pottery and Porcelain*. Magna Books, Wigston, Leicester, England, 1992, p. 4; A.W. Coysh and R.K. Henrywood, *The Dictionary of Blue and White Printed Pottery, 1780–1880*, Volume I. Antique Collectors' Club, Woodbridge, Suffolk, England, 1982, p. 402; *The Dictionary of Blue and White Printed Pottery, 1780–1880*, Volume II. Antique Collectors' Club, Woodbridge, Suffolk, England, 1989, pp. 211–212.

44. Noël Hume, *op. cit.* (note 40), p. 130; Salwen and Yamin, *op. cit.* (note 41), p. V-2.

45. George Miller, "Nineteenth century lists of cups from jobber's invoices." Unpublished listing table, 1994; Paul A. Shackel, *Personal Discipline and Material Culture—An Archaeology of Annapolis, Maryland, 1695–1870*. University of Tennessee Press, Knoxville, 1993, p. 112.

46. Salwen and Yamin, *op. cit.* (note 41), p. V-35.

47. Joan H. Geismar, "History and Archaeology of the Greenwich Mews Site, Greenwich Village, New York." Submitted to Greenwich Mews Associates. Copy on file, New York City Archives, 1989, pp. 73–94.

48. Jonathan Rickard, "Mocha ware: Slip-decorated refined earthenware." *The Magazine Antiques*

CXLIV, no. 2 (August 1993): 182–190.

49. George Miller, "Classification and economic scaling of 19th century ceramics." *Historical Archaeology* 14 (1980): 1–40; Rickard, *op. cit.* (note 48), pp. 182–190.

50. Sarah Peabody Turnbaugh, ed., *Domestic Pottery of the Northeastern United States, 1625–1850*. Academic Press, Orlando, Florida, 1985, pp. 209–229; William C. Ketchum, Jr., *American Country Pottery*. Alfred A. Knopf, New York, 1987, pp. 3–12; William C. Ketchum, Jr., *American Redware*. Henry Holt & Company, New York, 1991, pp. 15–45.

51. Olive R. Jones and Catherine Sullivan, *The Parks Canada Glass Glossary*. Canada Parks Service, Ottawa, Ontario, 1985, pp. 26–31.

52. *Ibid.*, p. 22.

53. Jean E. Howson, "The archaeology of nineteenth-century health and hygiene at the Sullivan Street Site, New York City." *Northeast Historical Archaeology* 21–22 (1992–93):137–160.

54. Cf. Diana diZerega Wall, *The Archaeology of Gender*. Plenum Press, New York, 1994.

55. Howson, *op. cit.* (note 53), p. 153.

Seventeen years excavating at Rose Hill Manor, Fordham University

Allan S. Gilbert
Roger Wines

In September of 1985, the first spadeful of earth was turned in the name of archaeology on Fordham University's Rose Hill campus. Pursued without fanfare but guided by great expectations, the act marked the start of a project designed to expose the buried remains of the Rose Hill manor, then believed to be Fordham's oldest building and one of the earliest colonial farmhouses of the central Bronx. Digging concluded in 2002, and now a general review of the investigation is in order to report on some of the details that have been revealed about the people and events connected with Rose Hill's past. After a description of the project's beginnings and what was initially known about the manor's form and occupational history, the reader will learn how archaeology, coupled with a fresh evaluation of the documentary evidence, has yielded new information to modify and substantially augment the traditionally accepted knowledge about Rose Hill. The account of the excavations takes a narrative form to illustrate something of the process of archaeological fieldwork, and in so doing, it also touches upon a few of the still unresolved problems that are the focus of continuing study.

THE ROSE HILL MANOR PROJECT

Exploration of the Rose Hill manor was planned in 1984 with two main objectives: applied teaching and historical research. As a teaching dig, the excavation would give Fordham College students an opportunity to study field methods under professional direction at the university's own historic site.[1] As a research project, it provided a means to illuminate through buried finds as well as written evidence the still dark areas of our knowledge about old Fordham and the history of the central Bronx. It also offered a chance to correct some of the "handed-down" local history that seemed less reliable at the end of the 20th century than it had when first set down in writing at the end of the 19th. Both an innovative educational experiment and a backyard historical self-study, the enterprise linked curriculum and research in a way that allowed its largely student participants to learn about the process of archaeological inquiry while pursuing a small part of that inquiry themselves.

At its start, the excavation was projected to last only a few years. After the old manor house was demolished in 1896, the site endured nearly a century of disturbances caused by construction, landscaping, and trenching for utilities. There was little basis for optimism about the extent of the manor's survival, and a campaign of short duration was presumed sufficient for the investigation. Though the manor's below ground remains did suffer some deterioration, they proved nevertheless to be extensive and very much intact, revealing layers of extraordinary complexity, foundation walls extending downward over six feet in places, and a considerable amount of information related to the minutia of everyday life in the past. Many of the archaeological findings described in the following pages may seem commonplace, but events too banal to have left a written record are among the most valuable historical gifts archaeology has to offer. Such discoveries afford a rare and intimate view of how things appeared in former ages as well as how they changed over the centuries. History is thereby personalized and its impact made more immediate and memorable.

Within the first few seasons of exploration, the magnitude of the site's buried information, as well as its challenges, became apparent. Fieldwork settled into a slow and controlled pace so that mistakes were avoided, and the full benefit of such archaeological detail was neither lost to the research effort nor denied to the educational exercise. In this way, 17 cohorts of Fordham students—and outside volunteers who eschewed more exotic locales for the ruins of early New York—have, to an extent that could not initially have been foreseen, mastered the rudiments of archaeological technique at Rose Hill.

THE ROSE HILL MANOR IN HISTORY

The first history of Rose Hill was compiled in 1891 by Thomas Gaffney Taaffe[2] to celebrate the 50th anniversary of St. John's College, the small New York Catholic school that would be rechartered in 1907 as Fordham University. Taaffe was an 1890 graduate of St. John's and had been editor-in-chief of the *Fordham Monthly*, the school's literary review, in his senior year.[3]

In about 1904, an account of the college was assembled by Rev. Patrick J. Cormican, S.J.,[4] a faculty member who gleaned from the older generation of Jesuit fathers of his day details relating to the college presidents and their official activities, the campus buildings, school organizations, and other administrators and benefactors. Cormican's text was never published, however, and the manuscript remains in Fordham University's archives in Walsh Family Library.

In 1939, noteworthy particulars excerpted from Taaffe's and Cormican's narratives were inscribed upon a commemorative bronze plaque affixed to a

Figure 1. Bronze plaque mounted on a granite boulder at the site of the Rose Hill manor.

granite boulder (Figure 1) at the site of the manor by Fordham's 25th president, Rev. Robert I. Gannon, S.J.[5] The information relating to early Fordham was then carried over with little alteration into Gannon's updated history of the university, which appeared in 1967.[6]

Despite the careful record keeping of Rev. Joseph Zwinge, S.J., Father Minister to the college at the time of Taaffe's research, the scholarship that gave rise to Taaffe's book was based upon a fairly cursory review of the relevant documents. Cormican reported that Taaffe was given a mere seven weeks to prepare a text for the printer.[7] Unverified assumptions led to inaccuracies, some of which were later memorialized in bronze, where they may still be counted upon to misinform visitors today. At the start of the Rose Hill manor project, therefore, retracing of available sources and careful re-examination of texts enabled a more reliable occupational history to take shape.[8] The discovery of new historical documents continues with the "excavation" of new archival collections and the sharing of information with other researchers, especially descendant genealogists of the principal families that formerly occupied the property. The sequence of ownership and uses of the manor house as it has been reconstructed from deeds, wills, and other records now appears as follows.

Fordham Manor

The Rose Hill campus of Fordham University was originally part of the Manor of Fordham, a 3,900 acre tract of the present central Bronx that, in 1671, became the first manorial patent granted by the British provincial government of New York.[9] In 1678, the Lord of the Manor, John Archer, sold into private hands several properties to raise cash. The sale included a 102-acre farm on "the great plain by the Bronx River," which was deeded to Roger Barton, an Englishman from the Town of Westchester. The designation "great plain" referred to the flatlands west of the river and south of the present New York Botanical Garden. The deed makes no mention of a house or improvements on Barton's land, however, the immediately adjacent farm of 103 acres contained a "dwelling house and other buildings, orchard, fencing, etc." Archer sold this improved farm at the same time to Thomas Statham.[10]

During the early 1680s, the Town of Westchester laid legal claim to the eastern parts of Fordham Manor.[11] Though Barton had acquired his farm by purchase from Archer, it lay within the disputed territory, and so Barton petitioned to secure his right of ownership from the new claimant as well. Court records of 1682 note that Westchester granted him land "where his now dwelling place is scituate on west bank of Brunxis River."[12] No information survives that relates anything about the appearance of Barton's house, but later deeds provide clues to its location.

When Archer died in early 1684, the unsold portion of Fordham Manor that remained under his lordship became the property of his creditor, Cornelis Steenwyck, one of the wealthiest men in the colony. But when Steenwyck died later that same year, the Manor passed to his widow, Margarieta, with a stipulation that it be deeded as an endowment to the Dutch Reformed Church.[13] The Church accepted the donation but did not assume proprietary status until after the litigation over ownership was finally resolved in 1693, and the Town of Westchester was denied its claim.[14]

The Michielsen and Corsa families, 1694–1787

After Barton's death (about 1688), Roger Barton, Jr. subdivided the property and, in 1694, sold the southern half to a Dutchman named Reyer Michielsen.[15] Michielsen had been a settler in Fordham Manor, and his father, Michiel Bastiensen, was one of the witnesses to Archer's manorial grant of 1671. The new Michielsen farm occupied essentially the core of the present university campus, and the deed contained no reference to a house. In 1704, and before moving to Eastchester, Barton sold the remaining northern half of his farm to William Davenport, Sr.[16] Davenport's deed specified that a house stood on the property, indicating that Barton's home was most likely built in the northern part of his farm. It was probably located somewhere near the eastern end of today's Bedford Park Blvd.

On the 1717 map of Fordham Manor commissioned by the Dutch Church and drawn up by Peter Berrien,[17] the separate boundaries of Davenport's and Michielsen's plots are recorded with Michielsen's right-of-way indicated, and the small stream flowing south across the west end of their farms (the Mill Brook in the 19th century) is labeled Reyer Michielsen's Brook[18] (Figure 2).

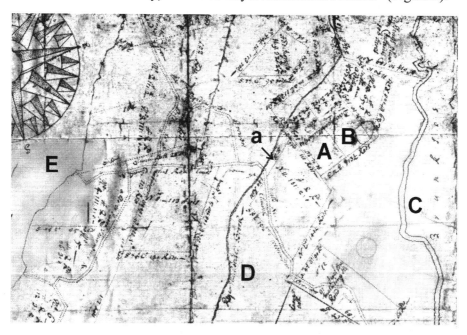

Figure 2. Detail of the map of Fordham Manor drawn up by Peter Berrien in 1717 showing the property boundaries of farms sold by Roger Barton to Reyer Michielsen and William Davenport, Sr., and the line of Reyer Michielsen's Brook. Key: A = Michielsen farm (a = right-of-way access); B = Davenport farm; C = Bronx River; D = Reyer Michielsen's Brook; E = Harlem River.

In his will of 1733, Michielsen stipulated that the farm should remain in operation until July 1, 1736, at which time it would be sold and the estate's worth apportioned among his heirs.[19] He passed away before the end of 1733, and after the sale date, Michielsen's son-in-law, Benjamin Corsa, took title to the property. A son of Dutch immigrants, Corsa had been a resident of New York when he was baptized in 1692, and he had married Michielsen's daughter, Jannetje, in 1718.[20] The couple's immediate post-marital residence is not established with certainty, but Corsa must have been in a position to purchase the estate from the other heirs, leading to his sole ownership from 1737.[21]

In 2003, Fordham University acquired through on line auction a water-color map of the Rose Hill campus (Figure 3). Written on its reverse side was a letter signed in January, 1841, that represents the latest possible dating for the map, which must have been drawn before the letter was penned and posted. Further investigation will be necessary before a detailed discussion of this oldest known plan of the campus can be published in full, but relevant to the issue concerning the Michielsen/Corsa domicile, it should be noted that the outline of a large structure, most likely a wood frame house, appears a short distance west of the Rose Hill manor and is identified on the drawing as the gardener's house. This building did not survive and must have been demolished when the Seminary of St. Joseph and Church of St. Mary were erected nearby in the mid-1840s. It was never documented in any later plans or drawings.

Over the course of its excavation, the Rose Hill manor yielded no artifactual material dating before the 1760s, and thus it became evident from the results of fieldwork that the manor was not likely the earliest house on the property. Acquisition of the watercolor map has provided a glimpse of the arrangement of earlier structures that were eliminated with the initial construc-tions of St. John's College. The gardener's house may have been the original Michielsen home and subsequently, the farmhouse of Benjamin Corsa.

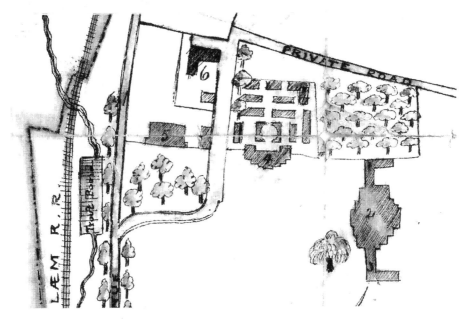

Figure 3. Detail of the 1841 watercolor showing the location of an earlier structure (no. 5) labeled "Gardner's House & Dairy" to the west of the Rose Hill manor (no. 4). This house, close to Reyer Michielsen's Brook and just south of the barns (no. 6), might have been the original Michielsen farmhouse. Courtesy of the Fordham University Archives.

In 1743, the Dutch Church offered Corsa additional land to the east in exchange for his common rights to other areas of Fordham Manor.[22] This new property extended his holdings as far as the Bronx River. He then bought another parcel of land, the location of which is unknown, in 1764. In 1766, he borrowed a sum of money from Robert Watts, a young lawyer and merchant from a well-to-do family of New York.[23] Construction of a second house may have been underwritten by this loan, as the farm was probably occupied by several of his children and their families at the time. It would appear that this second dwelling became the Rose Hill manor after the Revolution, and a 1760s date fits with the earliest ceramic evidence recovered archaeologically.

When Corsa died in 1770,[24] the farm passed to his son, Isaac, who faced the grim prospect of maneuvering his affairs through the turbulent times of the Revolution. Isaac Corsa supported the Crown and served in the local militia. Captured by a French and American raiding party, he endured 15 months of imprisonment before his release was arranged by exchange.[25] The location of the Corsa home is clearly labeled "Cusser" on a 1781 British field map from General Henry Clinton's headquarters[26] (Figure 4). The map was drafted to provide topographic details of southern Westchester as well as the distribution of

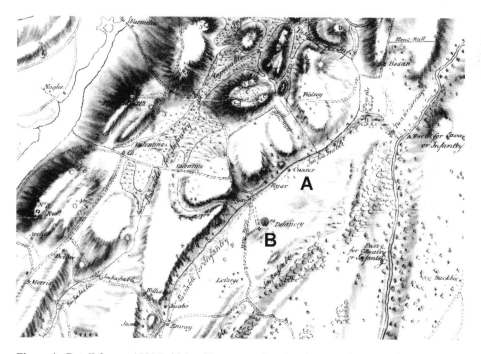

Figure 4. Detail from a 1781 British military map showing the central western Bronx and the location of the Corsa farmstead. Key: A = Corsa ("Cusser") farm; B = Union Hill farm operated by the Delancey family. Courtesy of the William L. Clements Library, University of Michigan.

farmsteads from which British troops might obtain supplies. Isaac's choice of the losing side led eventually to his being branded a traitor at the conclusion of the war, and he was forced to flee the new republic in 1783. Records indicate that he applied to the Loyalist Claims Commission in Nova Scotia for restitution of lost property, but the claim was dismissed when he failed to appear for his hearing.[27] Recent research by Marian Elder and Gale Corson suggests that Isaac Corsa eventually moved with his son, John Corsen, to New Brunswick, where their descendants still reside, as confirmed by DNA evidence. Isaac died "an old soldier of the Crown" around 1840.[28]

Isaac Corsa's son, Andrew, remained true to the American cause and even served the rebellion as one of the Westchester Guides.[29] Despite his patriotism, however, he was unable to retain the farm after his father's departure. In 1786, Robert Watts, the Corsa family creditor, sued for non-payment of his loan, and the next year, the estate was sold for debts.

The Watts family, 1787–1823

The legal particulars of the sale of the Corsa farm were handled by Robert's brother, John Watts, Jr., a prominent lawyer who had been the last colonial recorder of New York City under Governor William Tryon. John, Jr. eventually acquired the property himself, then transferred the title to his brother Robert's name. Robert then converted the old Dutch farm into a gentleman's country estate, and, just as his father, John Watts, Sr., had done with his own country house in Manhattan, Robert christened it "Rose Hill" after the Watts family's ancestral home in Edinburgh, Scotland. Robert then settled into the manor with his wife, the former Lady Mary Alexander, daughter of General William Alexander, Lord Stirling. For much of the rest of his life, Robert occupied himself with the management of his father's business interests and properties, left to him in 1775 when hostile mobs forced his Loyalist father to flee to England.[30]

Robert Watts died in 1814, and the estate passed to his son, Robert, Jr., who was at the time occupying the nearby Union Hill farm with his wife of three years, the former Matilda Sherborne Ridley of Livingston Manor. Union Hill bordered Rose Hill on the south (B on Figure 4). It had been a country home belonging to the Delancey family, and when Robert, Jr. moved in, he renamed the place "Sherborne" in acknowledgment of his wife's ancestry. Upon his father's death, Robert, Jr. rented out Sherborne, and the couple moved to Rose Hill with their first son.[31] They remained at Rose Hill until 1823.

In 1995, the project directors became aware of the existence of a water-color painting (see below Figure 42, p. 92) of the manor entitled "Rose Hill"[32] by the Scottish-American artist Archibald Robertson (1765–1835). An inscription on the back of the work dates it to 1815, which would make it the earliest known view of the house and its grounds. Presumably, Robertson was commissioned by the Wattses to create a formal record at the accession of young Robert, and it is almost certainly Robert and Matilda who are pictured standing in the broad field before their manor house.

Purchase of Rose Hill by the New York Diocese

With the departure of the Watts family in 1823, Rose Hill passed through eight successive deed transfers[33] until 1839, when the co-adjutor bishop of New York and later Archbishop, Rev. John Hughes (Figure 5), bought it for use by the Diocese. Once again, Rose Hill was transformed, this time from country estate to Catholic seminary and boys' college. When St. John's College opened its doors in 1841, its physical plant included buildings left by the Wattses and subsequent deed holders such as Horatio Shepheard Moat, an English physician and herbalist from Brooklyn. Dr. Moat had erected a new manor house in 1838, which survives today as the center hall of the university's administration building, Cunniffe House. The single story wings appended to Moat's original structure possessed classical columns and triangular pediments (Figure 6); these were replaced in 1869 by the existing two-story brick wings.

Figure 5. Rev. John Hughes, first archbishop of New York Diocese and founder of St. John's College.

The college soon added its own facilities. William Rodrigue, Hughes's brother-in-law, served as Professor of Drawing, Penmanship, and Civil Engineering, yet he also took on the role of architect, designing and building the college church (now university church) and the seminary building (now St. John's Hall dormitory) in 1844–45. He and his family lived in a small cottage (currently called Alumni House, or "Rodrigue's"), which had been previously built in 1840 (Figure 7; no. 9). Rodrigue also expanded the main college building (Moat's mansion) by adding large brick extensions on the east side to create a monumental complex in the shape of an "E." The

Figure 6. View of the St. John's College campus in the 1840s from a late 19th century engraving by Weldon McKeon that was based on an original drawing of 1845 by William Rodrigue.[34] The engraving first appeared in the St. John's College catalogue of 1876. Key: 1 = St. John's College buildings (Moat's mansion); 2 = Rose Hill manor; 3 = Seminary of St. Joseph. Courtesy of the Fordham University Archives.

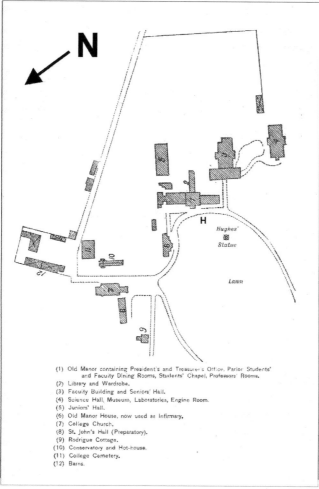

(1) Old Manor containing President's and Treasurer's Office, Parlor, Students'
    and Faculty Dining Rooms, Students' Chapel, Professors' Rooms.
(2) Library and Wardrobe.
(3) Faculty Building and Seniors' Hall.
(4) Science Hall, Museum, Laboratories, Engine Room.
(5) Juniors' Hall.
(6) Old Manor House, now used as Infirmary.
(7) College Church.
(8) St. John's Hall (Preparatory).
(9) Rodrigue Cottage.
(10) Conservatory and Hot-house.
(11) College Cemetery.
(12) Barns.

Figure 7. Plan of the Rose Hill campus in 1891 from Taaffe's history of St. John's College.
Current building names have changed from the original: (1) the second Rose Hill manor of Horatio
Moat with brick wings added in 1869–1870 [now the University's administration building,
Cunniffe House], (2) library and wardrobe; remaining one of three wings built at the college's
inception [all demolished], (3) Faculty Building and Seniors' Hall [now Dealy Hall], (4) Science
Hall and power plant [now Thebaud Hall], (5) Juniors' Hall [now Hughes Hall], (6) the old Rose
Hill manor and Infirmary [demolished in 1896 and recently excavated] with the small college ice
house immediately to its east [demolished], (7) College Church [enlarged in 1928, now the
University Church], (8) old Seminary Building [now St. John's Hall], (9) Rodrigue Cottage [now
Alumni House/"Rodrigue's"], (10) greenhouse [demolished], (11) College Cemetery [moved in
1890 from its original site in the New York Botanical Garden and used in its present location until
1909], (12) barns [demolished, present site of tennis courts]. Since 1949, the Hughes statue has
stood at the spot marked H.

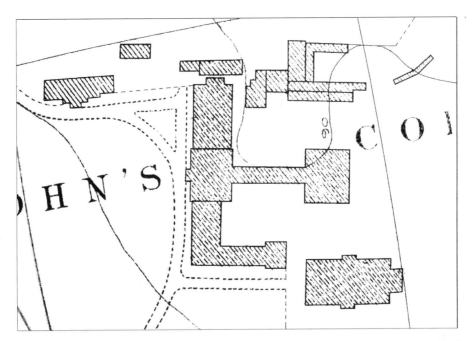

Figure 8. Plan of the St. John's College buildings taken from the Parks Department topographical map of 1873 showing the eastern extensions built by William Rodrigue in the 1840s.

1873 survey map of the Parks Department[35] shows this building configuration clearly (Figure 8). Part of the central extension can still be seen in Taaffe's 1891 plan (Figure 7; no. 2).

    Several sources provide notes on the manor's uses during the 19th century. The college first housed female servants there, together with some Sisters of Charity who handled domestic affairs.[36] The sisters managed the infirmary, wardrobe, refectory, and kitchen, and also assumed responsibilities for the youngest boys. The northern and western sides of the house had broad, shady verandas where tranquil relaxation could be taken by the sisters and the sick in their charge.[37]

    In 1845, Hughes sold the college to a group of Kentucky Jesuits, who moved to New York to resume their educational efforts in a new and promising location. The Jesuits arrived in 1846, and the formal handover took place after the July commencement of that year. With this administrative change, the manor continued as an infirmary staffed by Jesuit brothers but also as a domicile for scholastic novices, an arrangement that lasted until 1850, when the novices were sent to the Jesuit theological school in Montreal, Canada. To serve the infirmary and the nearby kitchen, an ice house was constructed a short distance to the northeast of the manor during the early 1850s (this ice house can be seen near the manor in the plans of Figures 7 and 8).[38]

In late 1855 or early 1856, major renovations were made to accommodate the Jesuit scholastics who were obliged to leave the seminary when Hughes's mounting disagreements with St. John's College caused a rift.[39] During this construction episode, a basement was excavated beneath the center hall to serve as a theologate (see below pp. 103ff. for the archaeological evidence of these renovations). The infirmary occupied much of the eastern part on the first floor,[40] and later, the manor also contained residences for several brothers. In October of 1891, the infirmary was moved to the second floor in the south wing of the administration building (now Cunniffe House),[41] where it remained until the 1960s. That same autumn of 1891, the brothers moved with the rest of the priestly community to the Senior Building (now Dealy Hall).[42] Prior to demolition in 1896, the cellar held a dairy, while the house above contained music rooms, workshops, workmen's quarters, and a paint shop.[43]

Despite significant improvements made by St. John's College to the old manor, its age and mounting maintenance costs became a cause for concern. Taaffe indicated that, despite "constant and costly repairs," the roof was "sagging in places and threatening to cave in."[44] Declaring the building not worth further repair, the Jesuit consultors finally recommended to the college president on April 30, 1895 that it be leveled.[45] The next year, Rev. Thomas J. Campbell, S.J., assumed the presidency and ordered the old house razed.[46] Cormican added that the manor's "unsoundness" was said to have been confined largely to its exterior, and that the wood of the interior was so well jointed and hard "that it had to be hewn to pieces."[47] Some of the wood was even cannibalized for use in a new ice house built to the south of present Dealy Hall.

Six years later, in 1902, construction began on Collins Auditorium, excavation for which destroyed much of the rear of the manor's buried foundations. In another five years, St. John's College was rechartered as Fordham University.

Returning to the commemorative bronze plaque, the text, cast all in upper case, should now be correctively annotated as follows.

1839   (Seal of University)   1939

ON THIS SITE STOOD THE FIRST ROSE HILL MANOR –
BUILT FOR THE CORSA FAMILY BEFORE 1692.

The manor was probably built by Benjamin Corsa during the 1760s. The structure labeled gardener's house on the 1841 campus plan is more likely to have been the first house on the property, possibly erected by Reyer Michielsen as early as 1694 when he purchased the farm from Roger Barton. Benjamin Corsa married into Michielsen's family in 1718 and could have resided in the earlier house prior to Michielsen's death, but he and his wife Jannetje likely lived there after he took over ownership of the property in 1737. Corsa may have put up a new house about 300 feet to the east using all or part of the Watts loan of 1766. This second house later became the Rose Hill manor. The plaque is correct about the house being the first Rose Hill manor, as Robert Watts gave it that name only after the Revolution. The third dwelling constructed was the stone house built by Horatio Moat in 1838. The first structure, or gardener's house, was probably demolished in the mid-1840s.

> - AT THE OUTBREAK OF THE REVOLUTION IT WAS OCCUPIED BY ROBERT WATTS WHO MARRIED LADY MARY ALEXANDER DAUGHTER OF LORD STIRLING A MAJOR-GENERAL UNDER WASHINGTON

Isaac Corsa occupied the manor during the Revolution and was forced to flee afterwards in 1783. Robert Watts had married Lord Stirling's daughter at Stirling's estate in Basking Ridge, New Jersey, on February 4, 1775,[48] but to the general's dismay, the newlyweds remained in British occupied New York City throughout most of the war.[49] To leave the city, they took a two year lease in 1780 on the Kingsbridge Heights farm of Mrs. Janet Montgomery, widow of the American Brigadier General Richard Montgomery, who was killed in the 1775 invasion of Canada.[50] They subsequently rented the Union Hill farm. Robert Watts assumed ownership of his newly christened Rose Hill estate only in 1787, six years after hostilities had ceased.

> AND TRADITION HAS IT THAT THE MANOR WAS STAFF HEADQUARTERS FOR THE CONTINENTAL ARMY.

On August 22, 1776, prior to the Battle of White Plains, Washington quartered a detachment of the Continental Army in Corsa's orchard.[51] His headquarters at the time were in the Roger Morris/Jumel mansion in Manhattan, but he may have visited the troop encampment. According to Andrew Corsa, Washington and the French general Rochambeau, commander-in-chief of the French Expeditionary Force, rode up to the manor's front gate at Mill Brook and Kingsbridge Road nearly five years later with a detachment of troops to pick up young Andrew, who as the youngest of the famous Westchester Guides, helped the party navigate about the Bronx during their reconnoitering of British lines during the Grand Reconnaissance of July 22–23, 1781.[52] Corsa reported that, on both nights of the maneuvers, the rebel army encamped on the high ground near the Valentine farm, west of Rose Hill.[53] No other direct mention of the manor has been found in any other documentary context related to the wartime activity of the Continental Army or General Washington.

> - IT IS ALSO SAID TO HAVE BEEN SELECTED BY JAMES FENIMORE COOPER AS THE SETTING FOR "THE SPY."

This is not certain, though Robert Bolton connects some events of the novel with the valley of the Mill Brook.[54] No further information suggests that the Rose Hill manor was more intimately involved in the story.[55]

> - PURCHASED FOR A FUTURE COLLEGE BY THE MOST REVEREND JOHN HUGHES IN 1839. IT WAS SOLD TO THE SOCIETY OF JESUS IN 1846 AND DEMOLISHED IN 1896.
>
> THIS PLAQUE WAS PRESENTED BY THE CLASS OF 1942 ON APRIL 30, 1939 TO MARK THE CENTENARY OF THE BISHOP'S FIRST STEP IN THE FOUNDING OF FORDHAM.
>
> A.   M.   D.   G.

This final part of the inscription is accurate. It was doubtless mere coincidence that the dedication of the boulder marking the site of the manor took place 44 years to the day after the consultors' decision to demolish it.

THE HOUSE

The Rose Hill manor faced southwest onto Fordham's oval drive. The main college buildings (Moat's mansion and its extensions) were adjacent on the east, and the college church was set back from the drive to the northwest. Late 19th century real estate atlases indicate that the house was a wood frame structure comprising a center hall with adjoining east and west wings. One insurance map rendered the manor in ground plan, showing that porches were built onto the ends of both wings as well as the rear of the center hall (Figure 9).[56] Apparently, the outer edge of the center hall's back porch was aligned with the rear walls of both wings, but as the construction of Collins Hall has completely destroyed this area, only documentary evidence presently illuminates the manor's rear appointments. The orientation and configuration of the building vary somewhat from atlas to atlas, indicating that the private grounds of St. John's College were not carefully mapped to scale by the surveyors. The topographic survey drawn by the Commissioners of Public Parks in 1873[57] is probably the most accurate map of the college and its surroundings (Figure 8).

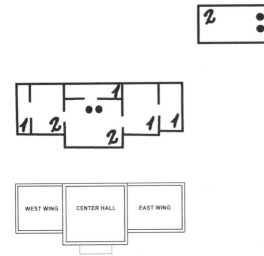

Figure 9. Redrawn plan of the Rose Hill manor and adjacent ice house from the insurance map of the 24th Ward of New York City dating to 1896; the manor ground plan shows the location of single-story porches at the ends of the east and west wings and in the rear, but both wings originally were one and one-half stories, not two or one.

Figure 10. Outlines of the Rose Hill manor based on dimensions recorded by Fr Joseph Zwinge, S.J., in 1894.

In 1894, Fr. Zwinge assembled a sketchbook of campus plans with the location of buried utilities. This small tome, preserved in the university archives, included on one page a simple ground plan of the manor with dimensions in feet.[58] Before excavations began, these maps, together with three photographs of the front facade also contained within the archives, conveyed most of the evidence about the manor's form and detailing just prior to its demolition.

On his sketch plan of the manor, Fr. Zwinge noted a length of 36 feet for the center hall, 32 feet for the east wing, and 26 feet for the west wing, while the front to back width for both wings was 27 feet. Excavations have confirmed Zwinge's east wing measurements and revealed the center hall width to be 33 feet. The manor's complete footprint therefore covered an area of 2,750 square feet during its college years (Figure 10), and it conforms proportionally to the 1896 insurance plan rendering almost exactly.

The photographs show a center hall of two-story frame construction with end gables (Figure 11). Both eastern and western wings were of one and a half stories, and both were set back about six feet from the center hall facade. The entire exterior was clapboarded in white. At the moment of demolition, the manor's low pitched roof was covered by interlocking galvanized steel shingles, dozens of which were recovered from the ruins. One of the photographs suggests that the house was roofed with wooden shingles (Figure 44), and thus this image may have been obtained prior to the installation of the metal ones in 1889.[59] Two rectangular brick chimneys with corniced tops rose above the roof ridge at each

Figure 11. One of three surviving photographs of the Rose Hill manor, viewed from the southeast shortly before demolition, probably taken between 1889 and 1896. Courtesy of the Fordham University Archives.

end of the center hall, and hundreds of brick fragments discovered where they had fallen among the foundations reveal average brick dimensions of about 8x4x2 inches, a canon typical of 18th century manufacture.

On the front facade of the center hall, four single windows spanned the second story, each containing movable double hung sashes glazed with eight rectangular panes held within wooden muntins. The three windows on the lower floor were larger in size and each contained two six-pane sashes. Both wings comprised a full lower floor illuminated on the front by two windows, as well as an upper half story with sloped ceilings under the eaves illuminated by a single, centrally placed, dormer window. All windows in the wings were glazed with six-pane sashes. The approach to the entrance led up several steps from road level to a small wooden porch covered by a flat canopy supported on slender poles. The porch was painted brown as was all the window trim.[60] In two of the photographs, two adjacent doors are just discernable within the shadow cast by the canopy (Figure 12). These two doors probably reflect a subdivision of the manor interior, most likely to isolate the infirmary on the eastern side from the living quarters on the west and upper floor. A late 19th century reference to the infirmary mused about the charm of "its uneven floors, its low ceilings, its narrow passages and cubby holes of rooms."[61]

Figure 12. Detail from the second of three surviving photographs of the Rose Hill manor showing two adjacent doorways beneath the canopy of the front entrance. Courtesy of the Fordham University Archives.

Excavated exposures have showed that the foundations were rubble walls of fieldstone, and the stucco that covered this masonry still adhered in places. The photographs reveal crawlspace openings in the foundations below each of the first floor windows (Figures 11 and 12). These gaps allowed air to circulate beneath the building to keep the wooden floor beams dry. Sills at the crawlspace openings and a few support points along the tops of the foundations were built of brick.

It had initially been thought, based upon Taaffe's comments,[62] that the wings were added to the old manor by the college, probably by William Rodrigue while he was building the church and seminary in 1845–46. No documentation directly confirmed the matter, but once digging had begun, the notion gained respectability because the east wing's yellowish and grayish mortars suggested a more industrial technology of hydraulic lime or natural cement. When the "Rose Hill" watercolor was examined for the first time in 1995, however, it became clear that the manor of Robert Watts, Jr., already had two wings of one and one-half stories that were similar to those in the St. John's College photographs (Figures 11 and 44). The house had therefore attained its winged form by 1815. In historical archaeology, documentary evidence often plays a crucial role in dating and attribution. In this instance, building materials were insufficiently diagnostic to assign the wing construction to the Wattses, and in all excavated areas, substantial modifications to the grounds immediately surrounding the house had destroyed the pattern of buried artifacts, leaving no clear indication of original construction dates.

Excavation began with some technical assistance. Given the numerous real estate atlases, photographs, and written descriptions of the manor, its location was never in doubt. The uncertain spatial relationships between campus buildings depicted on surviving maps, however, made it impossible to establish an exact position by triangulating from structures still standing. Instead of probing for buried walls in small test pits, a ground-penetrating radar survey was conducted on January 15, 1985.[63] A radar antenna—somewhat like a lawn-mower in appearance (Figure 13)—was slowly pulled across the site surface in parallel transects two and a half feet apart. Microwaves transmitted into the ground reflected off subsurface irregularities, and the echoes, when plotted, traced out the rear corner of the east wing. With this corner located, a site grid was laid down to obtain maximum exposure of the wing remains.

The dimensions recorded by Fr. Zwinge were later used to map out the former extent of the building on the modern ground surface based on the established corner point. As a result, the location of every part

Figure 13. Dr. Bruce W. Bevan of Geosight, Inc. conducting a ground-penetrating radar survey of the manor site in January of 1985.

of the foundations was known very shortly after the start of digging. Figure 15 (p. 60) shows Zwinge's plan of the manor, drawn where its remains lie beneath modern Collins Hall and its monumental stairway, with the excavation units (trenches) and the major remains to be described later in the text indicated.

THE EXCAVATIONS

A full narrative of the 17 years of fieldwork at Rose Hill must await complete publication of the project. Here, a series of vignettes is offered describing various episodes during the course of the excavations that illustrate the challenges of field exploration and the complexities involved in making sense of the recovered finds. Such discussions are rare in popular archaeology publications, but they illuminate aspects of life at the manor while simultaneously demonstrating how the evidence was uncovered and interpreted.

Ground breaking during the first field season of fall, 1985, initially followed the evidence obtained from the radar survey. Excavation units were opened directly over the rear corner of the east wing. Digging proceeded slowly, and by December, the corner emerged from its 89 year burial some 15 inches below the lawn. In summer of 1986, digging began within a new unit positioned over the diagonally opposite corner of the wing, the spot having been determined using Fr. Zwinge's dimensions. When this spot—where the front facade of the east wing abutted onto the center hall—was eventually exposed in fall of 1987, the junction was a mere three inches from the point calculated for it. Again, the accuracy of Zwinge's numbers was confirmed. Unfortunately, the wing and center hall exposures could not be joined because the sanitary sewer serving the university's Faber Hall (built 1959–60) was laid north-south through the middle of the wing, effectively cutting the manor deposits in two.

The depth of soil covering the manor varied. Close to Collins Hall, the ruins of the center hall were submerged more than four feet below an earthen embankment. Beyond the embankment, most of the east wing rested beneath a layer of grass and topsoil approximately 15 to 18 inches thick.

Though the total excavated area was limited, the deposits proved to be remarkably complex. In all places investigated, the uppermost preserved remains were obscured by jumbled debris from the moment of demolition. The tedious removal of only the tumbled stones eventually revealed the former ground surface and permitted a reconstruction of the manor's surroundings as they appeared at the end of the 19th century. Deeper penetration into the site showed that the lawn of today is perched high above several previous land surfaces. It lies two and a half feet above the 1896 level but nearly six feet above the soil layer that witnessed the first colonial settlement. This rapid rise in elevation may have been due largely to frequent landscaping with clean fill.

In places, trenching by the college and university during the late 19th and 20th centuries to lay utility lines disturbed the near-surface strata, making interpretation difficult. To understand the sequence of construction episodes, the project turned to a variety of scientific methods—such as chemical, mortar, and stone analyses—to help differentiate walls and associate parts of the structure that were erected during the same building operation. These techniques, together with the information obtained from historical documentation, permitted the separation of different building phases.

Figure 14. Students covering the wooden framework with a protective blue vinyl tarpaulin at the close of an excavation session.

During the project, none of the fragile remains exposed by digging could be left open to the elements. To prevent the crumbly mortars from disintegrating under the impact of rain, wind, and changing temperatures, the entire site was protected under blue vinyl tarpaulins supported on a lumber framework (Figure 14). Each excavation session began with the removal, and ended with the replacement, of a complicated array of struts, rafters, and plastic fabric, a task that became more laborious as the excavated area expanded.

Greater care was required in late November of each year to prepare the site for the four month winter hiatus. Exposed foundations were annually insulated with straw-filled plastic garbage bags to avoid irreparable damage from frost fracturing. Had these efforts not been applied consistently over the years, the subtle details that have yielded so much of the lost history of Rose Hill and its inhabitants would have been obliterated.

Over 17 years of digging, the sides of the excavation became severely weathered by seasonal temperature changes and alternate drying and wetting due to variations in ground water flow. These eroded sections were steeply sloped and fragile, and they looked nothing like the perfectly vertical and freshly trimmed sections of sites excavated over much shorter intervals. When sections were recorded at Rose Hill, they were indeed trimmed straight, drawn, and

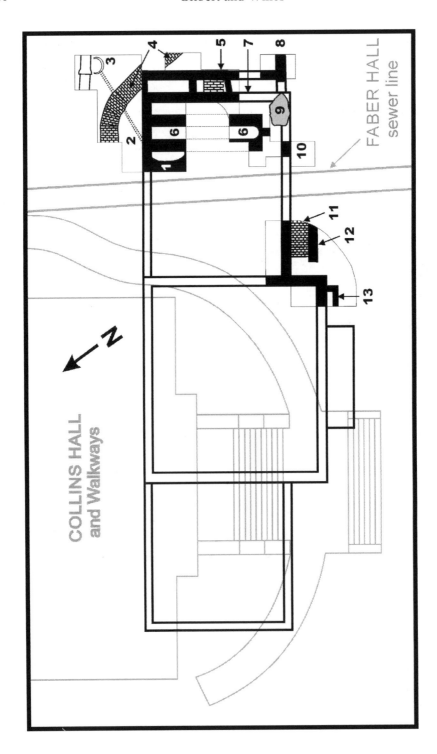

Figure 15. (Facing page) Schematic plan of the Rose Hill manor showing areas excavated, context of the buried remains, and the locations of structures mentioned in the text: (1) stone cistern, (2) conduit trench, (3) overflow barrel, (4) brick path, (5) end wall of Watts wing, (6) brick trough cistern, (7) foundation wall of 1855–56 porch, (8) stone yard wall, (9) commemorative boulder, (10) rebuilt foundations at the southern end of the brick cistern, (11) brick drywell, (12) retaining wall, (13) coal bin. Exposed walls are in solid black; modern facilities are rendered in gray.

photographed, but they could not be kept neat over the full duration of digging. Constant section maintenance would have wasted precious labor while steadily expanding the units beyond what could be easily covered and protected.

The college trash dump

In the summer of 1986, fieldwork at the manor site was interrupted by major construction on two new dormitories at the western end of the Rose Hill campus. The construction site had formerly been a dumping ground for St. John's College until the area was leveled and converted into terraced gardens in 1887 by Rev. Thomas J. Campbell, S.J., the 13th college president.[64] As foundations for the new buildings were being prepared, contractors permitted archaeological monitoring of the job site operations, and when the bulldozer uncovered several trash accumulations, time was allotted for sampling of their artifactual contents (Figure 16).

Figure 16. Salvage excavations, conducted while foundation work for the new Alumni Court North dormitory (now renamed Loschert Hall) was ongoing in June of 1986, uncovered trash accumulations that may have originally been heaps that were subsequently buried by later landscaping: (left) clearing of pit 1 immediately west of the university church, (right) flattened earthenware dishes in pit 2 to the northwest of pit 1 being removed by student Steven Wines (note the ashy soil with embedded coal in the foreground representing the fill of the pit).

Many pieces of ceramic tableware were retrieved from the dumps. Most specimens were of the earthenware variety commonly termed ironstone or white granite (Figure 17). Much ironstone was produced in England for export to North America, and it was popular from about 1840 until the end of the 19th century. Preserved makers' marks on the bottom of various dishes indicate that they were manufactured by many of the prominent English firms working in the industrial district of Staffordshire, including Davenport (1793–1887), T. & R. Boote (1842–1906), and Elsmore & Forster (1853–1871).[65]

Figure 17. Selection of white ironstone dishes recovered from the college trash: dinner plate by Wm Davenport of Longport, Staffordshire; saucer by John Maddock and Sons of Burslem, Staffordshire; handleless cup by an unknown manufacturer; and a condiment jar by Maling of Newcastle-upon-Tyne.

Figure 18. Base of an octagonal vessel from an English manufacturer bearing a registry mark dating to August 26, 1847.

A base fragment from an octagonal vessel (Figure 18), possibly produced by the manufacturer Cork & Edge (1846–1860), bore a stamped registry date of August 26, 1847. Registry stamps indicated the date on which a ceramic form had been legally patented to protect it from pattern infringement.[66] The protection lasted for a period of three years, and so the date stamp gives some indication when the piece in question was made. Other identifiable pieces were probably produced and used between the 1850s and 1870s, strongly suggesting that they represent some of the college's earliest dinnerware.[67]

The trash also yielded bottles that formerly held beverages and pharmaceutical preparations. Other discarded curiosities included personal grooming items, lead pencils, and various everyday objects, such as toothbrushes, dominoes, dice, buttons made of bone, and clay and glass marbles (Figure 19). Finds from the college trash provide a unique perspective on boarding school life in 19th century America.

Figure 19. A range of objects recovered from the St. John's College trash dumps; (upper left) beverage containers: (l. to r.) two wine/liquor bottles of green glass and a clear glass sarsaparilla bottle, the last distributed by Ayer's of Lowell, Massachusetts; (upper right) assorted pharmaceutical bottles, including patent medicines such as Dr. McMunn's Elixir of Opium (front row, extreme left), Ely Bros. Cream Balm (dark amber bottle in front row, right), Dr. August Koenig's Hamburger Tröpfen (front row, to the right of Ely Bros.), and Dr. Kilmer's Swamp Root Remedy (tall bottle in back row, extreme left); squat jar of clear glass in front row, third from left, contained Vaseline made by the Chesebrough Mfg Co.; (lower right) several pencil stubs made from extruded lead used to write on slates; (lower left) ceramic lids from shaving cream pots distributed by Philadelphia perfumer and cosmetics merchant Xavier Bazin.

The east wing

Excavation was initially focused on the end of the east wing, and by the close of the investigation, over 450 square feet were cleared. Cormican had suggested that modifications were made to the house by the college. Once the foundations were exposed, differences between the original structures and those added later showed he was correct. The most significant findings within this area have emerged from detailed examination of the cisterns, wall construction, window glass, and the late 19th century land surface.

The cisterns

Two cisterns built by two different owners were found within the foundations of the east wing; the earlier one was constructed of stone and the later one of brick.

The college cistern

As reported elsewhere,[68] the trough-shaped brick cistern was initially uncovered in 1987 (Figures 20 and 15:6). It was most informative about the building's plumbing and water containment system during the college period but also provided clues to understanding some of the modifications made to the wing. The cistern was exposed at its two ends; an unexcavated section was left in the middle. It ran across the wing from the rear wall in the north nearly to the front wall in the south. The interior was covered by a thin layer of smooth cementitious material, and the southern end was rounded with a metal drain opening into a large vitrified clay pipe. This drainage system led beneath the foundations and away from the house so the cistern could be emptied on its downhill end. The brick trough lay beneath the first floor, nestled between buttressing walls within the crawlspace, and its bottom rested a little over four feet below the modern ground surface. The trough measured about 2 feet 2 inches at its widest point, and the preserved height of the surviving brickwork gave it a depth of at least 3 feet. It could have held 1,000 gallons of water.

Small brick pillars were set about four feet apart on the trough's curved bottom (Figure 21), ostensibly to support outtake pipes (not recovered) that led most likely to manual pumps on the first floor. The support pillars insured that the pumps would not suck sediment through the pipes when the handles were cranked. The trough bottom was indeed blanketed by about two inches of sludge that had accumulated since the last periodic cleaning prior to demolition. Chemical assay of this sludge showed elevated levels of lead. Two samples, taken just above the floor of the trough, contained 1,538 and 1,629 parts per

Figure 20. Plan of the east wing showing location of the brick trough cistern (in cross-hatching).

Figure 21. Trough cistern of brick construction uncovered within the east wing crawlspace, showing brick pillars that probably supported outtake pipes for manual pumps on the floor above.

million: very substantial lead concentrations compared to natural soils, which rarely show levels in excess of 50 ppm in unpolluted, non-urbanized areas.

The source of the lead is still under investigation, but it is doubtless related to the plumbing system installed in the wing. With the advent of water closets in the 19th century, toilets could be flushed by gravity flow from attic reservoirs that were frequently fashioned of sheet lead. Water would be pumped up to the holding tank from underground facilities, or collected as rainfall draining through roof culverts, then filtered as it entered the distribution pipes. Overflow from above ground reservoirs was sometimes channeled into below ground cisterns such as the one unearthed.

Reservoirs made of sheet lead normally remained free of corrosion and developed a nearly insoluble coating of lead carbonate. Depending upon system residence time and acidity, however, water still might have accumulated dissolved lead that could have precipitated finally into the trough sediment if the cistern had been fed by attic overflow. Alternatively, overflow might have been directed down to the crawlspace basin through exterior downspouts, which are indeed visible on the archival photographs of the manor (Figure 11). If such pipes had been fashioned of lead, then seasonal expansion and contraction might have cracked off tiny flakes of crystalline carbonate adhering to the interior. Dislodged flakes could then have been washed down into the cistern where they would eventually settle within the sludge. Study of sludge samples with a scanning electron microscope has confirmed the presence of finely dispersed lead, but it has not yet isolated any lead-rich particulate matter that could be identified with a specific origin.

Prior to the arrival of city water in 1883,[69] several wells supplied St. John's College with clean underground sources. In 1846, one well stood immediately in front of the manor's western porch and another had been dug in the back yard.[70] Though there is no certainty that water from the cistern was ever consumed, curiosity nevertheless continues about the amounts of lead that might have leached into the cistern water from its toxic sediments. An experiment has therefore been projected for the future. Using the many bags of sludge collected, samples will be agitated in water of varying acidity until soluble components reach saturation. The U.S. Environmental Protection Agency currently requires that public drinking water contain lead levels no greater than 15 parts per billion at the tap. Lead assay of the water decanted from the sludge experiments may provide some idea of the range of possible dose rates per glass if, in fact, any dehydrated souls were tempted to quench their thirst at the old manor's pumps.

The cistern bricks held an added surprise in the form of brands, or impressed inscriptions, that were faintly visible in low relief on many loose specimens. The story, which appeared in a previous article,[71] is summarized here. In the New York area, branding is traditionally thought to have begun around 1850 as an advertising device for brickmakers in an increasingly competitive urban market. It involved carving the name, logo, or initials of the brickmaker into the bottom of each wooden brick mold so that the clay formed an impression when introduced. In the earliest brands, carving was done across the short dimension of the rectangular mold bottom, and the wet brick emerged with the letters in raised relief on a flat surface, but backwards—a mirror-image of the engraving.[72]

The cistern bricks spelled out (in reverse) the name REID followed by a 5-pointed star (Figure 22), an identifier unrecorded in any of the historic brand lists that have been compiled by historians and collectors.[73] The source of the bricks was eventually determined in another manner: by chemical analysis. The compositional profile that emerged from the assay of several specimens closely matched that of other bricks produced in the town of Haverstraw on the Hudson River in Rockland County.[74]

The U.S. census for 1850 revealed only one person named Reid residing in Rockland County. He was Patrick Reid, a 24-year-old Irish immigrant whose

1 INCH

Figure 22. Drawing of the REID brand impressed onto bricks used in the construction of the trough cistern.

employment was, incidently, as a laborer at a Haverstraw brickyard. Reid may have rented idle brickmaking machines on his employer's yard and output bricks under his own imprint, some of which ended up at Rose Hill in the construction of the cistern. Reid could not have been in business in Haverstraw after 1855 because, in that year, his name is absent from the state census rolls of Rockland County.[75] Ascertaining when Reid arrived in Haverstraw has been more difficult. Ships' passenger lists contain a number of Irish immigrants with the same name, and so far, none of them are recorded as having exactly the right age upon arrival. The candidate closest in age to the Haverstraw brickmaker arrived in New York in 1849 on board the ship *New York* bound from Liverpool.[76] Passenger Reid was 24 years old as of his voyage, which terminated on April 6, 1849, whereas brickmaker Reid was the same age on the 1850 census, which was recorded on September 6, exactly 17 months later. If the age discrepancy is accidental, and Patrick Reid did indeed disembark in America in spring of 1849, his brickmaking days in Haverstraw could not have begun earlier.

With this discovery, however, a chronological discrepancy arose. The east wing was built well before Reid could have made the cistern bricks. Reckoning based upon the date inscribed on the Robertson watercolor would place the wings as early as 1815, which is at least 35 years prior to Reid's brickmaking venture in Haverstraw and the advent of branding. The brick cistern must have been a later addition to an already standing structure. Like many archaeological problems, this one was resolved by further digging.

The Watts cistern

The brick cistern and its buttress walls were flanked on the east and west by two crawlspace compartments, both of which were eventually explored. After breaking through a hard, dark groundseal in the western crawlspace and clearing down into the underlying fill, it became apparent that, immediately beneath the brick cistern, a previous one had once existed (Figures 23 and 15:1). The

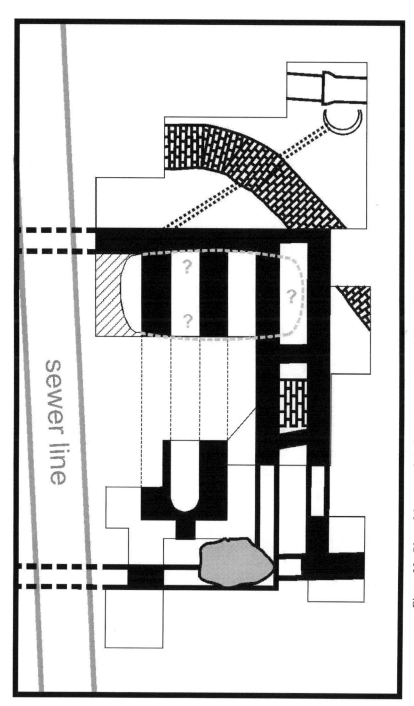

Figure 23. Plan of the east wing showing the location of the earlier stone cistern; the actual remains are in cross-hatching and the presumed perimeter of the former basin follows the dotted gray line.

sides of this earlier basin were built of fieldstones with a thick facing of what may be hydraulic lime plaster (Figure 24). Its floor, when encountered at a depth of four and a half feet below that of the trough cistern, was formed of tightly set bricks gently sloping eastward toward a presumed central low point. Complete exposure of this earlier cistern was not pursued, as removal of the brick masonry from the later trough cistern above would have been required, however, further excavation in the eastern crawlspace eventually made it clear that, except for its western end, the earlier stone-built cistern had been completely destroyed and removed. Apparently, the brick cistern had replaced the pre-existing basin, which was probably a water containment device built to serve the Watts family, as it lay beneath their wing. The first cistern was partly dismantled and buried, probably in the early years of St. John's College, when, for whatever reason, it proved inadequate or unusable.

Figure 24. View of the opening into the surviving western end of the stone cistern, probably built by the Watts family. The brick floor can be seen exposed at the bottom left, and the camera tripod legs rest on the buttressing wall west of the brick trough cistern.

Judging from the presence of Reid's brand on the bricks, installation of the new brick cistern must have occurred sometime around the 1850s. Suspecting that major remodeling must have been undertaken in order to insert new masonry into an existing foundation, a search for confirming evidence began.

Figure 25. The outer face of the east wing's rear foundation wall showing the original schist masonry below and to the right of the cistern patch; the patch begins beneath the curved cistern trough just visible at the top of the photograph and continues behind the five-foot range pole to the left edge of the photograph. The metal pipe (foreground) is a defunct utility line.

Wall construction

When the earth resting against the outside of the wing's rear wall was cleared, it became evident that this area had been exposed previously in order to gain access to the foundations for installation of the brick cistern. With complete clearance, two distinct masonry styles could be seen (Figure 25). The patch that sealed the end of the cistern contained large, mostly rounded stones accompanied by occasional brick fragments, all bonded with a dense, but now crumbly, gray mortar. The patched section also bulged noticeably, the thickening effected perhaps to support the weight of the impounded water (Figure 27:A). The original wing construction consisted of flattish schist stones with roughly squared edges held together by a yellowish, gritty mortar. No bricks or variant stones intruded into the stylistic uniformity of this wall, which began abruptly at the western edge of the excavation unit with a flat vertical joint (Figure 26) running through the preserved height of the foundation. The existence of this joint, with no dovetailing bonds connecting the stonework to any wall on the west, indicated that the rear wall of the wing had been built in sections, and the exposed part had been an add-on to an earlier, and shorter, wing. The wall

Figure 26. Western terminus of the east wing's rear wall at a flat vertical joint (right foreground); the rest of the wing to the west (to the right) was destroyed in 1959 by the cutting of a sewer trench. The Watts cistern lies just behind, and the brick trough cistern to the left. The location of the flat joint is marked by an arrow in Figure 27.

on the opposite (west) side of the flat joint, was unfortunately destroyed by the Faber Hall sewer in 1959.

The stonework immediately east of the cistern was continuous with the patch. It formed a stubby wall, only two feet in height, resting atop a thick base of brown sandy gravel that itself lay upon the original schist-with-yellow-mortar foundation. This upper wall continued several feet eastward to a corner, then turned south, still resting on its gravel base, to mark the end of the wing. Three Reid bricks (one with exposed brand) were mortared onto the cornerstone to support the cornerpost, and their presence indicated that the wall extension was built at the same time as the brick cistern (Figures 27:B and 35). With such minimal foundations, the superstructure resting upon the end of the east wing must have been of minimal weight. Most likely, it was the eastern porch.

These shallow foundations, on both the northern and eastern walls, also contained numerous large pieces of architectural brownstone in various neo-Gothic molding shapes (Figures 28 and 27:C). The cut stones form a motley assemblage of differing contours, each oddly oriented within the wall near the former ground level. One of them (on the wing's rear wall) had been set into the foundation with its former joint surface facing outward. Upon this surface, a previous mortar unrelated to that of the manor still adhered. Another molding stone (beneath the wing's end wall) retained a fragment of a metal cramp that had secured it in place within a pre-existing construction. These—and very likely all the other cut pieces—were doubtless part of an earlier building before ending up as footings for the end of the wing. It was suspected that they might have been remnants of the decorative brownstone moldings, stringers, and setback

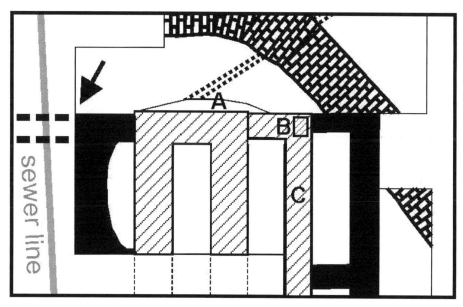

Figure 27. Plan of the northeastern corner of the east wing (with college period additions cross-hatched) showing locations of the flat vertical joint (arrow), the outward bulge in the foundation patch at the brick cistern (A), the REID brick cornerpost support (B), and the short porch support wall laid over neo-Gothic molding stones (C).

Figure 28. The eastern end of the wing, viewed facing west, showing its shallow foundation supported by neo-Gothic brownstone moldings set upon a gravel base (wall C in Figure 27).

caps from Rodrigue's construction of the church and seminary.[77] The signs of prior use might indicate that, after construction, they were deemed somehow unsuitable, removed, and set aside, to be enlisted as supports for the manor porch at a later date.

Normally, it would have been difficult to check this, as the original moldings on the church and St. John's Hall had long since crumbled, and all had been restored with a coating of cement stained the color of brownstone. During the major renovations of St. John's Hall in 1994–96, however, these cement patches were removed, exposing the stubs of Rodrigue's original detailing. Upon inspection, they were found to be a reddish brown sandstone sparkling with the vitreous luster of abundant mica. By contrast, the stones holding up what is thought to be the manor's eastern porch were darker in color and contained little mica, indicating that they probably did not come from the same source as Rodrigue's seminary trim. It therefore seems unlikely that the manor's molding stones had been originally prepared for the church and seminary. More likely, they derive from an as yet unknown structure. Possibly, they were dismembered parts of an early Rose Hill monument or second-hand scavenged pieces from a previous religious building that were brought to Rose Hill for examination, perhaps prior to work on the church and seminary. Brownstone is not found within the Bronx, and so both Rodrigue's ruddy micaceous trim and the manor moldings must be non-local.[78] If the porch footings were not part of some long forgotten early campus architecture, then records of the demolition of a nearby church around the 1840s or 50s could offer clues suggesting to which building they might have first belonged.

The brick cistern was thus confirmed as an invasive modification that replaced what had probably been the Watts family's stone cistern. Also, the shallow walls at the wing's east end were identified as the foundations for a porch. The brick cistern and east wing porch were apparently added at the same time by St. John's College, since Patrick Reid's brickmaking enterprise probably postdates 1849. The major renovations indicated by these findings likely occurred in 1855–56 as part of the provision of new quarters for the Jesuit scholastics who left Archbishop Hughes's seminary.[79]

Each building episode that contributed to the manor's final form involved the preparation of a fresh mortar mix, and it was assumed from the start that such sequential applications might be different in noticeable ways, and therefore distinguishable. Mortars and stuccoes were therefore exhaustively sampled, with care taken to obtain specimens intrinsic to the undamaged walls, not surficial repointings introduced during later repair. Preliminary microscopic examination has demonstrated that mineral composition of the aggregate does indeed vary. For example, the foundations directly connected to the brick cistern are held together with mortar that appears continuous with the cistern components, but not with other parts of the foundations, which have revealed different bonding materials.

An expanded series of mortar samples has also been analyzed chemically to see whether elemental assay confirms the microscopic findings. These comparisons are complex, however, because of wide compositional variability. Close similarities among mortars can suggest that they were part of a single application, but chemical differences do not necessarily prove that they derive from different building phases. Research on the manor mortars is still in progress, and a few walls remain undated with certainty because inspection of their constituent materials is still incomplete.

The drainage system for the Watts cistern

In 1993, excavations brought to light evidence of a filled trench that had been dug just behind the wing, but whatever had originally rested within it was missing. At first, it was assumed to be a robber trench from which a former wall had been "robbed out"—that is, its stones had been removed for reuse in some other construction. The line of the trench was clearly indicated by the orange color of the soil that filled it and by a trail of small stones left behind (Figure 29). The trench began at the rear wall of the east wing, and ran at an oblique angle (ca. 25°) from it in an easterly direction. The absence of mortar fragments appeared contrary to expectation for a robber trench, but it continued to be labeled as such in the field notebooks.

Probing through the bottom of the trench, a massive deposit of white clay was encountered (Figure 29). Unlikely to be a natural accumulation, the clay was eventually identified as a packing that lay just outside the east wing foundations constructed by Robert Watts, Jr., within which lay the stone cistern, and it formed a roughly semicircular shape in the surrounding soil. When the packing was cut in order to view it in cross-section, it could be seen that the depression into which the clay had been rammed tapered gradually toward the foundation wall with increasing depth. Presumably, the clay functioned as an impervious seal to prevent leakage from the cistern, but at its contact with the foundation wall, the dense and compact consistency became loose and discontinuous, with dark splotches of brown earth mixed in as if there had been substantial disturbance. The trench with the orange fill lay above this white clay and therefore had to be part of a later construction.

The significance of the trench remained a mystery until the summer of 1996, when investigation of its point of origin revealed a small hole in the wing foundations that appeared deep enough to have communicated with the stone

Figure 29. Looking down at the line of small stones (arrow) within the fill of the "robbed out" trench; the rear wall of the east wing runs parallel to the bottom of the photograph, just out of view. The white clay packing (wc) is visible peeking out from beneath the trench fill.

Figure 30. Brick path leading around the northeastern corner of the east wing; it was probably laid by Robert Watts, Sr.

cistern within. This hole was, unfortunately, obstructed on the inside by the later brick cistern, and exposure would have necessitated partial destruction and removal of the overlying brickwork. Assuming that the hole intentionally penetrated the wall and opened into the earlier basin, it became clear that the trench on the outside could have held a conduit of some sort to conduct overflow out of the east wing, over the white clay seal, and into a secondary containment system nearby.

About eight feet from its start, the conduit trench disappeared beneath a well laid brick path (Figure 30). During previous years, an exploratory sounding had been dug on the opposite side of the brick path, including the area where the trench and its possible conduit would have emerged. In this spot, located at the bottom of Figure 30, digging eventually led to the discovery of a backfilled pit. The sounding caught only a limited arc of the apparently round opening. The rest of its circumference lay outside the excavation unit and directly below a large 20th century fireclay drain pipe. To avoid the risk of undermining the pipe, only part of the pit was explored.

Figure 31. Two of the three bilge hoops belonging to the buried barrel exposed; the lower rim is visible at the bottom of the pit. The barrel was first thought to be a privy but eventually identified as a cistern drainage device.

As excavation continued down into this pit, the appearance of three thin iron hoops, clustered together and running horizontally about the pit margin, indicated that a large barrel had once been set within the hole (Figure 31). Stones had been inserted around the barrel to wedge it tightly into place, and since these had not tumbled in, it appeared that, at the end of its useful life, the barrel must have been intentionally filled with clean earth while the wood was still intact. During burial, the staves slowly decayed, and the hoops apparently slipped downward, their slide finally halted at the elevation of the lowest bilge hoop where the barrel diameter narrowed. None of the hoops could be removed in one piece without risk of undercutting the active drain pipe above, and their twisted condition provided no accurate means of calculating the barrel diameter based on measurement of the exposed arc. A rough estimate based on the curvature suggested a maximum bilge diameter of 29 inches, which would indicate a barrel about 38 inches tall based on traditional cooperage dimensions. If the hoop arc was wider, the barrel could have been of even greater size, however, possibly up to 48 inches tall.

About one and a half feet lower, the bottom rim of the barrel was reached. It comprised two superimposed hoops, tightly bound and now partly rusted together. This rim could not be removed intact either, and its diameter also proved difficult to estimate with any accuracy, so all hoops were cut to obtain samples. Below the rim was a natural deposit of glacial sand. The upper boundary of this sand, upon which the barrel was set, lay about 10 feet below the modern ground surface but almost six feet beneath the former ground surface at the time the barrel pit was dug.

When it was first discovered, the buried barrel was tentatively identified as a privy. Its location very close to the wing seemed odd, and it was therefore presumed to belong to an earlier period of occupation, prior to the wing's construction. Only later, when the barrel's clean filling cast doubt upon this identification, was a connection made to the conduit. Instead of a privy, the barrel might have served as a secondary, outdoor cistern to receive overflow from the stone tank. Once maximum fill level had been reached within the primary basin, excess water would have flowed out the hole into the conduit set within the buried trench. Water would have traveled just beneath the ground and under the brick path through the now missing conduit to an auxiliary under-ground reservoir in the form of a barrel. The need for such a barrel further implied that the cistern was engineered to fill automatically, possibly through a roof collection system. Microscopic examination of the deepest layers of loamy earth within the bottom of the barrel gave no hint of the vast quantities of pollen that normally precipitate to the bottom of "rainbarrels." If it was indeed a cistern, the sparse amount of pollen found within its basal sludge suggested that it was not the initial collecting device but a supplementary receptacle for fairly clear runoff from another one.[80]

Alternatively, the sunken barrel might not have been intended to con-serve water but instead to get rid of it. Without its bottom, such a barrel resting on an ice age sand bank would have efficiently drained away overflow into a ground water aquifer without creating a muddy mess at the ground surface. It was impossible to tell whether the barrel originally possessed its base or not, as no wood was preserved intact.

The orange fill within the trench did, in fact, serve as a support layer for what may have been a pipe. By summer of 1997, exploration of the trench profile where it disappeared beneath the brick path revealed a circular hole about four inches in diameter filled with sand and nestled within the "cushioning" layer of orange earth (Figure 32). Precise outlines of these features had been preserved in this spot because it lay beyond the area disturbed by the 1855–56 construction of the brick cistern. If this overflow conduit running through the trench and beneath the path had been a lead pipe, it could have been extracted easily,

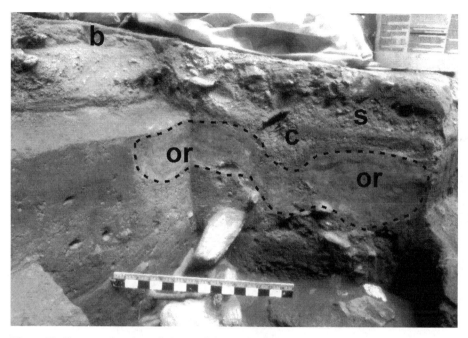

Figure 32. Cross-section through the conduit trench south of the brick path showing the level of the brick surface (b), the sand bed beneath the bricks (s), the silted up hole formed when the conduit was removed (c), and the orange soil filling the trench (or).

perhaps when the college built the new cistern. Removal of the pipe allowed the round cavity left behind to silt up with debris caved in from the overlying bed of sand beneath the brick path. A slight collapse in the bricks at the center of the path (Figure 30) just above the line of the conduit also suggests that, when the pipe was pulled out, sufficient settling into the hollow cavity occurred to disrupt the overlying brick surface.

The brick path was already in existence when the overflow pipe was laid and the barrel sunk into the ground. Evidence was found indicating that a section of path bricks was lifted to insert the pipe, then replaced. This modification was clearly seen in the above-mentioned sand bed. It was cut into and removed when the trench was dug, then relaid in multiple thin layers within the zone of disturbance before the bricks were reset. In all other places along the path exposure, the original sand bed was represented by a single, thick, continuous layer. One might reasonably presume that the path, conduit, and barrel were the work of the senior Robert Watts during his manor occupation (1787–1814), and that the pipe removal and barrel refilling occurred during the cistern replacement of 1855–56 conducted by St. John's College.

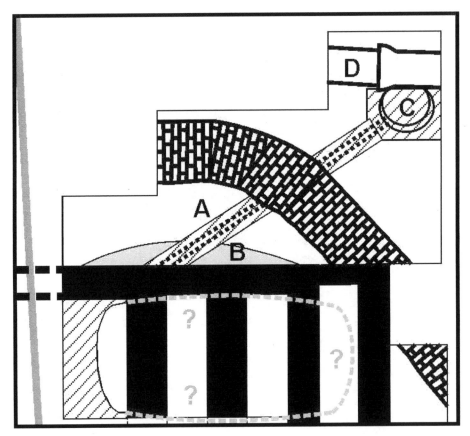

Figure 33. Plan showing the Watts cistern drainage system (cross-hatched), which included a white clay packing (B) on the north side of the cistern, a conduit (A) emanating from the cistern and running northeast below the brick path, and a barrel reservoir (C) for probable release of the excess flow from the main basin. The fireclay drainpipe preventing full exposure of the barrel lay above (D).

The complete plan of the cistern drainage apparatus is displayed in Figure 33, and a schematic section perspective viewed from the north showing the relationships in elevation between its various components appears in Figure 34. It is instructive to note that the hole in the schist wall enclosing the Watts cistern and through which overflow water entered the conduit was very close to ground level at the time, as represented by the brick path. It would seem that water level inside the cistern was intended to rise no higher than the backyard soil surface, possibly because winter freezing might block the conduit with ice if it were fully exposed to the elements. The clues that eventually explained the sequence of construction are reviewed in the next section.

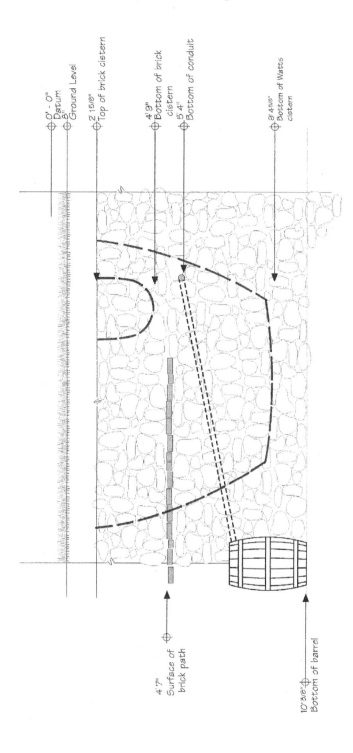

Figure 34. Schematic elevation of the east wing's rear wall showing how the two cisterns within the wing (hatched lines), the brick path, and the drainage system of conduit and barrel were spatially related. The tops of both cisterns were not preserved, so their uppermost configuration is unknown. All measurements are in feet and inches below the site datum, which was 8 inches above modern ground level. The barrel is here reckoned as having been 42 inches tall; a larger barrel would have reduced the slope of the conduit slightly. Drawing by Linda Dishner, architect.

The entire cistern drainage apparatus therefore involved several under-ground features that were discovered at different times during the 1990s. The process of making sense out of the orange-filled, oblique-angled trench occu-pied several years from its initial clearance and misidentification as a "robber trench" in 1993 to the eventual confirmation in 1997 that it held a pipe linking the stone cistern and the sunken barrel. Like most archaeological fieldwork, excavation at Rose Hill progressed exceedingly slowly, and new information emerged gradually over the course of many seasons. Generally speaking, most archaeologists do not find answers to be immediately forthcoming upon exposure of buried remains. Every sweep of a trowel does not bring instant historical resolution, especially when the remains under exploration have been disturbed or displaced. The "moment of discovery" can and commonly does encompass a continuous chain of procedures and results, each leading to a small gain in knowledge. This process may eventually lead to a final answer, but the investigation can last weeks, months, or, as in this case, years.

Grounds of the east wing

The clearest evidence pertaining to the grounds surrounding the house comes from quite late in the 19th century, just prior to demolition. This com-monly occurs with historic sites because extensive modifications over the years tend to disrupt prior landscaping. Excavations about the perimeter of the east wing did provide glimpses of previous land surfaces, however, and some details about earlier times can be reconstructed although exact dating and precise relationships with the house remain unclear. The complexity of the site and the difficulty of disentangling its many building phases provides an instructive story about how archaeologists work out *stratigraphic sequences*, archaeological jargon for the order in which the site was constructed, the layers formed, and the remains modified.

The pre-college years

The earliest structure behind the east wing appears to be the brick path. It entered the yard from the southeast, then turned 60° to the left and continued westward, parallel to the manor's rear wall (Figure 30). Perhaps it led to the back porch of the center hall. Bricks in the path were expertly laid, and all were of the common variety—soft, porous, and molded in the modern dimensions used since at least the 1790s: about 8x3½x2¼ inches. The upper surfaces of most were worn smooth, testifying to a lengthy interval of human traffic, while others were cracked and spalled from exposure to the climatic effects of freezing and thawing. The eastern porch foundations and the ground level that witnessed the demolition of 1896 are over a foot higher, and so the path must have been deeply buried when the college began operations in 1841.

The fact that bricks were lifted to insert the pipe, then replaced, indicates that the path was in use at the same time as the overflow drainage system. Curiously, the path must also be earlier than the east wing itself. This must be so because the original foundation of flat schist stones and yellow mortar—apparently belonging to the Watts occupation—continues about three feet beyond the corner of the 1855–56 construction and cuts into the path before reaching its own northeastern corner. In Figure 27 (on p. 73), the college additions are cross-hatched, and the parts built by the Wattses are in solid black. The northeast corner of the Watts's wing extended farther east than the one resulting from the renovations of 1855–56. It was built by excavating a pit and raising the walls from within it. When the already buried path was encountered as the pit was extended, only the bricks that intruded into the line of the new wall were plucked out. Relatively long and flat stones were then built up, their rougher, unfinished edges pushed against the outer sides of the pit, their inner edges more neatly dressed and thinly smeared with a now fragile and fugitive white plaster. The old path bricks that remained outside the wing space were left undisturbed, ostensibly because they had already become buried or thickly over-grown by this time. Construction of the end of the wing, therefore, nicked a path that had already become defunct and perhaps forgotten.

The plans of Figures 15, 20, and 23 (pp. 60, 65, and 69, respectively) show that a short section of brick path was exposed by excavations within the end wall of the east wing. These bricks implied that the path had branched several feet to the east, and a secondary walkway led westward, perhaps to a side door (Figure 35). The location of this brick surface *inside* the end of the wing further proves that it predated the wall that severed and enclosed it.

Resting atop the brick path as it skirted the manor on the east was about an inch of brown loam that was in turn covered by a thick layer of pinkish-gray cinder. Unburnt fragments of coal within this cinder clearly show the hard, shiny fracture surfaces of anthracite. St. John's College employed much anthracite in the fireplaces of its buildings, all of it doubtless mined from the coal seams of northeastern Pennsylvania. Ashy residue, including congealed globs of melted clinker and partly burned anthracite chips presumably swept from the college hearths, were spread about the campus to create paths throughout the late 19th century, and excavations have uncovered a number of these cinder surfaces that formerly led up to the manor. The cinder resting just above the brick path was the earliest encountered, and it had been spread well beyond the bricks, creating a broad road surface that was traced eastward at least another ten feet into an adjacent excavation unit.

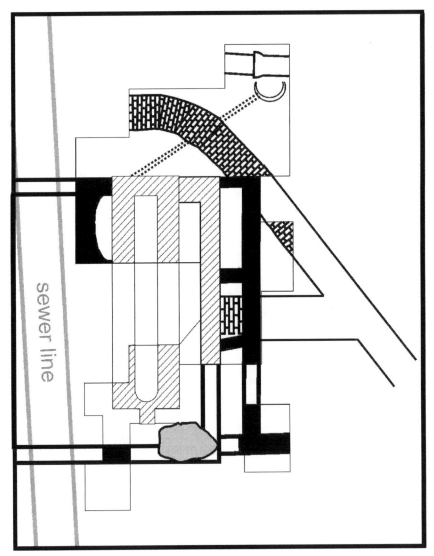

Figure 35. Plan of the assumed branch in the brick path east of the excavated units. This area was covered by coal cinder to form a broad driveway, probably by Robert Watts, Jr.

Embedded within this cinder was a U.S. penny, minted in 1803. The necessary implication of this find is that the soil which eventually covered this first cinder path when it went out of use must have been deposited in 1803 or later. But a more precise dating is afforded by the cinder itself, for unless the Wattses were importing anthracite at great expense from Europe, anthracite cinder would not have been available in the New York area until the Pennsylvania product began to enter the city's fuel market after 1812.[81]

This stratigraphic picture was consistent in some places but seemingly contradictory elsewhere. Clearly, the brick path is earlier than the cinder driveway, which must have been in use in the early 19th century. A puzzling paradox emerged, however: while the overflow system that drew water out of the stone cistern functioned while the brick path was in use, the end wall of the wing was constructed after the path had ceased to be. One scenario appears to explain all the conflicts while offering a plausible chronology for all the discoveries. It is the story that ties all the facts together.

Robert Watts, Sr. likely installed the brick path and the stone cistern during his early years at Rose Hill, after 1787. Since it was inserted beneath the brick path, the exterior overflow system was probably a later addition, but how much later remains unknown. There were no artifacts associated with the white clay packing that could provide a date, so the clay could have been applied to the outside of the cistern to act as a waterproof seal either at the time of its construction, or subsequently when the conduit and barrel were inserted. According to Robertson's "Rose Hill" watercolor, the manor's wings were in existence by 1815, but excavation has shown that the eastern half of the rear wall may have been an add-on: Figure 26 clearly demonstrates that the wall's flat vertical joint was not seamlessly bonded to the western half of the wing. One might assume, therefore, that the stone cistern was intended as an exterior facility at the time of its construction, perhaps provided with a roof and situated at the end of a shorter wing (now partly obliterated by the Faber Hall sewer). At the accession of Robert, Jr. in 1814, the cistern was likely "brought indoors" with the building of a wing extension to house it. Beginning at the flat joint, the new construction of schist fieldstones enclosed the water tank and increased the length of the wing. In the process, the rear wall construction chopped through the white clay sealing that enveloped the cistern and cut into the old brick path, which by that time was probably overgrown and perhaps partly buried. The conduit was left essentially to function as it previously had, since the enclosing wall seems to have been built around its connection to the cistern; it was this hole that was discovered during excavations in 1996.

Thus, an enclosing wall surrounded the cistern, and Figure 36 shows the configuration of the schist construction in black. It began at the flat joint and continued around the east end of the cistern, then turned another corner and headed back to the west along the southern side of the basin. When exposed by excavation, this southern side ended abruptly just underneath the college-built porch wall, its western continuation having been demolished together with most of the stone reservoir when the brick trough was installed.

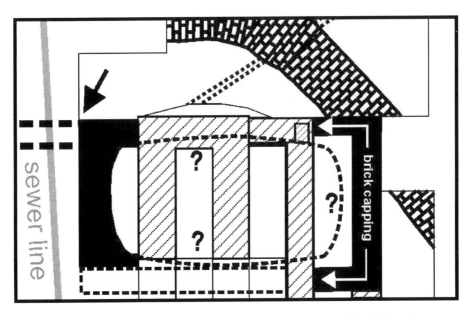

Figure 36. Plan of the schist wall that encircled the Watts stone cistern (all in solid black): it began in the northwest at the flat joint (arrow) and surrounded the stone basin. During the college period, its southern wall was partly removed for construction of the brick cistern and porch wall, and its eastern end was truncated to ground level and topped with bricks to form a border around a garden bed. Its southern side was removed west of the porch wall, a casualty of the brick trough installation.

There appears to be no justification for dating the first cinder use earlier than the occupation of Robert Watts, Jr., who might have employed the gravelly material to create a driveway surface after his arrival in 1814. If this was so, then the penny found in the cinders must have been in circulation for at least 11 years before it was lost on the roadway.

The college years
With the removal of the 1896 demolition debris, the grounds surrounding the end of the east wing were revealed as they appeared to the students and faculty of St. John's College. The porch that was added during the renovations of 1855–56 had left the newly refurbished wing about four feet shorter than Watts's earlier structure. The end wall of the previous wing was dismantled down to the ground surface, and soil was spread within the space between it and the newly built shallow porch foundation, ostensibly to create a garden bed (Figure 37). The stump of Watts's end wall was then capped with red bricks to form a decorative border, and beyond this border was strewn first pinkish-gray fireplace cinder, then, perhaps after some interval, crushed local marble to

Figure 37. View looking south showing the porch wall (right) with neo-Gothic stone supports and Reid bricks at the corner (lower right) and the Watts wall (left) dismantled to the former ground surface and topped with a brick border to enclose a garden bed (center).

produce a gleaming white gravel path running parallel to the end of the wing (Figure 38). White crumbs trailed off around the rear corner of the porch to the north, an area that had suffered repeated disturbances by later utility trenches. Most likely, the marble path had continued into the backyard just as the brick path had done over a half century earlier.

By the late 1800s, the building must have been in serious disrepair. In addition to the leaks and generalized decay described in written reports, the eastern end was probably sinking, judging by the substantial downward flexure of the porch foundation (Figure 39). Settling may have resulted from a combination of poor support at the east end (with its heavy brick trough cistern within) and the underground drainage. Ground water at Rose Hill flows generally from the higher elevation playing fields in the northeast (which were farmland until about 1912) toward the lowest elevation at the entrance to the oval drive (the Third Avenue gate at Fordham Road) in the southwest. This underground flow funnels past the eastern end of the manor, lubricating the soil profusely when runoff is heavy.[82] A building with shallow eastern foundations located where the manor stood might have settled into wet soil.

Figure 38. Stratigraphic section looking south showing the brick path (a) approaching the northeastern corner of the Watts wall with its later brick capping (b). The first cinder surface (c) rests atop the bricks, and above a thick layer of landfill, the white layer represents the college's crushed marble path (d) that skirted the garden. Above the marble lies destruction debris from the 1896 manor demolition (e).

Figure 39. Schist wall of Watts construction (left) that encircled the former stone cistern, garden bed (foreground), and shallow porch wall with its neo-Gothic undercourse sinking below the Watts wall, which represents its only firm support.

There is no indication that any major plan was implemented to stabilize the house. Both the historic records and the archaeological evidence suggest that some rehabilitation was attempted, including installation of a new roof and limited underpinnings, but the sagging end wall of the porch doubtless led to warping of the rigid frame above, and these indications were perhaps among the principal signs that convinced the Jesuit consultors in 1895 to recommend razing the Rose Hill manor.

Window glass

In addition to the inevitable scatters of broken window glass that permeate the grounds surrounding historic house sites, two places within the demolished manor contained massive piles of window shards.[83] The finding of occasional fragments of decayed wood among the pieces, and the fact that some shards were resting immediately adjacent to conjoining fragments from the same pane, suggested that the windows had been removed from their frames as complete sashes and intentionally buried within the ruins. In the wing, about 4,400 pieces of flat glass were found, nestled within the crawlspace area east of the brick cistern, a space that was probably the void beneath the eastern porch. Another 7,600 fragments were recovered in a different excavation unit near the center hall (Figure 40).

Figure 40. Looking down on layers of window glass shards representing sashes stacked within the porch crawlspace when the manor was demolished. Glass shards on the left; a preserved wooden window lath on the right.

Figure 41. Microscopic air bubbles trapped within the viscous glass as it was drawn downward by gravity into cylindrical forms during manufacture. Each elongated bubble is less than 0.01inch long.

Once the glass had been removed from the ground, close observation during cleaning yielded interesting details. Air bubbles were rare, but when they could be identified using a hand lens and a microscope, they were always long, thin ellipsoids with pointed ends, suggesting that the windows were produced using the broad glass method of manufacture (Figure 41). Previously during colonial times, glass windows were cut from "crowns" that were fashioned by swiftly rotating blown glass spheres to flatten them into large round disks from which panes could be cut. In the late 18th and early 19th centuries, glaziers adopted a different method of producing flat glass suitable for windows. They swung their glass spheres in pendulum fashion instead of spinning them, creating elongated, sausage-like cylinders that could be opened at the ends, slit length-wise, and eased flat to create a large rectangular sheet. This glass sheet could be cut into panes for insertion into window frames. Any spherical air pockets trapped in the molten glass were drawn downward into cigar-like or needle-like shapes by the increasing viscosity of the cooling material. These tell-tale bubbles identify broad glass manufacture and can also be used to help orient fragments during the mending process.

Mending has not yet begun in earnest. What may prove to be the "mother of all jigsaw puzzles" will require much time and patience, but once the panes are mended, observations and testing may furnish additional information about the glass making technology that supplied Rose Hill with windows. The restored pieces may be identifiable as having come from the lower or upper story on the basis of size when compared to the archival manor photographs.

Excavations in the center hall

Digging began in the area of the center hall in 1986, eventually exposing about 250 square feet of the southeastern corner and its abutment with the front wall of the east wing. A second buried pile of window glass was recovered in this unit, together with other interesting finds, including roofing shingles, a coal bin, the remains of a wood plank floor within the cellar, a pipe that may have brought the first city water into the manor, and two sections of brick chimney masonry with their interior plaster still intact and bearing faint traces of a wallpaper pattern that once decorated at least one of the manor's rooms.

The most curious aspect of the center hall investigations, however, was the degree to which renovations and landscaping during the 19th century had eliminated nearly all evidence of prior habitation. Modifications to the house apparently involved the stripping of soil layers to bedrock and their replacement with clean fill against the foundations. This was the case in all places explored. As a consequence, the initial phase of occupation in this plainly colonial house is underrepresented by clear artifactual evidence. Though the paucity of early finds has been a disappointment in the search for new knowledge about early Fordham, the massive earthmoving has illustrated the hitherto undocumented measures taken in the 19th century to preserve and modernize a structure that was at the time perhaps well over a century old.

Wall construction and the date of the center hall

Both the building materials and the architectural style suggest that the center hall was erected during colonial times. The walls were generally thicker than those of the wing, and the masonry also differed markedly, having larger, more rounded stones of diverse kinds held in place by a tough brown mortar composed of clay mixed with lime. Eighteenth century building technology commonly employed lime, but in places where the expense of pure lime was exorbitant or unnecessary, such as interior locations, clay or loamy soil would often be substituted, with lime added for hardness. This artificial marl, or lime-enhanced mud mortar, is frequently found in the earliest Dutch houses of the Hudson Valley, with a richer lime composition reserved for exterior exposures subject to weathering.[84] The center hall appears to be the product of colonial construction, probably during Benjamin Corsa's lifetime. Possibly, the Watts loan of 1766 helped pay for the construction.

Bricks associated with the center hall foundations also suggest an early date based upon their pre-Revolutionary dimensions: 8x4x2 inches on average. A dozen or so were found reinforcing the southeastern corner of the center hall, perhaps inserted as a repair, and hundreds of whole bricks and fragmentary bats recovered from the 1896 destruction debris represent the collapsed chimney that once stood at the eastern end of the center hall. All bricks found in association with the east wing conform to the modern, post-Revolutionary size.

Few artifacts of colonial date have been recovered anywhere within the entire site. In several locations, sherds of creamware, an English ceramic produced during the mid-18th century, have been found, meager indicators of a former colonial presence. Excavations were carried down alongside the center hall to the marble bedrock, which lies at a depth of nearly nine feet below present ground level, but no buried soil surface of colonial age was ever encountered. Instead, two thick layers of landscaping fill rest against the foundations, the lower one composed of river-rounded stones in a dark red sandy soil, and the upper one made up largely of fine red silty earth. Apparently, the walls were laid bare, then backfilled with the two artificial layers in sequence. This earthmoving might have been related to drainage, but at this time, it is neither fully understood nor precisely dated.

For the present, the most useful clues to the manor's pre-college construction history probably lie in the pictorial documentation rather than the archaeology. This evidence includes the Robertson watercolor of 1815 (Figure 42), the copper plate engraving by Weldon McKeon that was closely modeled after a drawing by William Rodrigue of the early college in 1845 (Figure 6, p. 48, and a detail showing the manor in Figure 43),[85] and the three archival photographs taken just prior to demolition (Figures 11 and 12, pp. 56–57, and Figure 44).

Figure 42. Watercolor titled "Rose Hill" by the Scottish-American artist Archibald Robertson, 1815. Courtesy of Mr. and Mrs. Stuart P. Feld, New York.

Figure 43. Detail of the Rose Hill manor from the engraving of St. John's College in 1845 by Weldon McKeon (Figure 6, p. 48).

Figure 44. Archival photograph providing a tree-obstructed view of the Rose Hill manor on the right and the former seminary building (now St. John's Hall) on the left, late 19th century. Courtesy of Fordham University Archives.

The depictions span the 19th century, and all reveal a curious stylistic blending of classic revival features with an asymmetrical door placement. The center hall's two stories, side-gabled roof with shallow pitch, denticulated cornice molding, end chimneys, and front porch were features frequently found on houses influenced by classical traditions, a trend that began in America as early as the first half of the 18th century. In general practice, this Georgian style manifested itself most commonly in an upper story of five windows with the door set beneath the central window. The Rose Hill manor differs in that four windows spanned its upper story, and the door was off-center. Such a first floor plan is typical of the earliest Dutch farmhouses in New Netherland[86] and would be unexpected for homes built after the mid-18th century.

Robertson's watercolor provides the earliest view of the manor, and if his rendition did not contain too many artistic liberties, then the differences between it and later representations must reflect modifications. Some liberties were surely taken, as the painting shows that chimneys once rose above the roof ridges at the end of each wing. No documents suggest that the wings were provided with chimneys during the college period, and the engraving does not show any. It is very unlikely that Watts-era chimney masonry was completely removed from the end of the wing in 1846; excavation in this area uncovered no deep root and suggested that no such stack ever existed there after the renovations of 1855–56. The wing chimneys may indeed have been invented by Robertson as embellishments for his painting.

The watercolor indicates that, originally, the canopy covering the graceful, wooden front porch was pedimented, not flat as in the college photographs. At the end of the west wing, Robertson drew a single wooden stair leading up to a door that passed into the wing to the right of the chimney. McKeon's engraving shows that, by 1845, the west wing was entered via two wooden stairs ascending perhaps three feet to a narrow porch without balustrade that was covered by a sloped roof supported on poles. Though doors were not indicated, the stairways presuppose two of them, one on either side. The presence of two doors in the west wing might also signal an interior subdivision of the wing. In the watercolor, the wings also lack dormer windows, modifications that do not appear on the manor in McKeon's engraving from 1845, but are clearly present through the trees in the third manor photograph from late in the 19th century in Figure 42. Most likely, the dormers were added by St. John's College during the renovations of 1855–56 as living spaces were added to the second floor.

Aside from the chimneys at the ends of the wings, there are only a few unexplained contradictions in Robertson's watercolor. The doorway of Watts's manor is placed below the middle window on the eastern side, yet the late 19th century photographs clearly show it on the west, together with an adjacent double door directly below the space between the two upstairs center windows (Figure 12, p. 57). This second entrance was probably inserted by the college to provide private access to the infirmary, which occupied the east side of the first floor. Minor discrepancies appear in the window treatments involving the number of panes in each sash. The wings of the watercolor contain windows with nine-pane sashes, and these could have been replaced by the more modern six-pane arrangement seen in the photographs. Robertson, however, placed six-pane sashes in the upper story of the center hall, yet the photographs plainly reveal that an older eight-pane style persisted there at the end of the century.

In its most significant aspects, then, the house in Robertson's artwork is very much the same structure recorded by Rodrigue at the inauguration of the college in 1841 and captured photographically on glass plate negatives toward the end of the century. Assuming that the basic plan of the manor has remained essentially the same since the Watts family's ownership, there are several possible interpretations of varying plausibility for the construction sequence.

The first is that the elder Robert Watts built the center hall in the 1780s after demolition of the old Corsa farmhouse. If so, then he erected a house that was architecturally at odds with the times in that it did not fully emulate the classically-derived form and detail of the then current Georgian and Adam styles. Furthermore, it also seems strange that the center hall mortar should reflect older colonial practice, whereas the wings used a newer lime technology.

A second possibility is that Watts made few alterations, and that the center hall remained essentially in its original form: a house that had been built and owned by a Dutch family of farmers. One suspects that a person of Watts's means would have applied his cachet in some fashion, but beyond this, features of the center hall do not entirely fit expectation for a Dutch colonial farmhouse. A two story structure and classical elements would be highly unusual.[87]

Though modifications could have been made by the Corsas with the rising popularity of Georgian style, major changes seem more likely to have been undertaken by Robert Watts, Sr., in 1787, or later by his son. This third possibility has always been the preferred explanation, but deciphering the pictures to determine what the pre-Revolutionary building might have looked like is fraught with difficulties, and the answer is still uncertain.

Speculating further, Watts's remodeling might have entailed the addition of a second story to a house built in the Dutch colonial style. Dutch farmhouses of the Hudson Valley were usually one and one-half story buildings in stone or wood frame construction. The half story was tucked beneath a steeply-pitched, side-gabled roof. If the door of the Corsa manor had been flanked by one window on the left and two on the right, then adding a second story with four

windows would have produced a house identical to the center hall in the old
photographs and, with the exception of the door being on the wrong side, the
watercolor as well. Classical features could have been added during the
alteration—the new roof might have been designed with shallow pitch, and end
chimneys could have been extended if they had been present in Corsa's house
or built in if not.

Grounds, renovations, and more glass

Knowledge about the grounds surrounding the center hall prior to the
establishment of St. John's College is extremely limited. Most archaeological
clues to the early manor were obliterated, and only the structures that existed in
the front yard at the very end of the manor's history, when demolition debris
covered them, are known with any confidence. Important finds from the excavated area included a coal bin, retaining wall, water pipe, and brick drywell.

Sometime after the introduction of coal into the New York fuel market,
a brick-built bin was set against the front of the center hall about three feet west
of the corner. It was embedded, pit-like, into the ground just below the easternmost crawlspace opening (Figures 45 and 15:13, p. 60). None of the archival
photographs provides any hints to its existence.

Figure 45. The Rose Hill manor coal
bin looking west along the center hall
facade (under the range pole); most of
the bin would have been underground.

When fully cleared, the
bin was about 5 feet 4 inches in
length, east to west, and extended outward a little more
than two feet from the center
hall foundation. It was found to
be brimming with anthracite
pieces that ranged up to three
inches in size. The coal was
likely delivered by wagon,
which pulled up on the nearby
oval drive, so that allotments
could be dumped into the bin,
which lay about 15 feet back

from the roadside. The coal would have been burned in the fireplaces of the manor as well as the basement furnace which served to heat the infirmary.[88]

Uncertainty still surrounds this seemingly ordinary structure. Prior to the demolition of the manor, the bin had been covered over with soil, evidently abandoned still containing a full load of coal. The covering soil was not a clean fill suggestive of a purposeful episode of landscaping, but rather a lawn or garden topsoil with abundant artifacts—white china, window glass fragments, rusted nails, shellfish remains, and occasional lost or discarded items such as marbles of glass and clay, bone and china buttons, and stubs of lead pencil.

It is possible that coal use became quickly obsolete in the various campus buildings when, in 1885, St. John's College built a power plant and steam heating system in the newly constructed Science Hall (built 1885–86, now Thebaud Hall). This project inaugurated what may have been the first electrical generator in the Bronx, and the steam produced in the boilers was conveyed throughout the college through pipes and tunnels.[89] If as yet undiscovered pipes linked the manor into this heating system, then the need for coal might have declined abruptly if it did not disappear altogether. The ultimate burial of a no longer useful coal bin was perhaps a by-product of trenching into the surrounding gardens to connect the steam pipes or lay other utilities.

A retaining wall was built about four feet in front of the east wing, running parallel to it (Figures 46:B and 15:12, p. 60). This wall of stones and brick came to an end less than two feet short of the center hall, leaving a gap, and it continued beyond the edge of the excavation unit to the east. Intended to lie below grade, the wall held up a narrow swath of front yard fringing the oval drive. Between it and the wing facade (Figure 46:C) was a brick-lined drywell recessed about 18 inches below yard level (Figures 46:D and 15:11). All bricks were modern in size, and their surface sloped very slightly westward toward the center hall. The bricks did not reach the center hall, however, but the paved surface ended as if it had been torn up. Most likely, the drywell and retaining wall were constructed as a unit in order to conduct rain or spillover from the roof gutters out through the gap, perhaps into a now missing culvert or drain.

Disruption of the brick paving was most likely due to the laying of what appears to be a water line. A two and a half inch diameter pipe (Figure 46:E) entered the excavation from the south, skirted the eastern side of the center hall and penetrated the wing wall. Within the crawlspace, the pipe zigzagged upward about 18 inches through two elbow joints, then passed out of the excavation toward the northeast, possibly to supply the infirmary with water. On the inside of the wall, the pipe protruded from a gray cement patch that sealed the hole punched through for its insertion. College records indicate that city water first entered St. John's in 1883, and the steam-producing plant followed closely in

Figure 46. View of the center hall excavations looking west, showing the coal bin (A), the retaining wall (B), brick drywell (D), front facade of the east wing (C), and the water pipe inserted through the wing foundations into the interior of the building (E).

1885–86. Subsequently, steam lines must have fed other campus buildings, gradually weaning the college community off of the fireplaces and coal-fired furnaces used previously. An 1880s steam line might also have entered the manor, explaining the abandonment of the coal bin. The intrusion of the water pipe disturbed the brick drywell and probably destroyed the original drainage apparatus that lay within the gap at the end of the retaining wall. It is unclear how residual water was eliminated from the drywell subsequent to this disturbance, for it seems the original installation was never restored.

The front facade of the east wing (Figure 46:C) near its abutment with the colonial center hall represents the only preserved exposure of the first wing construction, that is, the part that lay west of the add-on wall that surrounded the Watts cistern. All exposures of the joint between the early wing and its eastward extension—which were investigated along both front and rear facades—were obliterated by the Faber Hall sewer. Mortar analysis will be a critical aspect of the comparative study of all the building phases: those of Benjamin Corsa, Robert Watts, Sr., Robert Watts, Jr., and the college modifications. The information obtained may provide valuable diagnostics for characterizing and dating similar mortars in other coeval sites.

Resting on the brick drywell surface, another pile of window glass was uncovered. As with those in the east wing, these windows had been removed and buried at the time of demolition, but this deposit included special panes belonging perhaps to doors or cabinets. Only a portion of the total collection of shards could be retrieved. Much of the glass remains buried within the drywell to the east, beyond the limit of excavation. Among this debris, a fragmentary light bulb base and associated parts were also recovered.[90]

Covering this glass deposit were dozens of metal shingles that had been pried from the roof and used to cover and seal the glass, ostensibly preventing it from being unearthed accidentally (Figure 47). Patches of white oxidation product found amidst the iron rust on many specimens were identified as weathered zinc electroplating, or galvanization, that protected the underlying base metal.[91] A large piece of chimney masonry lay over the shingles (Figure 47, lower right), and the whole was buried under many cartloads of clean, yellow fill. As the 13x20 inch shingles were peeled up to expose the glass, their embossed patterns could be discerned: raised contours in the shape of an inverted "Y" for channeling rain, folded edges for interlocking with adjacent shingles, and a narrow panel at the upper end bearing an inscription that, in a few well preserved specimens, indicated a patent date of April 4, 1882.

The shingles were identified as Walter's Patent Standard Metallic Shingles (Figure 48) produced by the National Sheet Metal Roofing Company of New York City, and a company catalogue was located within the collection of trade papers archived at Avery Architectural Library of Columbia University.

Figure 47. Galvanized steel shingles as they were discovered resting on the glass deposit within the brick drywell near the center hall.

Published in 1890 and entitled "Practical Hints to Builders," the catalogue extolled the virtues of the metallic shingle and offered a description of its applications, installation instructions, and testimonials from satisfied customers. Among the satisfied customers were Jesuit officials of academic institutions such as the College of the Holy Cross in Worcester, Massachusetts, and St. John's College in Tremont, New York.[92] Replacement of the roof, therefore, must have occurred between the 1882 patent year and publication of

Figure 48. Drawing of interlocking Walter's Patent Standard Metallic Shingles showing the method of overlapping installation; a patent date was embossed between the first and second horizontal ridges on the upslope end of each shingle. Taken from the 1890 catalogue of the National Sheet Metal Roofing Company, preserved in Avery Architectural Library, Columbia University.

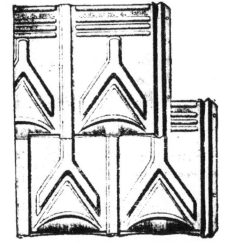

the catalogue in 1890. The Father Minister's diary notes that the roofing of the infirmary began on September 19, 1889,[93] a date that is perfectly bracketed by the known historical time markers. If the shingles had not been spread over the glass, they might have been sold for scrap or reused elsewhere. Their discovery indicated how the roof was covered, and the embossed patent date they bore plus the entry describing roof renovations in the college records made it plain that the shingles were still quite new in 1896 when the house was torn down.

Decorative elements: painted foundations and wallpaper

At some point during the late 1800s, the exterior surfaces of both center hall and east wing foundations on the front of the house were painted a maroon or dark red color. In places, the paint covers the original post-construction layer of white stucco, and in others, it coats the stones themselves. There is no mention of this decoration in college histories.

Nineteenth century house foundations were sometimes painted, and the job might have been ordered at Rose Hill to conceal the rough, crumbled, and patchy character of the old stucco through which the fieldstone core was apparently already beginning to show. Such a worn appearance can be seen on the center hall wall immediately beneath the range pole in Figure 46. The deep blush of reddish brown was eventually hidden beneath a smooth, gray coat of stucco. Two of the archival photographs must postdate this renovation since they clearly show the flat surface of this treatment over the foundations.

A small area was excavated within the southeastern corner of the center hall foundations, the only place where access into the interior was possible. Substantial amounts of broken brick representing collapse from the eastern chimney filled the space, which was originally part of the cellar excavated beneath the house in 1855–56. The architectural debris showed clearly that the

Figure 49. Section of chimney with interior plastering intact, showing the bricks held together with mortar that is continuous with the room's wall covering; the scored surface of the scratch coat and overlying smooth coat finish are clearly observable.

light brown mortar holding the brickwork together was also used to plaster the room interiors. This plastering showed the traditional three layer system of brown, scratch, and smooth coats used in early historic houses (Figure 49).

Surprisingly, two chunks of brick masonry covered with intact plaster surfaces still preserved images of a former wallpaper. Weathered and dirty, the printed designs were still faintly discernible in yellow and white floral and sprig motifs set against some form of wheel or fan pattern (Figure 50). Apparently, the paper fabric had decayed, yet the dry and thermally stable burial environment created in the pocket formed by the massive center hall foundations kept the mineral pigments that once adhered to the paper from disintegrating. Instead, the painted designs were transferred onto the underlying plaster surface.

Cleaning and stabilization by professional conservators began immediately after recovery,[94] and drawings were prepared to enable further study. Several students volunteered to pursue pattern searches, comparing the Rose Hill wallpaper to other historically-known designs using the wallcovering archives of the Cooper-Hewitt National Design Museum in New York City.[95] No exact match has been found yet, however, the individual motifs and their overall style fall within the Victorian fashion termed "Anglo-Japanese," which gained popularity between 1870 and 1890. Since the room in question was adjacent to the chimney, it had to be located at the eastern end of the center hall, and almost certainly on the second floor. The infirmary interiors, which occupied the first floor just below, were usually described in written accounts as having been whitewashed,[96] and many recovered fragments of room plaster were indeed coated with a thin white layer. Other pieces of plaster suggest that some walls were painted maroon, bright yellow, and even pale blue. Yet some fragments were unearthed entirely unadorned; the rooms in question may have been left plain, but it is also possible that these surfaces were originally covered by a now completely lost wallpaper. Such destruction is a product of time and the elements, and only the chance deposition of some intact pieces of plastered and wallpapered masonry within a burial environment protected from wide temperature variations and wet-dry intervals preserved their decoration over the intervening century.

The small corner of the center hall interior that was accessible to excavation was fully explored down to the underlying marble bedrock, upon which the colonial foundations were set. Just above the rock, remnants of a wooden floor were discovered (Figures 51 and 52). The floor boards had originally lain on sleeper beams that had elevated them several inches above the marble, but partial decay during burial and the weight of the fill above collapsed everything into a thin layer less than an inch in thickness that was dark and fragile but clearly showed the texture of wood.

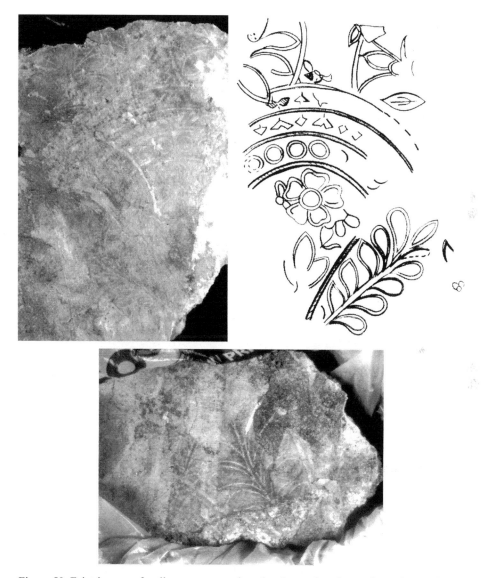

Figure 50. Faint images of wallpaper preserved on the plastered surfaces of two pieces of brick chimney masonry from the center hall fill; drawing of the larger piece (upper right) by Roberta Gardner.

Near the northern limit of this small excavation, the wooden floor showed evidence of a sheet metal covering, now fragmentary, pitted, and rusting. Digging could not be pursued any farther to the north (toward the upper right in figure 51), as it risked undermining a busy sidewalk used by persons entering nearby Collins Hall. For this reason, the metal cladding could not be investigated any more than the small hole already permitted. The root of the eastern chimney of the center hall also lay several feet beyond to the north and out of reach of safe archaeological study.

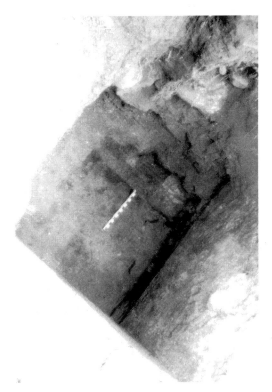

Figure 51. Photograph looking down into the exploratory excavation of the center hall's southeastern corner showing the cellar floor level (beneath the foot long ruler) and the marble bedrock below that (the light colored surface in the sounding to the right of the ruler). The southern facade of the center hall and its cellar window are at the lower left, and the coal bin would have been just outside, beyond the edge of the photograph; evidence for the metal cladding began beneath the northern (upper right) end of the ruler.

These discoveries may be explained by the following hypothesis. The area within the southeastern corner of the center hall foundations lay immediately below the basement window on the southern wall. This opening had likely been a crawlspace vent for the original colonial

Figure 52. Wooden residue of the cellar floor within the center hall (under the ruler) and the exposed marble bedrock upon which the floor remnants had settled (light colored stone surface to the right).

house and became a basement window when the cellar was dug in the 1850s. It can be seen on the archival photographs just above yard level on the outside of the colonial house. The coal bin was constructed just outside this window. Quite possibly, coal was delivered to the bin, then periodically shoveled through the window onto the wooden floor below. The metal cladding that covered the floor several feet to the north may have served to protect the wood from embers escaping from a furnace that may have been installed just beyond the excavated space. Such a furnace, or stove, might have been the principal heating device for the cellar and perhaps also for the infirmary on the first floor.

SUMMARY

Seventeen years of excavation at Rose Hill manor have yielded much information about the old house and its occupants, but there are many more details and extended interpretive discussions than can possibly fit into this report. These discoveries must await complete publication at a later date, after as many of the still unsolved mysteries surrounding the manor are answered with laboratory analyses still to come. More details will certainly emerge from the study of recovered artifacts, including ceramic fragments, window glass shards, nails, bones and shells, masses of architectural debris, and other items. Most were cleaned and inventoried as they were recovered, but all are as yet unanalyzed in more than a perfunctory manner. Sub-projects such as window glass restoration and mortar examination are also planned for the near future.

The present report has tried to place the discoveries made so far into preliminary historical perspective. Many of the finds have furnished insights into everyday life at the manor, illuminating details that received little or no mention in the traditional histories, such as the way coal was delivered to stoke the manor's furnace and the wall covering that decorated a room on the second floor. Aspects of house construction, its possible changes over time, and the design of the immediately surrounding grounds are among the most significant initial results. The east wing excavations revealed the water containment and drainage facilities installed most likely during the Watts occupation, as well as the substantial remodeling carried out by St. John's College during the 1850s, its second decade. Compositional analysis of the Reid-made bricks in the college cistern permitted the chronology of this construction to be established based upon the brickmaker's inferred years of production between 1850 and 1855, which dovetail neatly with the timing of the renovations according to archival documents. The recovery of metallic shingles patented in 1882 suggested that the manor underwent further restoration only a few years before its demise. It was finally razed in 1896, options or patience having run out on saving it. A further highlight of the wing excavations is that sediment collected from the bottom of the brick cistern may contain clues to the internal plumbing system through study of its high lead levels.

The center hall excavations revealed a colonial structure stripped of its surrounding archaeological evidence by large-scale modifications during the 19th century. Small finds left behind by the Michielsen and Corsa families may be buried in backyard trash pits or in the area to the west where the first farmhouse may have stood, but such deposits would be exceedingly difficult to locate given the restrictions posed by modern buildings and paved areas, and the fact that the current ground surface has been raised nearly five feet above colonial ground level by numerous episodes of landscaping.

Well-preserved and complex, the Rose Hill manor site will continue to provide new perspectives on 19th century school life, the rural gentry of early America, and eventually, perhaps, the lot of the Dutch colonial farmer. Archaeological exploration inevitably repays the prolonged time and exhaustive effort required to retrieve and analyze buried evidence. Like the intensive study of historical documents, careful examination of physical remains tells much about the past. Student participation at Rose Hill further multiplies the value of the project by providing a first-hand learning experience in the nature of original research. It will leave images of history that remain indelible on the mind long after other classroom memories have faded.

ACKNOWLEDGMENTS

Excavations were made possible through the sponsorship of Fordham University and the Bronx County Historical Society, and most generous support was received over the years from Fordham alumnus Richard B. Marrin (FC '67, LAW '70). The project directors offer their appreciation to past University president, Rev. Joseph A. O'Hare, S.J., for the opportunity to explore Fordham history from the ground up, and thanks are also due to Dr. Joseph R. Cammarosano, Dr. Brian J. Byrne, and the university's maintenance personnel for their cooperation and patient tolerance of the obstacle course that active excavation placed in the way of their grounds-keeping efforts. Much valued assistance in plumbing the depths of Fordham's own historical paper trail was provided by three generations of university archivists: the late Rev. Edward Dunn, S.J., the late Rev. Gerard Connolly, S.J., and Patrice Kane.

Many other people assisted in the successful research at Rose Hill, including Lt. Col. Frank Licameli, Prof. Elizabeth Kraus, Prof. Diana Bray, Prof. Lloyd Ultan, Dr. Gary Hermalyn, the late Daniel deNoyelles, the late Victor

Spaccarelli, Gale Corson, Joan King, Linda Dishner, Dr. Bruce Bevan, Patience Freeman, Roberta Gardner, Mr. and Mrs. Stuart P. Feld, James McCabe, Vivian Shen, the late Prof. Patricia Ramsey, the late Rev. Thomas Hennessy, S.J., and Msgr. Thomas J. Shelley. We also extend belated appreciation to Rev. Joseph Zwinge, S.J., the 19th century Father Minister of St. John's College who not only managed the affairs of his own generation at Fordham, including organizing the library and rudimentary archives of the College, but also provided us with detailed records of hundred-year-old minutia that became essential information to the excavation project; his accomplishments inspired the same careful observations and documentation during our own 20th century investigation.

Valuable assistance with historical sources was provided by several institutions, including the Bronx County Historical Society, the William L. Clements Library of the University of Michigan at Ann Arbor, Avery Architectural Library of Columbia University, the New-York Historical Society Library, the Beinecke Rare Book and Manuscript Library of Yale University, the New York State Library and Archives at Albany, the New York Public Library, the Thomas Paine National Historical Association, and the Westchester County Historical Society at Elmsford, New York.

During the 17 years of active digging, over 175 students worked at the site as part of their curricular studies, and dozens more volunteered their time as interns to share in the endeavor. Of course, nothing would have been unearthed without all these student excavators and volunteers who collectively served 17 seasons at hard labor, toiling under the Rose Hill sun.

ENDNOTES

1. Over 16 fall semesters beginning in September 1985, students of Fordham College were able to enroll in the course entitled Fieldwork in New York Archaeology, and for very nearly that many summer seasons, students and volunteers worked at the site until it was finally closed in 2002.

2. Thomas Gaffney Taaffe, *A History of St. John's College, Fordham, N. Y.* The Catholic Publication Society Co., New York, 1891.

3. *Catalogue, St. John's College, Fordham, N. Y. City, 1889-90.* The Bedell Press, New York, 1890. Many years later, the university newspaper reported that Taaffe's history of St. John's College had served as his masters thesis, and that he was "engaged in writing a new history of Fordham": "Taaffe on Fordham." *The Ram* 15, no. 25 (May 11, 1934): 2, col. 3. The fate of Taaffe's second history is unknown.

4. Patrick J. Cormican, S.J., "A Sketch of St. John's College, Fordham, N. Y." Unpublished typescript, Fordham University Archives, Fordham University, Bronx, New York, 1904.

5. The boulder of rose-colored granite was presented to the university by the freshman class on Parents' Day for Freshman Year: "The 1939 Commencement." *The Fordham Alumni Magazine* VII, no. 3 (October, 1939): 3.

6. Robert I. Gannon, S.J., *Up to the Present: The Story of Fordham*. Doubleday, Garden City, 1967.

7. Cormican, *op. cit.* (note 4), p. 1.

8. Vast amounts of information from municipal archives, church records, and other sources were compiled by Lt. Col. Frank Licameli, whose ability to navigate through all manner of document repositories, overcoming obstacles represented by misfilings, ancient scribbles of varied legibility, and overprotective curators, is acknowledged with appreciation and not a little awe. Licameli formerly served in the Fordham ROTC Program and is currently with the Center for the Army Profession and Ethic (CAPE) of the U.S. Military Academy at West Point.
A discussion by the present authors of Rose Hill history and archaeology that emphasizes college life of the 19th century has already appeared in: Allan S. Gilbert and Roger Wines, "From earliest to latest Fordham: background history and ongoing archaeology." In Thomas C. Hennessy, S.J., ed., *Fordham, The Early Years*. Something More Publications, distributed by Fordham University Press, Bronx, New York, 1998, pp. 139–176.

9. Jerrold Seymann, *Colonial Charters, Patents, and Grants to the Communities Comprising the City of New York*. Board of Statutory Consolidation of the City of New York, New York, 1939, p. 428; a full account appears in Lloyd Ultan, *The Bronx in the Frontier Era: From the Beginning to 1696*. Written in collaboration with the Bronx County Historical Society. Kendall/Hunt, Dubuque, Iowa, 1993, pp. 71ff.

10. John Archer to Roger Barton, November 20, 1678. Westchester County Clerk Deeds, Liber C, p. 68; for both Barton's and Statham's deeds, see Harry C.W. Melick, *The Manor of Fordham and Its Founder*. Fordham University Press, New York, 1950, pp. 92–93.

11. Ultan, *op. cit.* (note 9), pp. 128–133, 137, 141, 150–154; Harry C.W. Melick, "The Fordham ryott of July 16, 1688." *New York Historical Society Quarterly* XXXVI (April, 1952): 214–217.

12. Town of Westchester to Roger Barton, July 4, 1682. Westchester Town Records, Vol. 53, p. 105.

13. Melick, *op. cit.* (note 10), pp. 103–104.

14. Melick, *op. cit.* (note 10), p. 118.

15. George E. McCracken, "Roger Barton of Westchester Co., NY and some of his earlier descendants" http://www.rootsweb.ancestry.com/~genepool/bartonrog.htm; originally published in *New England Historic Genealogical Society* 106–107 (1952–1953); Roger Barton and Bridget Barton to Reyer Michielsen, June 9, 1694. Westchester Town Records, Liber 56, p. 206; see also Melick, *op. cit.* (note 10), 113, 118.

16. Roger Barton and Bridget Barton to William Davenport, Sr., February 26, 1704/5. Westchester County Clerk Deeds, Liber D, pp. 27–29.

17. The map is reproduced in Melick's book, *op. cit.* (note 10), opposite p. 120: "Map of the survey made by Peter Berrien, June 13, 1717." From the archives of the Collegiate Church of the City of New York.

18. In ancient times, the Mill Brook channel carried the main flow of the Bronx River, but a major fault and landslide blocked this route and forced it to find another path to the East River. The stream apparently shifted to the east, cutting a deep valley southward through what is now the New York Botanical Garden. Christopher J. Schuberth places this event about 15 million years ago: *The Geology of New York City and Environs.* Natural History Press, Garden City, 1968, p. 88. Charles Merguerian and John E. Sanders suggest that the carving of the gorge by the diverted river is a recent, post-glacial phenomenon that occurred within the past 13,000 years: "Bronx River diversion: neotectonic implications." *International Journal of Rock Mechanics and Mineral Science* 34, nos. 3–4, paper no. 198 (1997).

19. Reyer Michielsen's will of July 7, 1733 is in William Smith Pelletreau, *Early Wills of Westchester County, New York, from 1664–1784.* F.P. Harper, New York, 1898, p. 67.

20. Benjamin Corsa of New York married Jannetje Reyers of the Manor of Fordham in the Dutch Reformed Church, April 17, 1718: *New York Genealogical and Biographical Record* XII (1884), p. 194; see the Corsa family genealogy in Alvah P. French, *History of Westchester County, New York*, Vol. V. Lewis Historical Publishing Co., New York, 1925, pp. 90–95. The most current revised account of the Corsa genealogy was compiled by Mr. Gale Corson of the Corson/Colson Family Association in their publication, *Corson Cousins*: Jan Corszon (vol. 27, no. 1, January 2007a; vol. 27, no. 2, April 2007b; and republished article by Henry Hoff in vol. 27, no. 4, October 2007); Isaac Corsa (vol. 28, no. 1, January 2008a); Isaac Corsa and John Courser (vol. 28, no. 2, April 2008b, which also includes a republished article by Marian Elder); Benjamin Corsa (vol. 28, no. 3, July 2008c); and Andrew Corsa (vol. 28, no. 4, October 2008d).

21. Corsa purchased the farm for £339 from the three sons of Reyer Michielsen (Reyer, Jr., Frederick, and Tunis): Sons of Reyer Michielsen to Benjamin Corsa, April 26, 1736. Westchester County Clerk Deeds, Liber G, pp. 204–205.

22. On March 22, 1743, Benjamin Corsa exchanged his common rights in Fordham Manor for land adjacent to his farm: Acts of the Consistory of the Reformed Dutch Church in *Ecclesiastical Records of the State of New York* IV (1902), pp. 2793–2797.

23. The Dutch Reformed Church to Benjamin Corsa, July 18, 1764, for the sum of £157 7s 4½d: *Ecclesiastical Records of the State of New York* VI (1905), pp. 3941–3942. Corsa borrowed £155 from Robert Watts of New York City on November 8, 1766: New York State Archives, Albany, Mss. Chancery Court Records, J0065–W62 (back of p. 62), June 4, 1786.

24. Benjamin Corsa's will of October 1, 1770 is in Pelletreau, *op. cit.* (note 19), p. 241.

25. "Statement of Isaac Corsa," September 3, 1783, "Loyalist Transcripts–Royal Institution Transcripts," mss., VI, no. 21, 1783, New York Public Library; "Indictment of Isaac Corsa," August 23, 1783, New York Court of Oyer and Terminer, Mss. Records of the Supreme Court of the State of New York, New York City Hall of Records. Isaac Corsa was a captain in Maj. Bearmore's Westchester County Loyalist Militia and later served under James Delancey: John McLean McDonald, "The McDonald Interviews, mss.," "Interview with Dennis Valentine and

Andrew Corsa on August 26, 1844," p. 103, and "Interview with Frederick Valentine on August 24, 1847," pp. 482–483. Thomas Paine National Historical Association Library, New Rochelle, New York.

26. "A Map of the Country Adjacent to Kingsbridge, Surveyed by Order of His Excellency Sir Henry Clinton, K.B. Commander in Chief of His Majesty's Forces &c &c &c, 1781." Clinton Papers ms. map no. 152. William M. Clements Library, University of Michigan, Ann Arbor.

27. Isaac Corsa of Annapolis, Nova Scotia, Loyalist Claims, April 4, 1786, rejected for nonappearance, May 27, 1786: "New Claims at Halifax," Public Archives of Nova Scotia, Halifax, N.S., A/0 13, Halifax Loyalist Claims no. 162. See also Westchester Historical Society, "Andrew Corsa." *Quarterly Bulletin of the Westchester County Historical Society* 8, no. 2 (April, 1932): 55–58.

28. See *Corson Cousins* publications, *op. cit.* (note 20).

29. See Westchester Historical Society, *op. cit.* (note 27).

30. Harriet Mott Stryker-Rodda, *Watts; Ancestry and Descendants of Ridley Watts*. Polyanthos, New Orleans, 1975, pp. 22ff.; Clifton James Taylor, *John Watts in Colonial and Revolutionary New York*. Unpublished Ph.D. dissertation, University of Tennessee, Knoxville, and University Microfilms, 1981; [John Watts DePeyster], *Local Memorials Relating to the DePeyster and Watts and Associated Families Connected with Red Hook Township, Dutchess, NY*. 1881, pp. 1–6, 19–32.

31. Stryker-Rodda, *op. cit.* (note 30), p. 36.

32. The 1815 watercolor entitled "Rose Hill" by Scottish-American artist Archibald Robertson was studied and reproduced here with the kind permission of the owners, Mr. and Mrs. Stuart P. Feld of New York.

33. A complete listing of deed transfers following the occupation of Isaac Corsa is as follows.

| February 19/20, 1786 | Robert Watts to John Watts, Jr. | Watts Papers, MSS, New-York Historical Society. |

Westchester County Clerk Deeds:

| May 11, 1787 | John Watts to Robert Watts | Liber W, p. 330 |

Westchester County Clerk Wills:

| January 24, 1814 | Will of Robert Watts, Sr. | Liber D, p. 156 |

Westchester County Clerk Deeds:

November 17, 1824	Robert Watts, Jr. To Henry Barclay	Liber 26, p. 306
September 1, 1826	Henry Barclay to James Ponsford (Sherborne/Union Hill)	Liber 28, p. 80
May 1, 1826	Henry Barclay to Warren Delancey (Rose Hill)	Liber 31, p. 344
April 27, 1827	Henry Barclay to Robert Watts, Jr. (west end of Rose Hill)	Liber 32, p. 71

March 25, 1828   Robert Watts, Jr., to Jacob Berrian (west end of Rose Hill)   Liber 32, p. 240

Successive owners of the 106-acre Rose Hill estate after Warren Delancey are as follows.

Westchester County Clerk Deeds:

November 22, 1827	Warren Delancey to Samuel Fickett	Liber 29, p. 327
August 6, 1828	Samuel Fickett to Charles J. Hubbs	Liber 33, p. 157
December 29, 1829	Charles J. Hubbs to Henry Packard	Liber 39, p. 276
September 26, 1834	Henry Packard to Elias Brevoort	Liber 56, p. 189
April 1, 1836	Elias Brevoort to Horatio S. Moat	Liber 71, p. 102
May 11, 1838	Horatio S. Moat to Alexander Watson	Liber 81, p. 478
July 18, 1839	Alexander Watson to Andrew Carrigan	Liber 86, p. 115
July 23, 1839	Alexander Watson to Andrew Carrigan	Liber 86, p. 120
July 24, 1839	Horatio S. Moat to Andrew Carrigan	Liber 86, p. 124
August 29, 1839	Andrew Carrigan to John Hughes	Liber 92, p. 125
July 15, 1846	John Hughes to St. John's College	Liber 120, p. 489
December 1, 1854	John Hughes to the NY & Harlem RR Co.	Liber 334, p. 279
July 16, 1860	John Hughes to St. John's College	Liber 439, p. 347

This information will be found in Gilbert and Wines, *op. cit.* (note 8), n. 65, p. 174.

34. The McKeon engraving was produced several decades after the 1845 lithographic print by Rodrigue. A copy of this print is held by the Metropolitan Museum of Art. The on line catalogue lists it as: "St. John's College Fordham, New York" by William Rodrigue (1800–1867); Print Collection Accession Number 54.90.957, lithograph with tint stone. The inscription below the image reads: "Drawn from Nature by W. Rodrigue, Archt. / Lith by F. Michelin, 111 Nassau Street, N. York / Respectfully dedicated to the Right Reverend John Hughes D.D., Bishop of New York." The museum dates the print to 1846–1851, but a newspaper refers to its publication in 1845: "A good lithograph of St. John's College, Fordham has just been issued by C. Kuchel, John Street," Miscellaneous advertisements and notices in the *New York Herald*, July 25, 1845.

35. Sheet 6 of New York, Department of Parks, Topographical map made from surveys by the commissioners of the Department of Public Parks of the City of New York of that part of Westchester County adjacent to the City and County of New York embraced by chapter 534 of laws of 1871 as amended by chapter 878 or laws of 1872. Department of Public Parks, New York, 1873.

36. Cormican, *op. cit.* (note 4), p. 102.

37. Anonymous [Rev. Michael Nash, S.J.], "Fordham College and the way from New York City to it in the year 1846." *The Fordham Monthly* IX, no. 4 (January/February, 1891), p. 70.

38. Archival photographs and campus plans show a small rectangular building about 30 feet behind the manor's east wing that Fr. Zwinge identified as the college ice house in 1894 (see Taaffe's plan in Figure 4). Cormican—*op. cit.* (note 4), p. 15—wrote that the ice house was built by Rev. John Larkin, S.J., during his term as the fourth college president (1851–1854). The structure remained standing after the manor's demise, but by 1912, it too had been torn down.

39. Hughes succeeded John Dubois as Bishop of New York in 1842 and was elevated to Archbishop in 1850. He was a stern authoritarian dedicated to promoting Old World Catholic

tradition in the New World, and although his mood was exultant when the Jesuits took over the college in 1846, in ten years he had become thoroughly disappointed with their administrative practices and frustrated by his own loss of authority over the school he had founded. See Francis X. Curran, S.J., "Archbishop Hughes and the Jesuits." *Woodstock Letters* XCVII (1968): 5–56 (Reprinted in Thomas C. Hennessy, S.J., ed., *Fordham, The Early Years*. Something More Publications, distributed by Fordham University Press, 1998, pp. 177–221). See also Cormican, *op. cit.* (note 4), p. 102; and Christa R. Klein, *The Jesuits and Catholic Boyhood in Nineteenth-Century New York City: A Study of St. John's College and the College of St. Francis Xavier, 1846–1912*. Unpublished Ph.D. dissertation, University of Pennsylvania, Philadelphia, 1976, pp. 63ff.

40. Cormican, *op. cit.* (note 4), p. 102.

41. Rev. Joseph Zwinge, S.J., "Father Minister's diary," entry for November 11, 1891. Fordham University Archives, Fordham University, Bronx, New York.

42. *Ibid.*

43. *Ibid.*, entries for August 24, 1892 and August 7, 1893; Thomas Gaffney Taaffe, "The old manor house." *The Fordham Monthly* XV, no. 1 (October, 1896): 11.

44. *Ibid.*, pp. 10–11.

45. Jesuit Consultors, "Minutes of April 30." Fordham University Archives, Fordham University, Bronx, New York, 1895.

46. Cormican, *op. cit.* (note 4), p. 102.

47. *Ibid.* p. 103.

48. Kenneth Scott, compiler, *Rivington's New York Newspaper: Excerpts from a Loyalist Press 1773–1783*. New-York Historical Society, New York, 1973, p. 103.

49. Thomas Jones, *History of New York During the Revolutionary War*, 2 Vols. Printed for the New-York Historical Society, New York, 1879, II, p. 324; Alan Valentine, *Lord Stirling*. Oxford University Press, New York, 1969, pp. 235–236.

50. Stryker-Rodda, *op. cit.*, (note 30), pp. 23–24.

51. Continental Army, "Mss Orderly Book of the Continental Army," records for Kingsbridge, NY, August 22, 1776. Yale University Library, New Haven, Misc. Mss. 40, GP no. 352, Series XIV, Box 68, Folder 1488, p. 10.

52. John McLean McDonald, *The McDonald Papers*, ed. by William S. Hadaway, I: 75–80, II: 73–77. Westchester County Historical Society, White Plains, 1926–27. Also Lloyd Ultan, "The Grand Reconnaissance." *The Bronx County Historical Society Journal* 39, no. 1 (2002): 14–37.

53. John McLean McDonald, "The McDonald Interviews, mss., Interview with Andrew Corsa on October 27, 1851," p. 8. Thomas Paine National Historical Association Library, New Rochelle,

New York.

54. Robert Bolton, *The History of the Several Towns, Manors, and Patents of the County of Westchester, from Its First Settlement to the Present Time*, Vol. II. C. F. Roper, New York, 1881, p. 490.

55. Karolyn Wrightson reports that the former Cornelius Van Tassel house in Elmsford, Westchester County, has also been considered the model for Cooper's story: "Tracking down the history of the Spy House." *New Rochelle Standard Star* (September 27, 1997): Lifestyles, p. 1.

56. See, for example, Sanborn-Perris Map Co., Ltd, *Insurance Maps of the City of New York*. New York, NY, 1896, p. 269.

57. New York, Department of Parks, *op. cit.* (note 35).

58. Rev. Joseph Zwinge, S.J., "Maps of Property of St. John's College since the beginning by Father Minister," map labeled "Plan of College Before 1890." Fordham University Archives, Fordham University, Bronx, New York, 1893–94. The maps are available in the digital collections of the Fordham University Archives.

59. Rev. Joseph Zwinge, S.J., "Father Minister's diary," entry for September 19, 1889. Fordham University Archives, Fordham University, Bronx, New York. The roofing of the infirmary began on the date of entry.

60. The information comes from a poem written in memory of the demolished manor: F., '93, "Recollection! The old infirmary." *The Fordham Monthly* XV, no. 9 (April, 1897): 128–129.

61. One of the Old Boys, "More about the good old days." *The Fordham Monthly* XVIII, no. 3 (December, 1899): 153.

62. Taaffe, *op. cit.* (note 2), p. 13.

63. The radar survey was performed by geophysicist Dr. Bruce W. Bevan of Geosight, Inc., Pitman, New Jersey (now relocated to Weems, Virginia).

64. Taaffe, *op. cit.* (note 2), p. 116. After terracing the west campus and sealing the trash dumps beneath a protective layer of bricks, Fr. Campbell left St. John's College in 1888 to serve as Jesuit Provincial of the New York-Maryland province; he returned to serve a second time as president in 1896, just in time to receive the consultors' recommendations and order the demolition of the old manor. He must be credited with having created more archaeological deposits of significance at Rose Hill than any other single person.

65. Jean Wetherbee, *White Ironstone: A Collector's Guide*. Antique Trader Books, Dubuque, Iowa, 1996, pp. 18–21.

66. Tables for deciphering registry mark codes may be found in *ibid.*, pp. 14–15; also in Geoffrey A. Godden, *Encyclopaedia of British Pottery and Porcelain Marks*. Barrie and Jenkins, London, 1991, pp. 526–528.

67. Ceramic vessels emerged from the dumps not only in pieces but also with deep stains resulting from contact with corroding metal in the trash. Prof. Diana Bray of Fordham's Chemistry Department generously offered to "do the dishes" using various reagents to remove the intrusive oxides lodged beneath the crackled and worn glaze of some of the more reconstructable pieces. The project extends its appreciation to the entire Chemistry Department for its collegial hospitality in providing laboratory space and supplies to conduct other examinations of excavated materials.

68. Allan S. Gilbert, "Fordham archaeologists reach new depths." *The Ram* 70, no. 26 (November 10, 1988): 9, 16, 18.

69. *The New York Times*, "Above the Harlem River; the progress in improving the annexed district." April 29, 1883, p. 14.

70. "Fordham College and the way from New York City," *op. cit.* (note 37), p. 71.

71. Allan S. Gilbert, Richard B. Marrin, Jr., Roger A. Wines, and Garman Harbottle, "The New Netherland/New York brick archive at Fordham University." *The Bronx County Historical Society Journal* 29, no. 2 (1992): 51–67.

72. From 1850 to 1880, brick brands were transformed from reversed letters on a flat brick face to a legible inscription set within a rectangular recess. For an explanation, see Gilbert *et al.*, *op. cit.* (note 71).

73. See Daniel deNoyelles, IV, *Within These Gates*. Privately published, Thiells, New York, 1982.

74. Chemically matching an unknown brick to a particular source has been possible because of Fordham University's ceramic chemical data bank, a project that began in the mid-1980s. The material against which the Reid bricks were compared in order to establish their provenience consisted of a brick collection presently in excess of 3000 specimens, accumulated over the years from varied places and representing over 350 historically known brickmaking firms that formerly supplied the New York metropolitan area. The essence of chemical sampling, basic procedures, and technical details are available in Gilbert *et al.*, *op. cit.* (note 71) and Allan S. Gilbert, Garman Harbottle, and Daniel deNoyelles, "A ceramic chemistry archive for New Netherland/New York." *Historical Archaeology* 27, no. 2 (1993): 14–53.

75. Fordham student Nicole Raquet (FCRH '94), a native of Rockland County, took special interest in Mr. Reid, tracing leads and extracting much of the information now known about him through laborious research in the New City Public Library.

76. Ira A. Glazier, ed., *The Famine Immigrants: Lists of Irish Immigrants Arriving at the Port of New York, 1846–1851*, Vol IV. Genealogical Publishing Co., Baltimore, 1983, p. 31.

77. String courses are horizontal bands or moldings of stone, often high on a facade. Setbacks are places where the masonry surface steps back at intervals with increasing elevation. A capstone seals the top of the step, preventing the penetration of water into the wall.

78. Among the brownstone quarries functioning in the mid-19th century, Grand View-on-Hudson in Rockland County produced stone most closely resembling the seminary trim, whereas the manor moldings could have originated in the area of Little Falls, New Jersey (communication from Dr.

Sidney Horenstein of the American Museum of Natural History). It is unlikely that any of the stone came from more distant quarries within the brownstone belt, which extended from Gettysburg to southern Massachusetts, but the true sources remain unknown for the moment.

According to Fr. Zwinge's sketchbook maps, stone for the church and seminary facades was quarried by Rodrigue from a pit located on the campus and now buried beneath the university's Freeman Hall and adjacent seismic observatory. This material was largely metamorphic argillaceous limestone (technically a calc-schist), light in overall color but with abundant layering of varied shades. The stone is characterized in a description of the St. John's Hall restoration project: Pamela S. Jerome, Norman R. Weiss, Allan S. Gilbert, and John A. Scott, "Ethyl silicate as a treatment for marble: conservation of St. John's Hall, Fordham University." *Bulletin, Association for Preservation Technology* XXIX, no. 1 (1998): 19–26.

79. A more detailed discussion of the historical events and college documents relating to the renovations of 1855–56 will be found in Gilbert and Wines, *op. cit.* (note 8), pp. 57ff.

80. Dr. David Burney, a palynologist and, at the time, member of Fordham University's Department of Biological Sciences (now curator at the National Tropical Botanical Garden in Kaua'i, Hawai'i), generously offered to analyze pollen recovered from various manor site contexts.

81. Archaeologists use the Latin term *terminus post quem* to characterize objects that convey information about dating. The 1803 penny provides a TPQ for the soil layer overlying the cinder because it indicates a year "during or after which" the roadway must have been covered over. The cinder drive is not necessarily as old as 1803 because the penny could have been carried about in numerous pockets for a lengthy period before being dropped and lost.

As it happens, anthracite offers a later TPQ of 1812. Hard coal did not become a popular substitute for cordwood and charcoal until people overcame the difficulties of igniting it. Initial importation into New York was by coastal schooner from Havre de Grace, Maryland, but shipments of greater volume eventually followed the completion of a canal network, including especially the Delaware and Hudson Canal, in the 1820s. See Donald L. Miller and Richard E. Sharpless, *The Kingdom of Coal*. University of Pennsylvania Press, Philadelphia, 1985, pp. 11–12.

82. The northern and eastern sides of the excavation units consistently suffered progressive collapse after rainfalls due to loose sediment being dislodged by the "sweating" of ground water into the trench as it coursed in a southwestward direction. For this reason, it was impossible to maintain clean, straight sides in the excavation sections over all the years of digging.

83. First reported in a college newspaper article: Allan S. Gilbert, "The hole story." *the paper* 19, no. 2 (February 13, 1990): 10, 26.

84. Helen Wilkinson Reynolds, *Dutch Houses in the Hudson Valley Before 1776*. Dover Publications, New York, 1965 (orig. publ. 1929), p. 18.

85. The drawing by William Rodrigue is now preserved only in later reproductions as well as a copy in the Metropolitan Museum of Art (see note 34); the original is lost. The copper plate engraving differed only slightly from the drawing, and it included a legend in the center foreground identifying the principal school buildings. The engraving was published in Rev. Augustus J. Thébaud, S.J., *Forty Years in the United States of America*. Catholic Historical Society, New York, 1904, opposite page 214. The plate is now located in the university archives.

86. See examples in David S. Cohen, *The Dutch-American Farm*. New York University Press, New York and London, 1992, frontispiece depicting the Thomas Demarest house of Montville, New Jersey; Harrison F. Meeske, *The Hudson Valley Dutch and Their Houses*. Purple Mountain Press, Fleischmanns, New York, 1998, frontispiece of the Martin Van Bergen farmstead of Leeds, New York, and p. 122 of the Minnie Schenck house formerly of Manhasset and now in the Old Bethpage Village Restoration, New York. See also Rosalie Fellows Bailey, *Pre-Revolutionary Dutch Houses and Families in Northern New Jersey and Southern New York*. Dover Publications, New York, 1968 (orig. publ. 1936).

87. Reynolds, *op. cit.* (note 84).

88. An entry in the Treasurer's records for October 10, 1872, indicates purchase of fire clay for the infirmary's furnace: St. John's College, "Cash Book, October 1, 1871 to February 28, 1873." Fordham University Archives, Fordham University, Bronx, New York.

89. Taaffe, *op. cit.* (note 2), pp. 113–114. See also the recent paper summarizing the history of electrification at St. John's College in Roger Wines and Allan S. Gilbert, "St. John's College at Fordham and its pioneering electrification in the Bronx." *Bronx County Historical Society Journal* 51, nos. 1–2 (2014): 28–46.

90. The light bulb components provided significant clues for understanding the electrification of the St. John's College campus in 1888; see Wines and Gilbert, *op. cit.* (note 89).

91. Fordham student William C. Murray (FCRH '98) conducted an electron microprobe study of the metal roofing material to identify the electroplating technique. The white oxide encrusting many of the rolled steel sheets could have resulted from zinc galvanization as well as tinning and terne-plating (tin and lead), other electroplating techniques in use at the time. The massive presence of zinc confirmed that the shingles were galvanized.

92. Fordham student Patricia Fiorenza (FCRH '90) initially identified the shingles and discovered the catalogue, illustrating again the important research contributions made by diggers still learning the basics. The assistance of Avery Library in this matter is greatly appreciated. For more on sheet metal roofing, see Mary B. Dierickx, "Decorative metal roofing in the United States." In H. Ward Jandl, ed., *The Technology of Historic American Buildings; Studies of the Materials, Craft Processes, and the Mechanization of Building Construction*. Association for Preservation Technology, Washington, D.C., 1983, pp. 153–187.

93. See Father Minister's diary (note 58).

94. Archaeologist Patience Freeman initially noticed the patterns on the plaster in the field, and conservators Gary McGowan and Cheryl LaRoche from the cultural resource management firm of John Milner Associates, Inc., generously offered their expertise in treating the wallpaper, which would have deteriorated quickly if not attended to immediately.

95. Appreciation is expressed to Joanne Kosuda-Warner, formerly assistant curator of wallcoverings at the Cooper-Hewitt National Design Museum, for the help she provided to Fordham students researching the Rose Hill wallpaper.

96. See poem on the old infirmary, *op. cit.* (note 60).

4   Public archaeology in Riverdale Park[1]

Valerie Hauser

For a brief time in the late 1980s, the Bronx was host to a unique public archaeology project that provided many local residents and schoolchildren as well as tourists visiting New York with an opportunity to experience Bronx history first-hand. Unfortunately, the project was terminated in the wake of a city budget crisis, but the story of its origin and accomplishments illustrates how public involvement under professional guidance can make a difference in the study and preservation of the city's cultural resources.

ORIGINS OF THE PROJECT

In 1985, Wave Hill, a cultural and environmental center located on the heights immediately above the Hudson River in the northwestern Bronx, conducted a modest archaeological investigation of Riverdale Park, a narrow strip of city parkland fringing the riverfront. The effort was prompted by the knowledge that the New York City Department of Parks and Recreation (NYC Parks) was proposing to conduct major capital improvements in the park. Wave Hill's intention was simply to survey and locate archaeological sites that could be inadvertently destroyed during the rehabilitation if not identified beforehand. Wave Hill could then make recommendations to NYC Parks about integrating the cultural resources into the capital design, thereby preserving the sites from damage and providing a historical dimension to the green space.

The first stage of any cultural resource investigation is documentary research. In this case, records indicated the possibility of several historic period remains within the park, and an archaeological survey performed earlier had located several potential prehistoric sites.[2]

The next step in the investigation was field testing to verify the locations of the documented sites and identify others that might be as yet undiscovered. Wave Hill archaeologists began the survey process by staking out a map grid and digging small pits, or shovel tests, at prescribed intervals to search for signs of past human occupation. Such signs might include concentrations of artifacts or food remains (bones and shells, mostly), and evidence of razed structures. By the end of the first field season in 1985, nearly two-thirds of the park had been tested. Prehistoric and historic archaeological sites as well as a number of historic ruins were located.

It became evident during the survey that much of the archaeological record was threatened by erosion and the illegal activities of looters. The impact of these destructive forces was judged to be too severe to await the completion of the survey and the proposed capital improvements. In response, Wave Hill shifted the project's focus from surveying to management of the park's cultural resources. The first management task had to be salvage excavations to recover archaeological resources rapidly eroding out of steep, unstable embankments. The urgency was, unfortunately, twofold. While digging was being conducted at one severely eroding site, work had to be moved to another one that was being ravaged by looting. Field survey and archival research activities continued, but at a much slower pace considering the field situations requiring immediate attention.

THE PROJECT GOES PUBLIC

A commitment of this magnitude was ambitious for a small cultural center like Wave Hill. Because adequate resources and staff to handle a large-scale project were lacking, public archaeology programs were developed to address the need for increased labor to conduct the rescue operations. Wave Hill thereby added archaeology to its long list of public programs.

For the next four years, Wave Hill attempted with great determination to research, survey, salvage, and stabilize archaeological and historic sites throughout Riverdale Park. New public programs were continually developed not only to take advantage of novel and creative ways to augment the staff but also to provide an opportunity to include the public in the exploration of a public park. With each season, new cultural resources were recorded that required either immediate, emergency attention or, ultimately, long term management to ensure their preservation.

From the start, Wave Hill recognized the park's potential of harboring archaeological sites, but the extent of the resources found and their excellent state of preservation was a surprise. While only two-thirds of the park had been surveyed, five prehistoric and three historic archaeological sites were located. A number of historic structures, including a stone stairway and path, stone property walls, and stone retaining walls, were also recorded.

The prehistoric sites that were tested generally proved to be small shellfish processing stations[3] probably dating to the Late Woodland period (ca. A.D. 1000 to historic contact). One site curiously showed very little evidence of shellfish collecting but did exhibit signs of stone tool making and repair as well as possibly butchering. All the sites tested produced some artifacts, but it was clear that erosion had taken a toll in each case. Unless salvage excavations are conducted in the near future, the information these sites contain will be lost.

The historic sites, all dating to the 19th century, represented domestic occupations and industrial installations, the latter category including the remains of two kilns and a dock (Figures 1 and 2). Preliminary research indicated that the dock may be the oldest in New York's harbor that is still in its original context.

Figure 1. Eroding site surface covering the remains of a 19th century lime kiln in Riverdale Park; the crumbly, white stone is a limerock, probably Inwood marble, that was burned to obtain quicklime. Photograph by V. Hauser.

The greatest threat to these generally more recognizable historic sites is the continual burrowing by artifact collectors, who illicitly remove archaeological finds from city property. Much damage had been done before Wave Hill began its recovery work, but the theft persisted even while rescue efforts were under way, sometimes even in the archaeologists' very trenches after they had left for the day. The selfish desire to possess for personal use resources that belong to all still inspires some to destroy the city's limited archaeological sites. If such behavior is not checked, little of New York's buried past will be left for the future, and New Yorkers will benefit minimally if at all from the knowledge that controlled, scientific excavation might yield.

Wave Hill's first public program entailed an adult field workshop that eventually led to the formation of a corps of trained volunteers. These volunteers regularly assisted Wave Hill's archaeologists with all phases of research and fieldwork (Figure 3). The second program was a summer youth crew that employed and trained local high school students as archaeological technicians. The intent of the summer program was to introduce urban students to the range of problems and potential careers in environmental fields.

Figure 2. Offshore pilings from the former dock of the Dodge estate on the Hudson River. Photograph by V. Hauser.

Both initial programs were extremely successful, and a great deal of public and media attention was drawn to Wave Hill's archaeology project. Encouraged by this success, additional public participation programs were organized. These new endeavors included (1) a volunteer laboratory crew, (2) high school, college, and graduate internships, (3) weekend archaeology walks, (4) public lectures, and (5) a pilot curriculum in archaeology for elementary grades. Wave Hill felt that a project on public land should allow the public to share not only in the experience of archaeological exploration but also in the knowledge gained from the efforts.

The outstanding feature of Wave Hill's archaeology project lay not in the range of archaeological sites that were identified in Riverdale Park. Other city parks doubtless contain vestiges of the past, and some may reveal the same temporal span of Late Woodland to 19th century occupation. What made the

Figure 3. The author directing an adult field workshop in Riverdale Park. Photograph from Wave Hill archives.

Riverdale Park venture so exceptional was the successful combination of archaeology and public education that allowed the study and preservation of the park's cultural resources to be done by the public itself.

THE PROJECT ENDS

The public programs were rapidly expanding, and new ones were in development. Wave Hill was fulfilling its role in providing education programs unavailable at the time to the general public at other city institutions. Yet, the success of the public programs was in sharp contrast to Wave Hill's ability to care for archaeological sites along the riverfront. The demands of cultural resource management for a city park outstripped the ability of a small center with only two archaeologists and a corps of volunteers. The support of other city agencies, notably NYC Parks, was urgently needed, and increased funding to cover the expenses of site rescue and stabilization had to be found.

In summer of 1989, in the face of major funding cuts to all cultural institutions, Wave Hill was forced to begin phasing out the archaeology project. Recovered artifacts were washed, catalogued, and boxed. Records and photographs were organized and filed. By fall, the archaeology lab closed, and the program came to a halt. The untimely and abrupt termination made it impossible to analyze any of the finds or write any reports on the progress made. The information recovered from Riverdale Park for all to share was locked away with the artifacts and records in an underground building at Wave Hill.

In spring of 1995, while this report was in preparation, NYC Parks took possession of the archaeological collection from Riverdale Park. Together with its documentation, the material still sits in storage, this time in a Parks facility.

SUMMARY

Ironically, the fate of Wave Hill's public archaeology program parallels that of archaeology and historic preservation programs throughout the nation at this time. While local grass-roots interest in history, prehistory, and archaeology has always been strong, such programs are difficult to maintain without federal and local governmental support.

Spurred by the persistent federal budget crisis, there has recently been growing criticism by some that excessive public funds are expended on archaeology. A common perception supporting this criticism is that such funding benefits only a very limited archaeological community. Programs like those initiated at Wave Hill demonstrate that, although guidance and direction must be provided by professionals, there is substantial public interest in participatory local archaeology and extensive educational and community benefit to be gotten from it.[4] Nevertheless, even with public support, many programs find themselves, like Wave Hill did, in need of resources to maintain their projects and underwrite some of the material costs.

We expect the government officials who hold the public purse strings to act in fiscally responsible ways, yet we must also hold them responsible for learning what harm is done by an overzealous budget axe. Not only must they see what good can come of protecting, maintaining, and affording the means to study the archaeological record, but they must also know the ill effects of abrupt termination. Hudson River slope erosion will not wait for brighter economic times, and thus the halted rescue operation spells destruction for the soil, vegetation, and historic resources of a Bronx park. As it must do in connection with all government supervised, tax-supported services, the public must be ever vigilant and vocal in making certain that its elected leaders follow courses of action that properly balance the needs of preserving the environment and archaeological record as well as the bottom line.[5]

ENDNOTES

1. With only minor stylistic modifications and the addition of Figure 3, this article is reprinted from Valerie G. DeCarlo, "Public archaeology in Riverdale Park." *The Bronx County Historical Society Journal* 33, no. 1 (1996): 13–20.

2. Surveying in 1984 was conducted by Dr. Nan A. Rothschild of Barnard College, and a report was filed with Wave Hill.

3. Shell middens are common in many coastal areas of the world. In the New World, they are large—sometimes huge—accumulations of shell discarded by ancient Native Americans who collected the local species from shoreline locations for consumption or processing into subsequently consumable food. For general information, see Julie K. Stein, ed., *Deciphering a Shell Midden*. Academic Press, San Diego, 1992; Bretton W. Kent, *Making Dead Oysters Talk: Techniques for Analyzing Oysters from Archaeological Sites*, rev. ed. Maryland Historical and Cultural Publications for Maryland Historical Trust, Historic St. Mary's City, and Jefferson Patterson Park and Museum, Crownsville, Maryland, 1992. Sources more geographically focused on coastal New York include Lynn Ceci, "Shell midden deposits as coastal resources." *World Archaeology* 16, no. 1 (1984): 62–74; Lynn Ceci, *The Effect of European Contact and Trade on the Settlement Pattern of Indians in Coastal New York, 1524–1665*. Garland, New York, 1990; Carlyle S. Smith, "The archaeology of coastal New York." *Anthropological Papers of the American Museum of Natural History* 43, no. 2, New York, 1950.

4. Richard A. Wertime, "The boom in volunteer archaeology." *Archaeology* 48, no. 1 (1995): 66–73.

5. Interested readers can obtain more information about the nature and range of public archaeology programs in the U.S. from the following sources: Charles McGimsey, *Public Archaeology*. Seminar Press, New York, 1972; Alexandria Urban Archaeology Program, *Approaches to Preserving a City's Past*. Alexandria Urban Archaeology Program, Alexandria, Virginia, 1983; Parker B. Potter, *Public Archaeology in Annapolis: A Critical Approach to History in Maryland's Ancient City*. Smithsonian Institution Press, Washington, DC, 1994.

The business of archaeology:
Cultural Resource Management in the Bronx

Betsy Kearns *
Cece Saunders

During the past 50 years, Americans have grown increasingly concerned about preserving the past. The environmental movement of the 1960s and 1970s increased public awareness about historic preservation, and as a consequence, new laws were enacted to ensure that sites and historic buildings would receive appropriate study and evaluation of their archaeological and architectural importance prior to any development that could change, damage, or destroy them. In the case of archaeological sites, the legislation calls for testing, exploration, sampling, and analysis in order to learn as much as possible before construction-related disturbances take their toll. Most states and local governments, including New York City, now require that, under certain circumstances, certified archaeologists be hired to conduct work site investigations to determine whether development would pose a danger to any archaeological remains that might exist and, if so, to mitigate that danger in some way.

The emergence of preservation legislation spurred the growth throughout the U.S. of contract archaeology firms that bid on jobs in the same way other construction companies do. Cultural Resource Management, abbreviated CRM, is the field that has emerged to carry out such legally mandated research.[1] The authors' contract archaeology firm, Historical Perspectives, Inc., has been in business for 35 years, and in the process, studying Bronx history by conducting the archaeological assessments required by federal, state, or city regulations. Based upon the firm's experience and some specific cases, this paper describes CRM procedures and how they help to protect the borough's historic remains.

WHY CULTURAL RESOURCE MANAGEMENT?

The problem of preservation in the city

The intensity of urbanization in Manhattan has drastically modified much of the island's original topography, and buried remains of the past have

---

* In memory of Elizabeth "Betsy" Wright Kearns, d. 04.28.10.

often been destroyed or capped by tons of cement, asphalt, and stone. Except for the backyards of older houses, parklands, and other open spaces, what survives beneath the city's crust is mostly inaccessible and, therefore, safe until it is exposed in the continuous march of construction.[2]

The Bronx has suffered far less from intrusive urbanism than the densely packed cityscapes of Manhattan. It still harbors sites that lie relatively undisturbed just beneath the surface. Evidence of ancient Native Americans is not uncommon,[3] and vestiges of some of the fortifications that ringed New York during the Revolution have also been found.[4] Remains from the more recent past are even more plentifully distributed beneath many streets and shallow foundations of the borough's generally low skyline.

But like Manhattan, there are also places in the Bronx where the original landforms are almost impossible to imagine, and the extent to which anything from the past has survived is uncertain. The Kingsbridge and Spuyten Duyvil sections, for example, have undergone major changes. Prior to European settlement, the area contained forested uplands, extensive meadows, fresh and salt

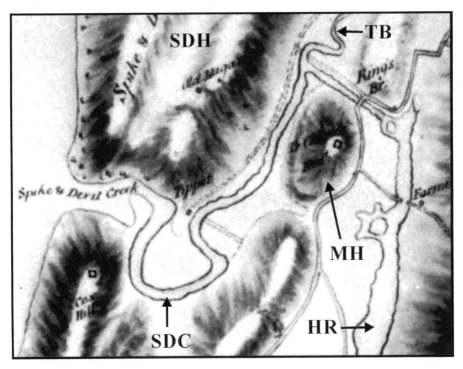

Figure 1. Detail from a 1781 British military map of the area surrounding Spuyten Duyvil showing the late 18th century landforms of northernmost Manhattan Island. Key: SDC = Spuyten Duyvil Creek; SDH = Spuyten Duyvil Hill; TB = Tibbett's Brook; MH = Marble Hill; HR = Harlem River. Courtesy of the William L. Clements Library, University of Michigan.

water marshes, shallow mud flats, tidal and fresh water streams, and a number of coves and bays. Native American groups visited the area seasonally, and colonial farmsteads later sprang up on its hills and plains. British occupation forces made it the northernmost defense perimeter for Revolutionary War New York. Figure 1, a detail from a British headquarters map,[5] illustrates the physical features, nearby farms, principal land routes, and the main military outposts. In the original landscape, Tibbett's Brook flowed south into Spuyten Duyvil Creek, a circuitous watercourse connecting the Harlem and Hudson Rivers, which rose and fell with the tides of the New York estuary.

In the 19th century, the Johnson munitions foundry established on the peninsula formed by the Creek spawned the industrial community of Spuyten Duyvil, which significantly and permanently altered the landscape (the atlas map[6] of Figure 2 shows the 1885 geography). Enormous amounts of landfill (much of it from excavations for Grand Central Station starting in 1903) were laid down to create space for extensive railroad tracks and freight yards. The

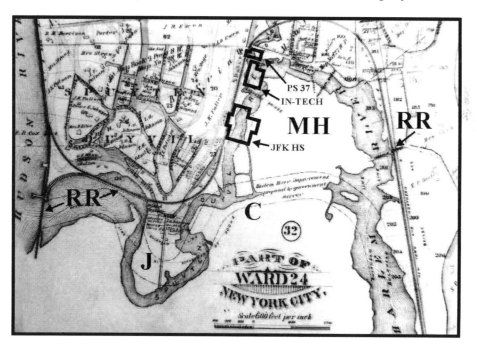

Figure 2. Map detail of late 19th century Spuyten Duyvil village north of the Johnson Foundry (J) showing the major landscape modifications produced by the shoreline railroad (RR), and the proposed Harlem River and Spuyten Duyvil Creek canal (C) that cut Marble Hill (MH) away from Manhattan and made it part of the mainland. Overlaid outlines of the current Primary School 37, In-Tech MS/HS 368, and JFK High School show the area surveyed as part of the Tibbett Gardens Project site in 1987 (see below).

cutting of a ship's channel separated Marble Hill from the tip of Manhattan, to which it had always been physically attached, while the infilling of Spuyten Duyvil Creek to the north joined Marble Hill to the Bronx mainland with which it had formerly been connected only by ferry and then by the "King's Bridge." Further modifications created the flat expanse at the end of today's Tibbett Avenue, which is now occupied by John F. Kennedy High School and the newer Primary School 37 and In-Tech Academy MS/HS 368 (footprints outlined in Figure 2). It was built up with landfill over the west-flowing Spuyten Duyvil Creek and the south-flowing Tibbett's Brook in addition to the removal of much of the slope of Spuyten Duyvil Hill just to the west.

Clearly, urbanized areas represent a diverse mosaic of neighborhoods with different occupational histories as well as historic remains in varying degrees of preservation. Layers of ever increasing complexity have been formed in step with the expanding population. Uninhabitable localities were transformed into marketable real estate, and parcels of land were subdivided and consolidated over many episodes of reuse.

Modifications inflicted by city growth are apparent everywhere. Places where original land surfaces have been removed have usually also been stripped of the archaeological clues that inform us about the past. Places that have been buried under landfill theoretically still preserve historic information, but the often formidable depth of the fill can render archaeological investigation next to impossible even with a backhoe in support of the traditional trowel and brush.

The practice of CRM has helped local administrators determine which job sites contain archaeological remains that have been previously destroyed, which ones cover layers of cultural significance that are deeply and safely entombed well below the maximum depth of planned construction, and which ones hold part of the national or local heritage as intact archaeological deposits, vulnerable and in need of rescue, just beneath the surface.

The legal dimension of CRM

Because various governmental bodies have become major catalysts for archaeological research, particularly in urban settings, many archaeological studies now conducted in the U.S. are done to fulfill a legal requirement. Regulations that pertain to archaeology customarily direct public agencies and private developers to hire qualified archaeologists to carry out the requisite investigations. ("Qualified" has usually referred to certification by RPA, the national Register of Professional Archaeologists, or meeting the professional standards set by the National Park Service.) Many projects in the Bronx are sponsored or licensed through various levels of government, which sometimes provide financial support or regulatory oversight. In such cases, cultural resource studies must be conducted if they were stipulated by the conditions under which the project was approved. As part of this process, contracted archaeologists file cultural resource reports on the work they perform, and sometimes, they must recover samples of the buried remains through archaeological excavation before a new sewer line is installed or a new building foundation is laid.

The cost of a CRM investigation is borne by the developer and is usually only a small fraction of the total price of development. As the law sees it, this expense is justified in the interest of providing the public with a way to preview the ground and what lies beneath it in order to save historical remains of consequence. The conditions under which CRM must be employed are narrowly defined, however, and an investigation is not always mandated.

In New York City, developers who build within zoning guidelines at their construction site usually need not underwrite a cultural resource study. Any archaeological remains within the ground may legally be obliterated, except if (1) federal, state, or city funds are being used, or (2) the site contains a designated historic landmark (described below). Should either or both of these conditions occur, or should a developer seek a variance in order to build outside any zoning restrictions, the request triggers an evaluation by the City Environmental Quality Review, or CEQR (regulations listed within the CEQR Manual).[7] CEQR entails various environmental studies, including a CRM assessment to determine the archaeological sensitivity of impacted areas. Entire city blocks, street beds, manufacturing complexes, parklands, industrial waterfronts, or private holdings may be subject to CEQR, and CRM research must be conducted to identify, evaluate, register, and treat significant archaeological and other cultural resources within the project area.[8] CEQR provisions are also activated for any proposed changes to a property that is listed as a historic resource: a city landmark of any kind, a site scheduled for landmarking, a site listed as a State or National Register Property, or a site eligible for inclusion on any historic registry.

CEQR regulations have no jurisdiction outside New York City, but state and federal laws will still apply. For example, federally-assisted projects obligate compliance with federal statutes if they impose any effect upon a district, site, or structure included in (or eligible for inclusion in) the National Register of Historic Places.

Undertaking a CRM study in an urban area transcends the popular perception of archaeology. The digging takes place first in archives, libraries, and by interview to record the memory of eyewitnesses before a spade is ever placed in the ground. The focus of the inquiry may not be a lost culture but an existing reservoir or a historic residence, backyard, graveyard, or even a commercial site.

THE CRM PROCESS

The CEQR Manual describes the steps involved in archaeological evaluation within New York City. A helpful companion to the CEQR Manual, first published in 2001, is the *Landmarks Preservation Commission Guidelines for Archaeological Work in New York City.*[9]

Documentary study

The initial objective for an urban archaeological research team is to conduct a *documentary study,*[10] the aim of which is to delineate, prior to any digging, specific areas of the overall project site which might contain deposits that are potentially "archaeologically sensitive." It would be impossible to know whether the site contained actual deposits that were archaeologically sensitive unless a probe or sounding (a small excavation) were conducted, but field testing is generally not undertaken right away. Documentary studies on city sites are typically reviewed by the Landmarks Preservation Commission, the city agency responsible for facilitating the preservation of archaeological and historic properties affected by development.[11]

Extant documents often contain much relevant information bearing upon the history of the locality, e.g., maps, deeds, wills, census records, etc. The documentary study relies upon such sources to assess the likelihood that archaeological remains of significance, historic or prehistoric, might exist within the work site in question. If it appears probable that such remains have also survived the many waves of urban disturbance, such as construction, demolition, landscaping, road building, or utility line placement, then the documentary study might also establish a need for subsurface investigations.

A wide range of sources are employed to assemble documentary evidence. Many archaeological sites have already been found and are listed by the City's Landmarks Preservation Commission or other agencies, such as the SHPO (State Historic Preservation Officer). These sites, in addition to any historic structures that remain standing in the immediate vicinity, are important indicators of the potential sensitivity of a work site.[12]

Other archaeological resources might nevertheless exist that have not previously been consulted, or even acknowledged. Therefore, further research based on archival records, library materials, historic maps and atlases, as well as field inspections are necessary. Sometimes interviews with eyewitnesses or technical specialists provide a preliminary evaluation of the original landforms, history of use, and degree of previous disturbance to the project site.[13]

The report generated by this effort enables a monitoring agency, which is often the Landmarks Preservation Commission in New York City, to determine how likely it would be to find archaeological resources in the path of destruction. If it is deemed necessary, a second stage of examination—archaeological field testing—is recommended to verify the existence of buried remains and ascertain their significance.

Archaeological significance is judged on the basis of whether any contribution to current historical knowledge is likely to accrue from further investigation. Criteria for assigning significance change as our knowledge of the past increases, but in general, sites from poorly known periods, or those possibly containing historic remains that have rarely or never before been explored archaeologically would be considered highly significant because of the completely new information they might reveal.

When documentary research determines that potentially significant archaeological resources may lie within a work site, the impact of proposed construction upon those potential resources must be assessed. The archaeologist compares the "future no action condition"[14]—what the future impact to the buried resources might be in the absence of any impending modifications—with the "future action condition"[15]—which evaluates what disturbances or other "significant adverse impacts" the proposed action might impose upon those resources. If the proposed action would irreparably change the appearance, integrity, or historical significance of the buried remains, mitigation measures must be undertaken, which commonly involve further archaeological exploration.

Testing and mitigation

Mitigation[16] usually begins with *field testing* to locate and evaluate the buried remains.[17] Field testing consists of limited subsurface probing with digging tools. If no important resources are encountered, then archaeological consideration of the site is completed. If, however, the testing determines that historically significant remains do indeed exist, then succeeding steps in the CEQR review may take one of two courses. Either the construction project undergoes *redesign* to avoid impacting the buried remains, or, if this is not feasible, a program of fieldwork is developed for *data recovery*, i.e., retrieval of a broad enough range of archaeological materials through full-scale excavation that will form a suitable sample for historical study.

Excavations[18] are typically planned in connection with the overseeing agency.[19] This is the most intensive phase of mitigation, and it begins only after agreement is reached concerning the goals, research issues, level of field effort, treatment of recovered finds, character of the final report, and duration of the project. The collections of artifacts that result from the CRM study are eventually placed in a repository that may curate the material and provide access to other scholars who might wish to conduct subsequent analyses.[20]

Excavation may be required by law in many situations, but in an urban context, fieldwork presents many complications and hazards. The everyday problems include site and personnel security, safe passage for passersby, and the halting or redirecting of traffic. The obstacles unique to urban digging usually involve locating and avoiding active underground conduits and other utilities that form part of the dense maze of subsurface infrastructure. Among the many hazards are the risk of uncovering toxic materials, the height of the water table in certain places, and the potential for trench collapse of loosely packed landfill or other cultural debris, especially when it is rendered unstable by the vibrations created by mechanized transportation. Urban excavation thus presents special challenges that must be overcome in the interest of legal compliance as well as historic preservation.

CASE STUDIES

The Tibbett Gardens Project Site

Historical Perspectives, Inc. was contracted to evaluate the archaeological potential of the Tibbett Gardens Project site (Figure 3). Located north of John F. Kennedy High School at Spuyten Duyvil, the site includes the street

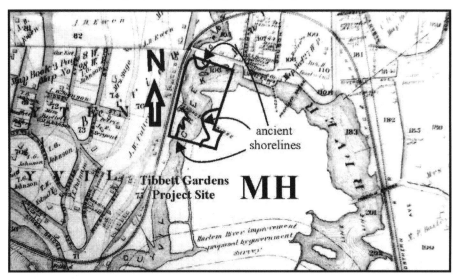

Figure 3. Location of the Tibbett Gardens Project site, superimposed over the confluence of Tibbett's Brook and Spuyten Duyvil Creek on the atlas map of Figure 2. The shorelines indicated were considered archaeologically sensitive because they might have been shallow enough to be impacted by construction.

frontage now occupied by Primary School 37 and In-Tech Academy MS/HS 368.[21] Formerly, the channel of Tibbett's Brook discharged into Spuyten Duyvil Creek at this spot (see Figure 1), but the present land surface is elevated far above the former stream beds. Little original landscape was left to survey, and an unknown depth of fill covered what might be archaeologically sensitive riverside sites dating to prehistoric and early historic times.

A geologist (Prof. Dennis Weiss, formerly of City College, CUNY[22]) was therefore called in to analyze 181 soil borings (Figure 4) that had previously been obtained in connection with the earlier construction of JFK High School to the south. Each boring contained a sequence of subsurface sediments, which by their characteristics and depth of the strata, as well as the placement of the core, could inform about the changes in ancient topography over time. In this way, the original shorelines could be located based on the distribution of sediments at the same depth, and a visual image of what the streams looked like at any given date

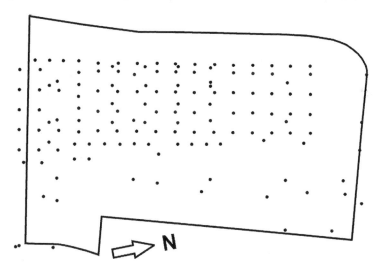

Figure 4. Locations of boreholes from the Tibbett Gardens Project site. Layers of sediment recovered from the cores provided evidence permitting reconstruction of former landforms now deeply buried below the modern land surface.

could be recreated.[23] If these buried landforms were sufficiently deep or peripheral to the construction site, then foundations for new buildings might not endanger any potential archaeological deposits. If, however, such landforms were close to the modern surface, their exposure in the course of building could then be carefully monitored for signs of cultural remains. Use of geological techniques to help answer archaeological questions has grown over the past four decades. Such innovations have led to the emergence of an interdisciplinary

Figure 5. (Facing page) Paleogeographic maps of the subsurface sedimentary record beneath the Tibbett Gardens Project site (horizontal cross-sections at 1:60) indicating landforms existing at (a) 10 feet below modern ground surface dating to *ca.* 2000 years ago, (b) 20 feet below modern ground surface dating to *ca.* 4000 years ago, and (c) 30 feet below modern ground surface dating to *ca.* 6000 years ago. Legend:

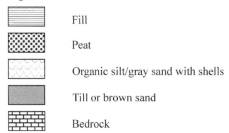

Fill

Peat

Organic silt/gray sand with shells

Till or brown sand

Bedrock

specialization called *geoarchaeology*, which has introduced new methods and new kinds of training and expertise that have fostered closer ties between archaeology and the earth sciences.[24]

A similar sequence of strata was found in most of the boreholes. The bedrock was either (1) Fordham gneiss, which underlies Spuyten Duyvil Hill to the west, (2) Inwood marble of Marble Hill to the east, or (3) another rock body, the Lowerre quartzite. Resting upon the bedrock in many places was a brownish sand containing gravel, boulders, and silt that was identified as glacial till, i.e., materials transported by the Pleistocene ice sheet and dumped in an unsorted jumble. Above the brown sand appeared a series of other sands, organic silt, and peat layers, sometimes interbedded with one another and often repeated through the column of sediment. Spread over everything was a thick layer of modern fill that marked the final interment of Spuyten Duyvil Creek as Marble Hill was connected to the Bronx.

It was assumed that sediments revealing organic silt, peat, or a grayish sand with shells had been deposited within an ancient tidal estuary where freshwater streams emanating from the Bronx had met the brackish backflow of the Hudson and Harlem rivers. The brown sand and bedrock projections appearing in the cores were presumed to represent dry land formerly perched above mean high tide levels.

Over the approximately 6000 years represented by the cored sediments, estuarine conditions apparently increased as more of the lowlying land surface was covered by water due to the rising sea level that accompanied the melting of the Pleistocene glaciers. At a depth of some 30 feet (Figure 5c), cores revealed the presence of a small embayment that may have been surrounded by a sandy beach, bedrock outcropping from beneath glacial till, and perhaps tidal marsh, all dating to about 4000 B.C. At about 20 feet in depth, probably reflecting conditions of about 2000 B.C. (Figure 5b), the estuary or tidal inlet had spread

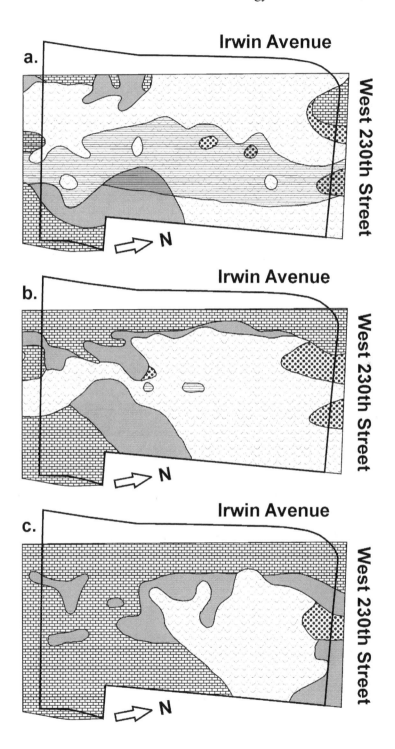

through the center of the site, leaving potential shoreline habitats for prehistoric human habitation along the west and southeast. At a depth of about 10 feet (Figure 5a), terrestrial deposits dating probably to 2000 years ago that could have been archaeologically sensitive were revealed in the extreme northwestern, southwestern, and southeastern corners of the site, and running through the length of the site lay the beginnings of the massive fill of the late 19th and early 20th centuries that had engulfed Spuyten Duyvil Creek and forever changed the modern landscape.

The core analysis had not discovered any artifacts, but it did show where sites might have been located, and consequently where attention would have to be focused if construction were eventually to impact those places.

The old St. John's College cemetery

In the early 1990s, Historical Perspectives, Inc. conducted a document-ary study of the archaeological potential of the New York Botanical Garden (NYBG) in conjunction with the NYBG's preparation of a master plan for the future.[25] This study was not legally required, as no immediate construction plans were in place, but it was commissioned in order to obtain a professional eval-uation to use in planning. Research confirmed earlier archaeological reports[26] that had identified zones of probable prehistoric occupation (such as caves) along the Bronx River.

In addition, documentary evidence indicated the former existence of a burial ground that once contained the graves of Jesuit faculty, students, and hired workers from St. John's College, the Bronx school that opened in 1841 and eventually became Fordham University. The southern part of the NYBG had been the property of the college, but in 1884, the city's Department of Public Parks included this land within the boundaries of its proposed Bronx Park. The college was forced to sell the property, some 30 acres, which included the cemetery plot it had used since its inception.

At the end of 1889, the Department gave permission to St. John's to exhume the burials and move them westward across Southern Boulevard for reinterment within the main part of the Rose Hill campus.[27] Rev. Joseph Zwinge, S.J., Father Minister to the college, was in charge of the operation (Figure 6), and his record of the event included plans of the old cemetery and the new one that was established immediately east of the college church of Our Lady of Mercy,[28] as well as a daily journal that reported the removal of bodies between January 21 and 28, 1890. The work must have been arduous, as a *New York Times* feature[29] reported a severe cold snap beginning on January 22 with temperatures plummeting to 18° F and winds gusting to 60 miles per hour. Presumably, the frozen ground was pierced by the diggers to remove the human remains, and

Figure 6. Map detail of 1868 showing location of the burial ground belonging to St. John's College from which burials were removed in 1890 for reinterment alongside the church. The map appeared in a real estate atlas published by F.W. Beers.[30]

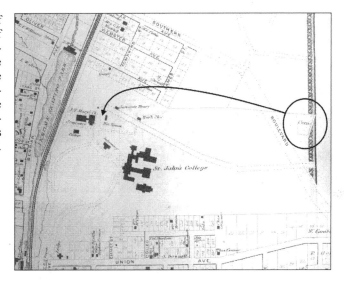

the dipping mercury could have been a blessing in the case of some bodies that had been buried for less than a decade, especially for one whose funeral had taken place within the past year.

According to Zwinge, 78 bodies were interred within the new cemetery. Of these, 74 had been brought over from the old burial ground within the area of the future NYBG. Zwinge's terse summation on the old cemetery plan was that not all of the bodies had been found. Brother Joseph Creedon, S.J., and a servant named Joseph Kessel remained unaccounted for. Thus, two occupied graves might still lie within NYBG property. Zwinge had mapped the location of Creedon's grave, the first Jesuit interred within the cemetery (he died on July 10, 1847), but as his body was not found, the remains could have deteriorated within the ground, making them difficult to discern. Kessel's grave was not indicated on the cemetery plan, though his marker had been restored in 1865, 10 years after his death in 1855. Had the grave's location been lost, the diggers would have faced a serious obstacle probing the frozen ground. Despite the efforts to find and exhume him, Kessel had not been recovered either.

An in-depth documentary study (officially, a "topic intensive study") combining archival research, interviews, and careful cartographic comparisons was conducted.[31] The approximate areal extent of the old cemetery was plotted based upon its appearance in several 19th century atlases and a map book drawn by Fr. Zwinge,[32] and aligned stones just visible at the lawn surface were identified as probable remnants of boundary walls for the burial plot (Figure 7). Evidence of subsurface disturbances and installation of a water system as well as an asphalt path indicated that some intrusive penetration into the former cemetery had taken place over the past century.

Figure 7. Stone alignment at lawn level within the New York Botanical Garden that likely marked the perimeter of the former burial ground of St. John's College. Photograph by A.S. Gilbert, October 19, 1995.

Considering the uncertainties surrounding the whereabouts of the two undiscovered burials, the NYBG was advised that it might wish to avoid subsurface impacts in the immediate vicinity of the former cemetery. If development of the area ever became necessary, close monitoring of any earth-moving by certified archaeologists would probably ensure retrieval of any human remains encountered so that the marooned of St. John's might be reunited with their long departed colleagues across the street on the Fordham University campus.

The Shorehaven Beach Club condominium complex

Field testing and subsequent mitigation stages, whether by shovel or backhoe, verify the predictions of an archaeological documentary study. These excavations are not intended simply to locate pretty objects for display but to attempt to answer specific questions concerning how and why occupation at a particular site took place as it did. Artifacts and features recovered during excavations take on meaning in relation to their potential to contribute to the identification and understanding of past cultural practices.

Sometimes, excavations produce significant amounts of informative remains, but occasionally they have unexpected results. For example, field excavation in preparation for the development of a condominium complex at the southern end of Sound View Avenue, near Clason Point, was designed to answer questions regarding Native American life along the East River. The documentary study[33] had determined that aboriginal groups formerly occupied the high sandy knolls along this section of the river. "Snakapins," a Native American village that may have supported over 300 persons, was located just one-half mile from the tip of Clason Point. During excavations here by Alanson Skinner in 1918,[34] the site yielded over 60 earth ovens, human and dog burials, stone tools, and fishing implements. Pre-colonial shell middens (i.e., concentrated piles of the discarded remains of shellfish) have also been recorded in the vicinity of Clason Point—in Castle Hill, for example. As late as the 1970s, parklands along Pugsley Creek in this coastline community of the Bronx were still yielding Early Archaic workshop sites for making stone tools.[35]

The documentary study also indicated that the long arm of Robert Moses had been at work, and that up to 30 feet of modern landfill had been dumped on or at the periphery of the site. Known areas of landfill were avoided during subsequent mitigation,[36] but nevertheless, a backhoe had to remove up to 10 feet of broken brick chimneys, coal ash, and huge boulders before test units could be dug. It was necessary to climb down ladders into trenches inundated with the tides. Mud and water sometimes rose to knee-high levels (Figure 8).

There was great excitement the day one archaeologist located a large cache of broken white clay pipe bowls and stems (Figure 9). The long stemmed pipes were a ubiquitous part of colonial life and are often encountered in excavations of 17th and 18th century sites. Dates of occupation can even be roughly calculated by an analysis of the borehole diameter of the pipe stems. Excitement was short lived, however. When the historic documents were re-examined, it was discovered that the *ca.* 1910 amusement park on the tip of Clason Point had game booths that gave away quite modern long-stemmed white clay pipes as prizes! Continued testing revealed only more evidence of the 20th century grading, filling, construction, and total destruction of what had once been a bucolic setting peopled by Native Americans.

SUMMARY

The contracted research described in this paper does not rival the spectacular finds familiar from broadcast reports, magazines, films, and popular books. Other projects undertaken by Historical Perspectives, Inc. have been more traditional in their exposure of ruins and recovery of artifacts requiring cleaning, cataloguing, and analysis. The examples provided here were chosen especially to make the point that CRM exists to protect the archaeological record, not necessarily to find the best sites and dig them up.

In the Tibbett Gardens site, land surfaces that were exposed after the Ice Age and possibly inhabited by ancient Native Americans or early colonists proved to be blanketed by a thick protective layer of fill. Construction activities did not endanger these buried landscapes, and as a result, no excavation to

Figure 8. Shorehaven Beach Club exploration, Area B, Trench 7, Unit 1, showing seepage into the excavation units. Photograph by Historical Perspectives, Inc.

Figure 9. White clay pipe fragments, including stems, decorated bowls, and spur sections, representing prizes from a midway booth of an early 20th century amusement park; recovered from the Shorehaven Beach Club exploration. Photograph by Historical Perspectives, Inc.

explore and sample archaeological materials in the impacted area was necessary. Determining this, however, did require pre-construction investigation using geoarchaeological techniques to facilitate the archaeological assessment.

The former burial ground of St. John's College, presently located within a public park, should have been a historical curiosity were it not for the unfortunate fact that the recovery operation of 1890 did not successfully locate all the recorded graves, a situation that potentially complicates development by the NYBG in the vicinity of the cemetery. Locating the boundaries of the plot with as much precision as possible using documentary sources provided NYBG administrators with the means to make informed judgments about managing the area. Quite possibly, the bodies in question were no longer recoverable at the moment of exhumation, but in the event that any modification of the grounds proved necessary, close monitoring of excavations would be the next step in dealing with this 120-year-old missing persons mystery. During the summer of 2007, in connection with an expansion of the Children's Adventure Garden, a deep backhoe excavation was conducted in what may have been the southern portion of the former burial ground. It is not known whether archaeological oversight was involved.

The Shorehaven Beach Club construction project appeared destined to disturb land with a proven link to Native American habitation, yet the digging conducted through upwelling mud proved to be unproductive of any archaeological information reflecting aboriginal life. The effort was necessary, however, because the probability of prehistoric remains being destroyed by development had to be assessed before construction could begin. It is the responsibility of CRM archaeologists to make appropriate evaluations of a site's archaeological potential regardless what form of "romantic allure" the site may exude.

ACKNOWLEDGMENTS

We appreciate the expertise of Dr. Dennis Weiss, as well as the patience and cooperation of Patrice Kane and Vivian Shen (Walsh Library Archives of Fordham University). HPI's excellent team on many Bronx projects has included Faline Schneiderman, Sara Mascia, Richard Schaefer, Nancy S. Dickerson, Martha Cobbs, Barbara Magee, and Julie A. Horn.

ENDNOTES

1. Many CRM firms are small businesses that engage in local archaeological and environmental studies, but some are archaeological subdivisions of major engineering corporations with nationwide and international branches and clientele. For additional information, see H. Cleere, ed.,

Approaches to the Archaeological Heritage: A Comparative Study of World Cultural Resource Management Systems. Cambridge University Press, Cambridge, 1984; S. Hunt, E.W. Jones, and M.E. McAllister, eds., *Archaeological Resource Protection.* National Trust for Historic Preservation, Washington, DC, 1992; Jordan E. Kerber, ed., *Cultural Resource Management: Archaeological Research, Preservation Planning, and Public Education in the Northeastern United States.* Bergin and Garvey, Westport, CT, 1994; Thomas W. Neumann and Robert M. Sanford, *Cultural Resources Archaeology.* AltaMira Press, Walnut Creek, CA, 2001; Thomas F. King, *Thinking About Cultural Resource Management: Essays from the Edge.* AltaMira Press, Walnut Creek, CA, 2002; Thomas F. King, *Cultural Resource Laws and Practice: An Introductory Guide*, 2nd edition. AltaMira Press, Walnut Creek, CA, 2004; Thomas F. King, *Doing Archaeology: A Cultural Resource Management Perspective.* Left Coast Press, Walnut Creek, CA, 2005; Lynne Sebastian and William D. Lipe, eds., *Archaeology and Cultural Resource Management: Visions for the Future.* School for Advanced Research Press, Santa Fe, 2009.

2. Bert Salwen, "Archeology in megalopolis." In *Research and Theory in Current Archeology*, ed. by Charles L. Redman, pp. 151–163. John Wiley and Sons, New York, 1973.

3. Edward J. Lenik, "Native American archaeological resources in urban America: a view from New York." *Bulletin and Journal of the New York State Archeological Association* 103 (1992): 20–30; Faline Schneiderman-Fox and A. Michael Pappalardo, "A paperless approach toward field data collection: an example from the Bronx." *Bulletin, Society for American Archaeology* 14, no. 1 (1996): 1,18–20.

4. Julius Lopez, "History and archeology of Fort Independence on Tetard's Hill, Bronx County, N.Y." *Bulletin and Journal of the New York State Archeological Association* 73 (July, 1978): 1–28. (Edited posthumously by Stanley Wisniewski.)

5. "A map of the country adjacent to Kings-Bridge surveyed by order of His Excellency General Henry Clinton" and drawn by Andrew Skinner and George Taylor in 1781. William L. Clements Library, University of Michigan, Ann Arbor. Map detail courtesy of the William L. Clements Library.

6. E. Robinson and R.H. Pidgeon, *Robinson's Atlas of the City of New York.* E. Robinson, New York, 1885, plate 40 (Spuyten Duyvil, Kings Bridge, Jerome Park, Fordham).

7. City of New York, *City Environmental Quality Review Technical Manual.* Mayor's Office of Environmental Coordination, New York, 2014.

8. City agencies, e.g., the Department of Parks and Recreation and the Department of Transportation, are also responsible for assessing project impacts to cultural resources. CRM firms are often hired as consultants for such city agency projects.

9. The most current version of the Guidelines is available through the New York City Landmarks Preservation Commission website: http://www.nyc.gov/html/lpc/downloads/pdf/pubs/ayguide.pdf.

10. Outside New York City, the documentary study is termed a Phase 1A assessment by archaeologists working under state authority: see New York Archaeological Council, *Standards for Cultural Resource Investigations and the Curation of Archaeological Collections.* New York Archaeological Council, Rochester, 1994; New York Archaeological Council, *Cultural Resource Standards Handbook.* New York Archaeological Council, 2000; New York State Office of Parks,

Recreation and Historic Preservation, "State Historic Preservation Office Phase I Archaeological Report Format Requirements." Peebles Island, Waterford, New York, 2005.

11. Some state agencies—e.g., the Dormitory Authority of the State of New York and the School Construction Authority—have legislated authorization to coordinate all reviews through the State Historic Preservation Office and are thus not directly subject to CEQR even though their projects may be conducted in New York City.

12. CEQR Manual, *op. cit.* (note 7), section 321.1. The NYCLPC's library of prior archaeological studies in the city, as well as evaluations of historic structures, is available on their website: http://www.nyc.gov/html/lpc/downloads/pdf/pubs/ayguide.pdf. Cultural resources data on file with the New York SHPO can be accessed through the agency's electronic system: https://cris.parks.ny.gov/.

13. *Ibid.*, section 321.2.

14. *Ibid.*, section 321.3.

15. *Ibid.*, section 321.4.

16. *Ibid.*, section 510.

17. Field testing is referred to as Phase 1B in the state terminology: see New York Archaeological Council, *op. cit.* (note 10).

18. Excavation is categorized as a Phase 2 assessment according to state law: *ibid.*

19. CEQR Manual, *op. cit.* (note 7), section 512.2.

20. See the discussion in this volume by Amanda Sutphin on the matter of an archaeological repository for New York City.

21. Historical Perspectives, Inc., "Phase 1A Archaeological Assessment Report for the Tibbett Gardens Project, Bronx, New York." Prepared for Allee King Rosen & Fleming, Inc. Copy on file, New York City Landmarks Preservation Commission, 1987.

22. Dr. Weiss retired in 2015 as Dean of Natural Sciences and Mathematics at Stockton University in Galloway, New Jersey.

23. Dennis Weiss, "Paleo-Environmental Interpretation of the Tibbett Gardens Project Site, Bronx, New York." Submitted to Historical Perspectives, Inc. and Allee King Rosen and Fleming, Inc. Copy on file, New York City Landmarks Preservation Commission, August 26, 1987.

24. For an overview of geoarchaeology, see George Rapp, Jr., and Christopher L. Hill, *Geoarchaeology: the Earth-Science Approach to Archaeological Interpretation*, 2nd edition. Yale University Press, New Haven, 2006; Paul Goldberg and Richard I. Macphail, *Practical and Theoretical Geoarchaeology*. Blackwell, Malden, MA, 2006; and Allan S. Gilbert, ed., *Encyclopedia of Geoarchaeology*. Springer, Dordrecht, 2017.

25. Historical Perspectives, Inc., "Stage IA Archaeological Assessment for the New York

Botanical Garden, Bronx, New York." Prepared for Vollmer Associates and the City of New York Department of Cultural Affairs, 1993.

26. Sherene Baugher, Edward J. Lenik, and Daniel N. Pagano, "Design Through Archaeology: An Archaeological Assessment of Fifteen City-Owned Cultural Institutions." Prepared for the New York City Dept of Cultural Affairs, on file at the New York City Landmarks Preservation Commission, 1991.

27. City of New York, Department of Public Parks, *Minutes and Documents of the Board of Commissioners of the Department of Public Parks for the Year Ending April 30th, 1890*. Martin B. Brown, New York, 1890. The request of St. John's College to exhume and move the bodies was heard at the commissioners' meeting of December 16, 1889 (p. 316), and formal permission was recorded at the meeting of February 26, 1890, a month after the exhumations took place.

28. Materials relating to the old Jesuit cemetery are kept in the Archivist's Files, Cemetery Lists folder, Walsh Library Archives and Special Collections, Fordham University, Bronx, NY. See also Nicholas Falco, "The old cemetery in Fordham University." *The Bronx County Historical Society Journal* 8, no. 1 (1971): 20–25.

29. "Winter weather at last." *The New York Times* (Thursday, January 23, 1890): 8, col. 1.

30. F.W. Beers, *Atlas of N.Y. and Vicinity*, F.W. Beers, A.D. Ellis, and G.G. Soule, New York, 1868, plate 11 (Fordham).

31. Historical Perspectives, Inc., "Stage IB Topic-Intensive Research: Jesuit Cemetery on the Grounds of the New York Botanical Garden." Prepared for Vollmer Associates and the City of New York Department of Cultural Affairs, 1993.

32. Rev. Joseph Zwinge, S.J., "Maps of Property of St. John's College since the beginning by Father Minister," map labeled "Part of Property beyond Boulevard." Walsh Library Archives and Special Collections, Fordham University, Bronx, NY, 1893–94.

33. Historical Perspectives, Inc., "Phase IA Archaeological Assessment Report on the Shorehaven Project, The Bronx, New York." Prepared for Soundview Associates. Copy on file, New York City Landmarks Preservation Commission, 1987.

34. Alanson Skinner, "Exploration of aboriginal sites at Throgs Neck and Clasons Point, New York City." *Contributions from the Museum of Natural History* 5, no. 4 (1919). See the chapter by Robert Grumet (this volume) for information about the term "Snakapins" and the absence of reliable documentation for its aboriginal use.

35. Michael Cohn and Robert Apuzzo, "Pugsley Avenue site." *Bulletin and Journal of the New York State Archeological Association* 96 (Spring 1988): 5–7.

36. Historical Perspectives, Inc., "Shorehaven Project, Phase IB Archaeological Fieldwork Report, Fall 1987." Prepared for Soundview Associates. Copy on file, New York City Landmarks Preservation Commission, 1988.

A turtle in the garden

Allan S. Gilbert, Jeremy Tausch, and Patrick Brock

Years ago, the image of a turtle was carved into the surface of a boulder in the central Bronx. The rock lay alongside the Bronx River within the grounds of the New York Botanical Garden (NYBG), and upon discovery, the carving was identified as an aboriginal petroglyph that may have served as a trail or territorial marker for Lenape (Delaware) Indians between A.D. 1000 and 1600. Press coverage,[1] a news feature in a popular archaeological magazine,[2] a children's book,[3] and several scholarly discussions[4] appeared in print soon after formal curation of the boulder began in the late 1980s, and thus a sense of legitimacy has surrounded the carving from its initial public recognition.

Unfortunately, authenticating this petroglyph as the product of a pre-contact Native American is not a simple matter. Its age was roughly estimated and based on the association of turtle imagery with the Late Woodland period of prehistory, not on any scientific analysis. Indeed, circumstantial aspects of the find suggested to some that the incised turtle might be far younger in date and perhaps the handiwork of a relatively recent Citizen American. This chapter will review the petroglyph's discovery, describe the stone and carving in detail, and explore the issues relating to its antiquity.

THE DISCOVERY

The glyph was first brought to the attention of the archaeological community by the late Bronx Borough Historian and founder of the Bronx County Historical Society, Dr. Theodore Kazimiroff (Figure 1). It is not clear how long Kazimiroff knew about the turtle, but in 1976, he showed it to Prof. Ralph S. Solecki of Columbia University.[5] Solecki noted the location of the boulder (Figure 5), as well as the condition and general configuration of the carving, but he did not publish anything, expecting that Kazimiroff would wish to exercise his priority as discoverer to describe the find in print. Kazimiroff died in 1980, however, without having written a word about the turtle, and so over the following years, Solecki prepared a short paper on the glyph, working from the plans, drawings, and photographs made during his visit.

Before completing his manuscript, Solecki sent a draft of it to two archaeologists who possessed expertise in local prehistory: the now late Prof. Herbert C. Kraft of Seton Hall University and Edward J. Lenik, an archaeologist

Figure 1. Dr. Theodore Kazimiroff preparing the turtle petroglyph for drawing and photography in 1976. Photograph by Ralph Solecki.

from New Jersey with knowledge of rock art in the northeast. Both Kraft and Lenik are acknowledged for their comments in Solecki's final publication.[6]

A decade later, Lenik was granted an opportunity to apply the tip he had obtained from Solecki. As part of an archaeological survey team assembled in 1987 by the New York City Landmarks Preservation Commission (NYCLPC), he was assigned the task of locating sites of archaeological significance within public lands across the city's five boroughs.[7] While investigating the NYBG, he found the boulder (Figure 2). Lenik obviously knew of the object's existence but may have been unaware of its exact location. In his own published paper,[8] he describes himself as the discoverer (p. 17) yet acknowledges the information obtained from Solecki (p. 20). Kazimiroff was mentioned only as "a local avocational archaeologist who reported finding pottery fragments and projectile points" within a nearby rockshelter site (p. 19).

By 1987, the boulder was heavily covered with graffiti, and a decision was made to move it indoors to protect it from further damage. Dr. Sherene Baugher, the director of archaeology for the NYCLPC at the time, consulted the Native American Community House of New York City to discuss the need to place the boulder out of harm's way and into a protected setting.[9] Presuming the petroglyph to be genuine, the city invited local Native Americans to participate in the planning process, as they would surely have had an interest in the disposition of a relic left by their ancestors. Recently, archaeologists have recognized the value of being responsive to the public, and especially descendant groups. In the past, decisions involving the significance of sites, approaches to their investigation and preservation, and display of their finds were almost always

Figure 2. Edward Lenik examining the boulder in its place of discovery in 1987 during the survey of the NYBG. Photograph courtesy of the New York City Landmarks Preservation Commission.

made by the investigators themselves, with little consideration for any input from the contemporary cultural representatives who might have interests based upon their own traditional or religious perspectives. Now, it is a matter of ethics to share research strategies and results, giving concerned non-archaeologists greater access to the field in order to demystify its methods of recovery and solicit advice in matters of interpretation and exhibition. In addition, wider participation by the public may foster greater awareness of archaeology and preservation as well as increased respect for ancient and historic remains.[10]

By mid September, 1987, the NYBG had moved the boulder to its Operations Building.[11] Conservation of the stone was performed there by Marie Sarchiapone, then of the NYCLPC. Her efforts focused specifically on cleaning the accumulated marker graffiti by carefully applying a series of alkaline and solvent-based paint removers using a soft brush, then hosing the material off with a gentle water stream after several minutes. Beneath the top layer of marker ink lay many others, which were removed in turn using the same process.[12] The repetitive buildup of messages indicated that the boulder had been continuously inscribed by many visitors, among whom figured a person who recorded the name "Shorty" several times to ensure its continued visibility (Figure 3). As

Figure 3. Photograph of the boulder's upper surface in 1987 showing the scratches and marker graffiti before conservation. Photograph courtesy of the New York City Landmarks Preservation Commission.

soon as the boulder was free of graffiti, and the loosely adhering grime had been washed from the rest of the rock surface, the glyph could be observed more clearly and in greater detail.

The stone was then launched on an odyssey of display venues within the NYBG. It was first placed under plexiglass in the lobby of the Watson Building in 1988 but was later transferred to the GreenSchool in the early 1990s, where it contributed to the Garden's childhood education program. In 2005, it was moved to a room adjacent to the school and placed on permanent exhibit within a skylit niche at the foot of a stairwell leading up to the Enid A. Haupt Conservatory.

DESCRIPTION OF THE PETROGLYPH

The boulder rested on a hiking trail (Figures 4 and 5) that followed the left (eastern) bank of the Bronx River within the gorge, a stretch of river where the flow has entrenched itself deeply into the schistose bedrock. The sides of the gorge rise up on either side, steep and abrupt on the west, more open and gradual on the east. Travelers on foot, both ancient and recent, probably followed the valley bottom northward or southward along the river's eastern bank, as it afforded an easy transit route through the forested countryside. The boulder lay squarely in the center of the path, yet it left sufficient clearance on either side for people to pass. The turtle had been carved into the upper surface of the stone, and thus many passersby might have noticed it over the years.

Solecki described the boulder as basalt; Lenik called it granite, as did the NYCLPC report written subsequent to the survey.[13] It is, in fact, diabase, an igneous rock chemically identical to basalt but with larger crystals due to its having cooled intrusively—that is, slowly below the earth's surface. The source

Figure 4. Petroglyph boulder resting on the hiking path in 1976. Photograph courtesy of Ralph Solecki.

of the stone was the Palisades formation, an eroding ridge of Triassic age that forms a precipice overlooking the Hudson River in northern New Jersey and southern New York. The glacial advance that brought Palisades diabase to the Bronx surged into the region from the northwest perhaps 40,000 years ago, representing the next to final spread of continental ice over the metropolitan area.[14] It plucked pieces of diabase from exposed cliff faces or debris piles at the cliff base and, together with other rocks picked up on its long southeastward slide, transported them into the Bronx. When climatic warming brought about glacial retreat, these boulders were dropped by the ice, then collected or dispersed by the dynamic forces of outwash rivers, proglacial lakes, and post-glacial erosion. Once the ice had abandoned them, these residual boulders, or erratics, were

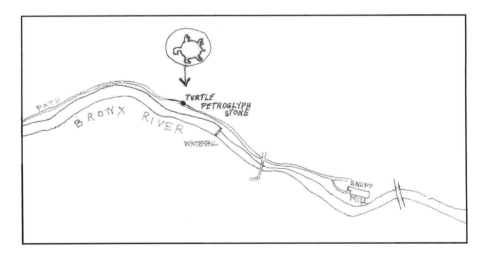

Figure 5. Ralph Solecki's 1976 traced and hand-drawn map showing the location of the boulder with respect to the dam and Lorillard Snuff Mill downriver. Courtesy of Ralph Solecki.

rounded by spheroidal weathering, a process of chemical breakdown that alters surfaces and gradually wears them down. It progresses more rapidly at corners and edges, where water penetration is greatest, and results over time in rounding of the boulder through a slow reduction of its surface. Such erratics are common throughout the meadows and forests of Bronx and Westchester counties, so much so that in earlier times, farmers of New York and northern New Jersey could claim, like their neighbors in New England, that the best crop to emerge from their fields was sometimes stones.

Lenik wrote that the boulder "was in its original position, that is, it was dropped here by the retreating ice sheet about 13,000 years ago."[15] A minor additional detail would be that the final glacial advance of the Pleistocene (the Woodfordian stadial, *ca.* 25,000 to 13,000 years ago) entered the area from the north-northeast. While it brought its own erratics, it did not transport diabase boulders into the Bronx but only covered, reworked, or rearranged those that had already arrived millennia earlier.

One more matter complicates the issue of the boulder's original position. Merguerian and Sanders have proposed that the lack of evidence for glacial abrasion within the Bronx River gorge suggests that the steep valley was created by riverine erosion entirely during the post-glacial period.[16] If this is true, then the boulder was not left within the gorge by retreating ice because, at the time, the gorge did not yet exist. Instead, the boulder must have come to its resting place either as colluvium—debris slipping downhill as the ravine deepened and widened through the agency of stream down-cutting—or as an artifact brought to its present spot by people.

Viewed from above in its original orientation, the boulder is roughly rectangular—approximately 28 by 34 inches (71 by 86 cm)—though its southwestern corner is missing (Figure 6). A large spall has cracked off the side near the northwestern corner. The turtle was carved next to the northeastern corner, its tail to the south and its head turned to the west as if looking in the direction of the river. The glyph follows the curvature of the stone, so that the head and neck curl downward over the rounded northern edge.

The carved lines are narrow and relatively shallow, cut at most 1/16 of an inch into the rock (Figure 7). They are discontinuous, indicating that the overall design was engraved in segments that were not seamlessly merged together at their ends. Most of the incisions seem to have been made by scratching and gouging, with perhaps only a small amount of initial pecking to establish the lineations. There are no areas that are continuously pecked to create a solid fill. Extraneous scratches make it difficult to determine exactly which lines were original to the glyph and which represent prior or subsequent marring of the boulder's surface, but a best estimate using low-angle lighting over many visits between 1997 and 2005 yielded the new drawing of Figure 8.

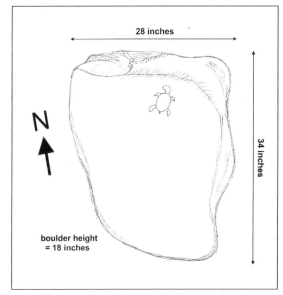

Figure 6. Sketch of the boulder from above showing its overall configuration, size, original orientation when discovered, and location of the petroglyph on its upper surface.

The grooves of the carving are lighter in color than the surface of the stone, possibly due to crushing by the engraving tool of the crystalline constituents of the rock (largely plagioclase feldspar and pyroxene).[17] The overall stone surface is smooth, but upon close examination, it appears quite irregular, with tiny peaks and valleys. The top half of the boulder is grayish-yellow in color, the effect produced by an orange coating that covers the low-lying areas between protruding mineral grains of the underlying rock. (This coating will be discussed later, pp. 164ff.) Along the bottom, the boulder is redder, and the upper boundary of this color change appears to mark the former soil level. Oxidation was intensified here because this part of the stone lay below grade, exposed continuously to moisture and acidity through contact with the wet earth. The soil level must have risen from northwest to southeast, following the rise of the gorge slope, and as a consequence, the reddish oxidation climbs higher on the boulder's southeastern side. When Solecki recorded his visit to the site with Kazimiroff in 1976 (Figures 1 and 4; also Figure 2 from 1987), ground level along the path had already been reduced by erosion well below this previous grade indicator, suggesting that the boulder was somewhat less firmly embedded in the soil than it had formerly been.

The carving is undeniably a turtle, but the image is nevertheless not a very naturalistic portrait. Solecki pointed out that the forelegs emanate from the carapace too far behind the neck to match the true proportions of a turtle skeleton.[18] The turtle's "gait" is also curious. Both right appendages appear to be advancing into the next stride, as they are both drawn farther forward than the appendages on the left. If the animal was meant to be in motion, then an accurate depiction of the turtle's movement would show opposite legs (e.g., right front and left rear) placed forward. In addition, the head is rendered in an impossible position for a living animal: the neck bent sharply to the left but also twisted so that the left eye faces upward. The pattern of scutes (scales) on the carapace is spare and unlike that of any known species; nor does it correspond to any plastron pattern, should one imagine that the turtle is really upside-down and lying on its back. The glyph might represent an artist's unfinished work, but after much observation and discussion about which parts of the carving were original and which ones random marrings of the surface, the shell pattern began to resemble somewhat the numbers 53 or 59 (Figures 7 and 8). If this identification is correct, then the case for a prehistoric origin cannot be sustained.

The turtle's dimensions, measured along the convex surface, are as follows.

Dimension	inches	cm
Top of the head to the tip of the tail	5 3/8	13.7
Length of the carapace	3 7/8	9.8
Maximum width at front legs	4 1/2	11.4
Maximum width at rear legs	4 1/8	10.5
Carapace width midway between legs	2 13/16	7.1
Head length, mouth to back of head	1 1/4	3.2

Figure 7. Photograph of the turtle petroglyph by A. S. Gilbert.

Figure 8. Drawing of the turtle petroglyph by D. F. Gilbert, 2005.

Consultation with herpetologist Peter Brazaitis[19] drew the comment that the turtle carving is not an accurate rendering of any particular species but an impressionistic averaging of the features of several local possibilities (Figure 9), including the Eastern painted turtle (*Chrysemys picta*), the red-bellied turtle (*Pseudemys rubiventris*), and the wood turtle (*Clemmys insculpta*). The blunt head, short tail, and shell shape make these species the most likely referents for the glyph, but in general, the carving reflects neither a naturalistic depiction nor an abstract simplification of essential traits. Instead, it seemed to Brazaitis like a caricature, carved from a mental image of a turtle cartoon. The anthropo-morphized head and neck, turned like a human craning to the left, gives a whimsical appearance reminiscent of an animated character.[20] The shell design is unrelated to natural scute patterns and does not even resemble an unfinished attempt at reproducing them. Overall, one is struck by the degree to which the artist was either *unfamiliar* with turtle anatomy or intent upon modifying it.

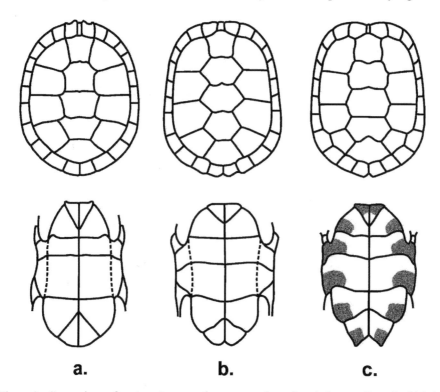

a.   **b.**   **c.**

Figure 9. Comparison of scute patterns on the carapace (upper) and plastron (lower) of (a) the Eastern painted turtle (*Chrysemys picta*), (b) the red-bellied turtle (*Pseudemys rubiventris*), and (c) the wood turtle (*Clemmys insculpta*). Redrawn from Heinz Wermuth and Robert Mertens, 1961. *Schildkröten, Krokodile, Brükenchsen.* Gustav Fischer Verlag. Jena, pp. 54 (*Chrysemys*), 150 (*Pseudemys*),and 50 (*Clemmys*).

LOCATION OF THE BOULDER

The bucolic setting of the Bronx River gorge appears at first glance pristine and secluded, and one might imagine it to be sufficiently isolated to conceal a prehistoric artifact for centuries. The gorge, however, lies within a public park (Figure 10) and has hardly been untouched by the intrusiveness of society or industry. It may have been a very busy place during the last 200 years.

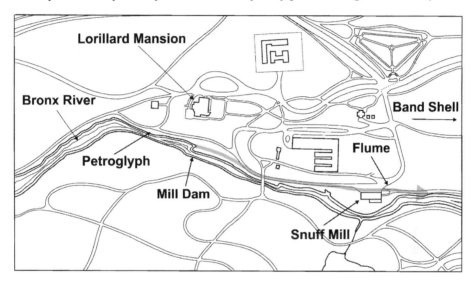

Figure 10. Map detail of the southeastern part of the NYBG from a plan of 1920. The petroglyph's location as well as that of the Lorillard mansion, mill dam, snuff mill, and infilled flume are indicated. Redrawn from "General Plan of the New York Botanical Garden 1920." *Bulletin of the New York Botanical Garden* 38 (1920):Appendix B.

The earliest substantial development occurred in the late 18th century. In 1792, Pierre II and George Lorillard moved their family's tobacco processing plant from lower Manhattan to an old grist mill located downriver from the site of the boulder. They subsequently added to their initial purchase of land and buildings, eventually accumulating an estate hundreds of acres in size. A larger mill for producing snuff was constructed of local fieldstone in 1840, and this structure persists today as the landmarked Lorillard Snuff Mill,[21] the oldest extant facility in the U.S. that was designed for tobacco processing. It drew water to turn its millstones through a long flume, now infilled, that emanated from a pond impounded behind an artificial dam that still exists as a waterfall less than 400 feet south of the boulder (Figure 11). The Lorillards amassed great wealth through their industrial efforts. The census of 1850 assessed the estate of Pierre Lorillard III (son of Pierre II) at $600,000, and upon his death in 1867, its

Figure 11. Photograph of the Lorillard mill dam looking north, with the footbridge above and the mansion on the bluff in the background; from Randall Comfort, *History of Bronx Borough, City of New York*, p. 86. North Side News Press, New York, 1906.

Figure 12. The Lorillard mansion from the southeast; from the *New York Botanical Garden Journal* XVI, no. 191 (1915), plate 229. Photograph courtesy of the LuEsther T. Mertz Library of the New York Botanical Garden.

estimated value had grown to over $1,000,000.[22] The stone mill continued to process tobacco products until 1870, when the Lorillards moved their manufacturing activities to Jersey City.

In addition to their commercial venture, the Lorillards built a 45-room stone mansion in 1856 on the eastern edge of the gorge immediately above the dam (Figures 11 and 12).[23] From the bluff where the mansion stood, the boulder site would have lain only 400 or so feet away, being perhaps visible in winter with the disappearance of obstructing foliage. The mansion was accompanied by stables to the southeast, a gate house at the driveway entrance (now near Fordham Road), and a "studio" that formerly stood at the river's edge. Randall Comfort recorded a photograph of the studio (Figure 13a), "a most romantic little building, with Gothic windows, set with diamond-shaped panes," but while admiring the picturesque location within earshot of the falls, he speculated more mundanely that the house might have been a laundry judging from its basement tanks, proximity to the riverbank, and the small spillway between the mill flume and the river that passed by the southern side of the building (Figure 13b).[24] The mansion remained within the family's holdings after the company left the Bronx in 1870, and in 1884, the City of New York purchased 661 acres of Lorillard land, including the mansion and mill, to create Bronx Park.

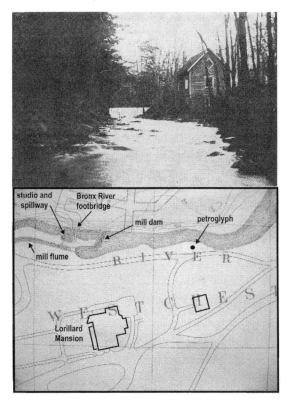

Figure 13. (a) The Lorillard studio from the south; from Randall Comfort, *History of Bronx Borough, City of New York*, p. 47. North Side News Press, New York, 1906; (b) Map detail from the 1873 survey of the 23rd and 24th wards by the New York City Department of Parks (Sheet 6) showing the location of the studio, the falls, the mill flume, and footbridge. Outlines of the mansion and footpaths on the unsurveyed eastern side of the river were transferred from the NYBG plan of 1920 in Figure 10. The 1873 map detail is courtesy of the New York Public Library Map Division.

The NYBG was established in 1891, but the land was allocated by the state legislature only in 1896. Botanist Nathaniel Lord Britton left Columbia University to be its first director-in-chief (1896–1929). The NYBG initially occupied the northern part of Bronx Park; the southeastern corner, including the Lorillard mansion and snuff mill, remained within New York City Parks Department jurisdiction. The mansion was used as a station house for the Parks Police (probably 1887–1903), and the Lorillard stables sheltered police horses, the most efficient means for officers to patrol large parks.[25] A January 25, 1899 report of the Torrey Botanical Club indicated that the more than 65 officers occupying the structure had made "a new and wholesome water-supply necessary."[26]

The Parks Department also built a band stand (Figure 10) on the grounds south of the mansion,[27] and concerts were held that drew large crowds of listeners. In the summer of 1900, average attendance at the 12 Sunday concerts was estimated at 7000.[28] In a letter of complaint to the *Bronx Home News* published Friday, July, 19, 1907, one reader and Bronx resident wrote:

> This summer, for the first time within my recollection, the band stand is vacant and the large audiences which gather are sent home in disappointment and with no better explanation for their disappointment that "the commissioner has more important business to attend to than arrange band concerts on Sunday afternoons." This was the only satisfaction I could obtain when last Sunday in Bronx Park I sought from a park employee a reason for the absence of the usual concert.[29]

Misappropriations may have depleted the park budget, leading to the musical cancellations on Sundays. According to an article in the *Bronx Home News* for Friday, June 5, 1908, the commissioner subsequently resumed concerts in all Bronx parks to appease the dismay of music lovers.

The popularity of park use is also apparent in Mrs. Mary M. Hopper's early 1890s petition to the Commissioners of Parks requesting permission to sell refreshments at the Lorillard Mansion,[30] as well as the case of clandestine partying recorded in the densely wooded areas north of the mansion:

> Horrified at the discovery of a shrine dedicated to Gambrinus, the inventor of lager beer, in the woods back of the old Lorillard mansion in Bronx Sunday afternoon, Detectives Horrigan and Kelly of the Park Police Station seized the altar to the Teuton benefactor, a full keg of beer, and arrested ten of his devotees. But Magistrate Walsh, in the Westchester Court yesterday, was more tolerant. He told the Gambrinus worshippers that if they could smuggle a keg of beer into the park, past the noses of the police, they deserved to be discharged. He let them all go with reprimands.[31]

Provision was made for the relief of all revelers, lawful and otherwise, by the construction of "comfort stations," one for men and one for women, within small buildings in the vicinity of the mansion.[32]

Accommodations were continuously made for the ease of movement of visitors within the grounds. The terrain was graded, landscaped, and provided with roads and bridges throughout the decades of the 1890s and early 1900s, and contractual matters involving bids and authorizations were entered into the commissioners' minutes,[33] while the expenses were summarized in the department's annual reports. The significance of these indications for the present investigation of the turtle carving is the substantial seasonal visitation that must have occurred. Very likely, people coursed in and out of the park and along its various paths as early as the 1890s. A petroglyph in plain sight should have been easily seen, yet it wasn't.

In January of 1915, the Parks Department released its final land holdings, together with the mill and mansion, to the NYBG. On the authority of the Garden's board of directors, space within the mansion was provided to various departments and outside groups subsequent to renovations. Carpentry, paint, and plumbing shops were set up in the basement, a lab was established on the second floor to prepare plant labels, the Horticultural Society of New York was permitted to use several offices, and the Bronx Society of Arts and Sciences (which had contributed toward underwriting the renovations and was already using the mansion on Parks authority for exhibit space) was allowed to use a second story room to display American paintings loaned by the Metropolitan Museum of Art.[34] In 1935, a WPA grant permitted major renovations and alterations to the NYBG, including "rip-rapping along the Bronx River,"[35] which might have brought riverbank contractors within a few feet of the petroglyph.

The mansion burned accidently on March 26, 1923. The fire ignited from sparks escaping the boiler chimney, with the result that the roof and upper story sustained heavy damage.[36] Initially, city assistance was sought to restore the house,[37] but by resolution of its Executive Committee on May 21, 1924, the NYBG authorized the razing of the "unsightly, useless and dangerous" ruins of the mansion because the building bore "no architectural interest," its location was objectionable as the "only available sewage outlet was the Bronx River," and according to many experts (including Frederick Law Olmsted), the landscape would benefit from its removal and "restoration of its site to the natural conditions which surround it."[38]

In 1941, a new NYBG facility, the Ruth Rea Howell Family Garden, was constructed on the site of the destroyed mansion. The largest residual feature of the house is the debris dump from the demolition, a low mound immediately southwest of the original location.

When it was discovered, the boulder had been engulfed by graffiti, most of it applied with felt-tipped markers (Figure 3). A number of ♂ loves ♀ messages appeared on the exposed northern end, and unfortunately, a sharply incised—and thus irreparable—circle with three equidistant lines crisscrossing through the center was gouged into the petroglyph itself, directly over the turtle's right "shoulder" area (Figures 3 and 7). The boulder was not, however, the only recipient of graffiti. Additional records left by amorous couples were cut into several nearby trees, especially the smooth-barked beeches that are easy to carve and display their message prominently for years. Some of the tree dedications were accompanied by dates (1988 to 1994 according to a late 20th century inspection), and since these messages of fidelity probably outlasted the relationships they describe, one wishes the trees had been spared the burden of long-term advertising for essentially ephemeral human affairs. The important point, however, is that both boulder and trees participated in the self-promotion. Though the graffiti are not necessarily linked to the earlier creation of the glyph, the markings demonstrate that the place has attracted substantial human traffic in recent years.

It should be evident that the Bronx River gorge has been occupied and exploited commercially and recreationally for over two centuries. Doubtless, the path on which the boulder rested has been frequented by many modern Americans, any one of whom could have noticed an ancient petroglyph in plain view years before Dr. Kazimiroff did.

COMPARABLE PREHISTORIC EASTERN U.S. ROCK ART

Petroglyphs are uncommon in the eastern U.S., and to date, no local examples have been found that bear the image of a turtle. Many more rock art sites are known in the western part of the country because (1) the generally drier climate leaves a greater expanse of rock surface free of vegetation cover, (2) weathering does not destroy the engravings—or pictographic paintings—as quickly, and (3) the surficial coating (referred to as rock varnish in arid regions) grows slowly, allowing the carved lines to remain lighter in color and prominent against the darker stone for a long time. In contrast, the northeast of the country experiences moist, temperate conditions as well as the impact of acid rain, both of which hasten the weathering process by eliminating painted decoration and wearing away glyphs more rapidly.[39] In addition, the luxuriant foliage of open forests hides rock surfaces in many places, prompting some to propose that, like the amorous couples of recent decades in the NYBG, Native Americans must have commonly applied markings to trees in the form of dendroglyphs,[40] though no aboriginal tree evidence persists today aside from documentation of the the practice in historic times. Rock art sites, wherever they are located, are nevertheless deteriorating, often at an accelerating rate due to the influence of climate change, development, and tourism. It has thus become crucial to find, record, and, if possible, preserve these remains if there is ever to be a chance of understanding them. For this reason, the boulder was treated with great care.

Are there any commonalities that the turtle petroglyph shares with other carvings? Stylistic similarities have long been sought among rock art sites in an attempt to discover patterns that might reflect cultural connections or meanings. It remains very difficult, however, to determine which stylistic variations might be caused by (1) cultural changes over time, (2) different aboriginal groups, (3) the particular sculptor, or (4) the purpose for which the markings were made. Style does vary, but little significance can be assigned with certainty to such variation.

Chippindale[41] notes two kinds of interpretive methodology for rock art: formal and informed. Formal methods include comparison of iconography and style, specific locations and regional distribution, and any other analyzable attributes that can be studied from the sites or carvings themselves. Informed methods rely on additional information from informants, ethnohistory, and documentary records that reflect upon the potential importance of the sites or designs to their probable creators. Lenik and Solecki used both methods in their search for evidence to support the turtle's aboriginal origin.

Lenik wrote in the abstract of his published paper that the carving may represent either a trail or territorial marker, but he appeared more confident that its pedigree descends from prehistoric Delaware Indians:

> The turtle petroglyph is a Native American rock carving that was executed at some time between c. A.D. 1000 and 1600. Although its meaning and purpose are not known, the turtle design may represent the turtle phratry or clan of the Munsee-speaking Delaware Indians who once occupied this area prior to the coming of the Europeans.[42]

His assignment of a Late Woodland period date was based on formal archaeological comparisons, as well as informed ethnohistoric information. He invokes three lines of evidence to reinforce his identification, and although these represented the best clues then available, they remain nonetheless circumstantial. First, he pointed to the nearby rockshelter excavated by Kazimiroff, who removed aboriginal artifacts from the site.[43] Second, he noted that turtles played a significant role in the cosmology of Delaware Indians, figuring prominently in their creation myths as the progenitor of dry land, which took shape as the rounded carapace of an earthly turtle emerged from primordial waters.[44] Finally, he referred to two other turtle carvings found within the coastal New York area that have been dated to late prehistoric time: a slate gorget from Nassakeag Swamp in Setauket, Long Island (Figure 14) and a turtle head pendant or effigy of sandstone, recovered in Staten Island (Figure 15). Solecki added in his paper that, according to Kraft, the turtle, wolf, and turkey were lineage markers for

Figure 14. Gorget (L 8.0 cm, W 4.0 cm, T 0.4 cm), ground slate, perforated, with an incised turtle, recovered from Nassakeag Swamp in Setauket, New York; collection of the National Museum of the American Indian, Smithsonian Institution, no. 184705.000. Photograph published with permission of the National Museum of the American Indian.

Figure 15. Turtle head pendant (H 7.2 cm, W 6.6 cm, D 10.2 cm), red sandstone, Late Woodland (*ca.* A.D. 1300–1500), found at Howland Hook, Staten Island, New York; currently in the anthropological collection of Seton Hall University, no. 1579. Photograph from Brawer, Catherine Coleman, ed., *Many Trails: Indians of the Lower Hudson Valley*, p. 44. The Katonah Gallery, Katonah, New York, 1983; published here courtesy of The Katonah Gallery and Seton Hall University.

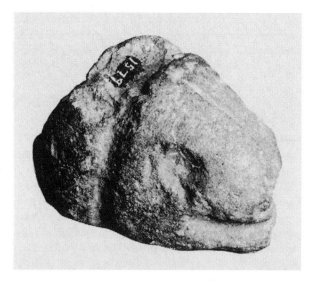

various Native American groups throughout the northeast.[45] None of this evidence, marshaled in support of the glyph's authenticity, constitutes proof. It still leaves open the possibility that the rockshelter, other Late Woodland finds, and symbolic use of turtle imagery are unrelated to an essentially modern carving. Playing devil's advocate to the formal artifact comparisons, one could point out that the turtle of the Bronx petroglyph differs from the other turtle carvings in significant ways. For example, the Setauket gorget renders more accurately the carapace scute pattern possessed by nearly all woodland turtles: a central row of vertebral scutes flanked by one row of pleural scutes running from the head to the tail (Figure 9). It omits only the marginal scutes that encircle the shell's edge. Further, the neck of the turtle on the gorget is straight, with the head pointing forward, and, viewed from above, both eyes are seen, one on either side of the head. The pendant from Staten Island also contains realistic elements reflecting a skull configuration that is generally anatomically correct. Though the Bronx turtle's idiosyncrasies do not invalidate its antiquity, as they might be the first discovery of such stylized features, one might be happier with such quirks if some of the prehistoric finds used as ancient comparisons included similarly odd anatomical inventions.

A WORD FROM THE ARTIST?

Shortly after his paper was published, Solecki heard that, upon seeing the boulder on display in the Watson Building, a visitor to the NYBG had remarked that he had made the carving himself as a young boy scout. In a letter dated February 3, 1993, Solecki brought this information to the attention of Bruce K. Riggs, who was at the time Manager of Horticultural Interpretation and Plant Records at the NYBG.

> Somewhere recently I heard that a former boy scout had confessed that he had pecked out the petroglyph himself. The man was reported to be quite elderly. My question is, was there such a happening, and would you have the identity of this individual? It is quite important for the archaeological record to have the truth known.[46]

Riggs had been instrumental in the recovery of the boulder and its initial indoor installation, and in his reply to Solecki, he wrote: "In response to your question about the rumor that a Boy Scout had pecked out the turtle design, I know of no such occurrence."[47]

An anonymous claim without corroborating details should not be accepted automatically, though it does cast additional suspicion. Such an admission, if verified, would invalidate any aboriginal identification and render all the efforts to preserve, display, and publicize the turtle essentially a gratuitous waste of time. The turtle's odd pose might then be explained as mimicry of the eagle on the Boy Scout emblem—wings and talons outstretched with the head turned to the onlooker's left. No additional information was provided by the claimant, possibly because a former boy scout did not wish to be associated with an act of vandalism in a public park that, inadvertently, came to be designated the creation of ancient indigenous people. Yet, some pride in the accomplishment must have encouraged the statement of responsibility in the first place.[48]

The second-hand assertions of a mysterious stranger are hearsay, however, and they should not be granted unconditional admissibility until the carving is proven to be recent by independent testing or its creator, if he is able, owns up with a satisfactory account.

RESOLVING THE UNCERTAINTIES

Ideally, what is needed is an independent means of determining from the glyph itself whether its antiquity is high or low. If an approximate age for the carving could be established, then the uncertainty surrounding its authenticity might be resolved. Unfortunately, the dating of rock art is still an evolving field; in the late 1980s, when the glyph was publicly acknowledged, rock art dating was essentially embryonic, and few reliable avenues to age estimation were available.

Coatings

Relative ages have been obtained at some rock art sites by comparing glyphs according to the coatings within their carved lines.[49] Rocks exposed to the elements in arid areas develop what is called desert varnish, a microscopically thin surface layer composed largely of clay with elevated levels of manganese that may be partly biochemical in origin or related to humidity levels. This layer is removed when the lines of a glyph are incised. Over time, the fresh surface created by the engraving becomes recoated, and so greater varnish regrowth within the incised grooves should reflect longer intervals of post-carving exposure.

Rock surfaces of the northeastern U.S. do not develop the varnishes of arid lands but instead a variety of other coatings. The diabase boulder in the NYBG bears a rough, discontinuous reddish-orange coloration due to the presence of iron oxide. Initially, this was thought to be a silica glaze. Such glazes form on the surfaces of exposed rocks in many geographic settings—from polar to arid to equatorial zones—and they consist of an amorphous accretion of silica containing oxides of aluminum and iron.[50] They are also usually quite thin (less than 200 μm in thickness) and appear as relatively lustrous whitish, brown, or orange deposits. In many rocks, they originate from the dissolution of phyllosilicate minerals (i.e., sheet-structured silicates such as micas) with precipitation of the product as aluminum-silicon complexes. The minerals comprising diabase are all chemically unstable to some degree and weather fairly readily, especially the olivine and plagioclase but also to an extent augite, pyroxene, and magnetite. This surficial instability makes it difficult for glazes (or desert varnishes in arid areas) to form, since dissolution or fragmentation renews the surface before sufficient time passes to allow the accumulation of significant coating. This surficial erosion represents the spheroidal weathering process described earlier as the cause of rounding among glacial erratics.

Had this coating been a glaze, some dating strategies might have been possible. In temperate parts of the northeastern U.S., any glaze buildup within the carved lines of a petroglyph might have helped to establish an approximate age in three ways. First, the thickness of the glaze might be directly related to the duration of exposure, though calibration of glaze depth with the amount of time gone by would have been hard to establish with accuracy. Second, any chemical or particulate contaminants of industrial origin trapped within the glaze would have implied growth of the coating during the late 19th and early 20th centuries, a time when rapidly expanding factories and urbanization filled the air with pollutants that had never before been generated in such quantities. Third, coating regrowth could also have created an opportunity for radiocarbon dating. The newly carved lines of a petroglyph are sometimes colonized by tiny algae or fungi that penetrate into the rock along microfractures produced by the pecking and engraving, or by subsequent freeze-thaw seasonal cycles. If a rock coating then encapsulates these colonizing organisms, sealing them in and preventing continued metabolic exchange of carbon dioxide with the air, then even minuscule amounts of biological material recovered from within the glaze can be radiocarbon dated using an accelerator mass spectrometer.[51]

In the end, none of the three options involving the investigation of glaze buildup proved feasible. Close observation of the petroglyph boulder and another similar but smaller diabase erratic from the Bronx revealed no glaze formation on the exposed surfaces. Hand lens examination of the boulder by Tanzhuo Liu (geologist and paleoclimatologist at Columbia's Lamont-Doherty Earth Observatory) in 2007 and by Patrick Brock (co-author and retired geologist at Queens College, CUNY) in 2009 revealed no signs of glaze on the boulder's surface or glaze redeposition within the lines of the carving. Without glaze formation, there is no depth to measure, no impurities to discover within the coating, and no carbonaceous organisms to find embedded within it. The absence of glaze within the turtle design suggests a very recent cutting—even if the rock surface was stable enough for a glaze to develop.

Instead of glaze, the outer surfaces of both boulders were marked by mineral crystals in the process of chemical decomposition. Figure 16 shows the surface of the other diabase boulder, which could be destructively sampled to demonstrate the dynamic process of surficial decay. The outlined triangular area belonged to a crystal that is now oxidizing into a reddish-orange byproduct through chemical breakdown. To its left, the circle encloses a tiny plant tendril still clinging tenaciously to the rock surface years after the boulder had been taken indoors...and cleaned. (Organic residues of this nature, engulfed by glaze, could have provided a radiocarbon date for the time of its entrapment, but in this case, there is no glaze to bracket it as older than simply modern vegetation.)

Figure 17a and b are photomicrographs of a thin section cut from the same boulder specimen photographed in Figure 16. In both a and b, it is clear that not only are surficial crystals succumbing to oxidation weathering, but deeper ones are also deteriorating as indicated by their opaqueness in the section.

Figure 16. Photomicrograph of the surface of a diabase boulder similar to the one bearing the petroglyph showing a triangular area of decay representing surface deterioration (light reddish-orange in color) of a crystal surrounded by darker, protruding, intact mineral components of the rock. In the circle to the left is a remnant plant tendril still clinging to the exterior stone surface. Distance across the image is about 2.5 mm.

Further, small microcracks can be seen penetrating deeper into the rock along weakened crystal boundaries where further chemical breakdown can be seen in the darker oxidation traces.[52] The surface of the boulder is bumpy and irregular, a condition created by the occasional crumbling or dropping off of deteriorating mineral crystals, especially after cold season freeze-thaw dynamics that expand the moisture continuously seeping into the small cracks. In this way, the diabase boulders show signs of an unstable surface that would not sustain glaze accumulation over lengthy periods of time. The gradually receding surface would be unlikely to preserve in sharp detail an ancient petroglyph over the course of centuries; more likely, the clarity of such a carving would be steadily reduced, leading at some point to total effacement.

Figure 18 shows a wider image of the outer surface of this diabase specimen. The irregular topography indicates how gradual loss of crystalline components creates the roughened outline seen in the cross-sections of Figure 17. It is likely that any incision into the stone, as in the carving of a petroglyph, would over lengthy periods of time steadily lose definition leading to eventual disappearance of the design.

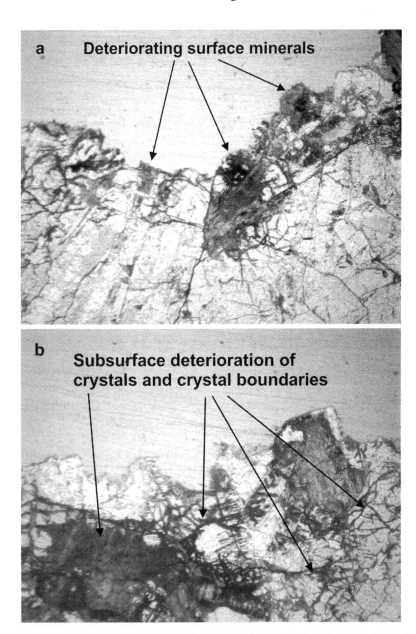

Figure 17. (a) Photomicrograph of a thin section (30μ thick cross-section viewed in plane polarized light, or ppl) of the boulder fragment in Figure 16 showing the crystalline subsurface. Note the decaying mineral crystals darkened by the oxidation of iron. The other intact minerals are mostly transparent under ppl. The uneven surface indicates where crystals have been loosened by erosion and fallen off. (b) Photomicrograph of the same thin section but at an adjacent part of the surface showing larger crystals eroding well below the surface and lines of deterioration penetrating deeper into the rock along crystal boundaries. Photomicrographs by Patrick Brock.

Figure 18. Photograph of the surface of the diabase specimen of Figures 16 and 17 showing the irregular topography produced by attrition of crystal components of the rock over time. Width of the image is about 5 mm.

Microerosion

In the absence of glaze, weathering of the mineral crystals within the lines of a petroglyph also conveys information that might be relevant to dating. Microscopic wear, or microerosion, of the crystalline components of the rock exposed by the glyphic artist may indicate something of the passage of time since the carving was executed.[53] Bednarik has developed a technique of assessing micro-wanes, or the degree to which the sharply angular protrusions of mineral grains from hard rock become reduced and rounded through weathering. When a petroglyph is cut, the fractured grains within the carved lines are prominent and pointy, but time gradually wears them down to bumps of progressively lower and rounder relief. In some localities, Bednarik has had moderate success in calibrating the extent of micro-waning to the passage of time, thereby yielding age estimates.

For the wide range of rocks in the world's diverse regions, determining age from microerosion will depend not only on climatic conditions but also on the stability of the minerals in the rock and the degree of surface weakness. Potential complications include the fact that many micro-fractured rocks will pit and lose their crystalline components under the erosive impact of wet-dry and freeze-thaw cycles during normal seasonal change, possibly leaving no time for rounding of grains—and this is likely the case for the Bronx diabase erratics.

Also, the crystals or grains making up rocks have different degrees of resistance to the forces of weathering and dissolution. Again, there are no universal rules for gauging the age of a surface based on the extent of microerosion.

In order to assess the degree of microerosion, the petroglyph had to be investigated up close. Hand lens examination made some details apparent, but imaging of the petroglyph was eventually pursued using two methods—confocal microscopy and close-up light photography.

With the cooperation of Prof. Timothy Bromage, director of the Hard Tissue Research Unit of the New York University College of Dentistry, parts of

Figure 19. Imaging of the petroglyph with a confocal microscope. Prof. Bromage sits at the computer that registers the imaging process; Dr. Jeremy Tausch leans over the boulder positioning the microscope, assisted by Dr. Bin Hu. Photograph by A. S. Gilbert, September 23, 2008.

the carving were imaged using a confocal microscope (Figure 19). The goal was to obtain three-dimensional views of the rock at the bottom of the grooves to determine if evidence of a tool could be detected or the roughness of the carved surface could be gauged. Dr. Jeremy Tausch, a co-author of this chapter, assisted.

Confocal microscopes have been in use since the late 1950s. They achieve high resolution of the target by imaging a very small area at a time, each image capturing a limited part of the surface lying within the microscope's optical focal plane.[54] These small images, all in sharp focus, are then spliced together to form larger mosaics in which everything is at maximum resolution. A three-dimensional effect can be created when the small images are collected from locations at varying elevations. Traditional wide-field microscopes differ because they take in a broader area at once, including surfaces that are higher or lower than the optical focal plane and thus not in sharp focus.

The mosaic images obtained this way cannot be reproduced in this book since they are in 3D. The information gained was instructive, however, and indicated that the bottom of the engraved lines possessed small depressions and occasional micro-grooves. The depressions could have resulted from the popping out or weathering of the smallest mineral grains, either during the act of engraving itself or later as climatic conditions eroded the crystalline components that had been loosened or otherwise compromised by the act of carving. The micro-grooves could have been produced by a thin tool like a sharp chisel (though no metal residue was found within the imaged areas) or by dislodged mineral grains pushed along to create a furrow. Surfaces that appear smooth to the eye can show topographic irregularities at the very close ranges afforded by the confocal microscope, and thus the images that were obtained proved difficult to interpret. They did not lead to an unequivocal determination of whether the incising took place recently or at some time earlier.

Publishable images of the micro-topography were obtained by the use of light photography at close range. Figure 20a (below) illustrates the locations on the turtle glyph where the following two figures (20b and c) were taken.

Though confocal imaging demonstrated that rough surfaces exist at very small scale, plain light photography demonstrated that the groove bottoms and some sides are relatively smooth and minimally eroded; small crystalline rock components protrude from the smooth surfaces because they were either too hard to incise or the grooves were cut in non-continuous sections.

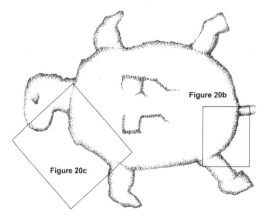

Figure 20b

Figure 20c

Figure 20. (a, facing page, bottom) Locations on the glyph where photographs in b and c were taken; (b, this page, upper) photograph of the shell edge between the tail and left hind leg showing a few mineral crystals protruding at the bottom of the groove within the area of the white square; (c, this page, lower) photograph of the shell edge between the neck and left foreleg showing that the incising was done in discontinuous segments (indicated by dotted arrows) leaving uncarved material in between the depressions (indicated by solid arrows). The lower sides of the groove segments are brightly lit, revealing a smoothness probably produced by a sharp chisel that had been directed downward into each segment, shaving the inclined slope flat.

The most telling aspect of the carving is the smooth, flat incline of many groove segments, readily seen in Figure 20c and in the left leg incision on the right side of Figure 20b. A sharp steel chisel with a width equal to the length of each segment could produce this effect if directed downward at an angle into the weathered surface of the stone. The slope parallel to the cut appears to have been shaved smooth, and the opposite slope roughened as mineral crystals fell off with each blow.

SUMMARIZING THE EVIDENCE

Investigation of the turtle petroglyph led in several directions and used both physical and historical evidence. The significant findings are summarized in the table of evidence on the next page, grouped according to whether they support or undermine the attribution of antiquity for the rock carving.

Clearly, the evidence supporting a prehistoric origin for the petroglyph is relatively weak and based on the location of the boulder along an old Indian trail and the link to Native American turtle imagery. One might add another poorly supported justification for identifying the carving as genuine in the fact that petroglyphs are not commonplace features of modern American society, and the discovery of one might immediately conjure up an ancient context even though it could be considered an unusual example of contemporary graffiti.

The two or three lines of weak evidence in favor of an ancient origin are more than outweighed by six lines of moderate to strong evidence suggesting that the petroglyph is a relatively recent carving produced by someone in modern times. This evidence is *historical* (carving of the glyph on a movable boulder that escaped notice within a busy industrial and recreational area over the course of two centuries), *iconographical* (the glyph reveals unusually narrow lines and peculiarly unnaturalistic rendering), and *physical* (no traces of silica glaze have been found within the grooves of the carving, which shows relatively smooth bottoms in contrast to the pock-marked exterior surfaces that have apparently experienced rapid surficial weathering over a lengthy interval).

CONCLUSION

Genuine rock art discoveries in the eastern woodlands are uncommon, and this one reveals not only unusual stylistic aspects but also a surprising location in plain view within a glen that has witnessed over two centuries of substantial modern human presence. If, despite much evidence to the contrary, the glyph is truly ancient, then the people of America, native and immigrant alike, owe the city and NYBG personnel who found and curated it a debt of

Table showing weak, moderate, and strong evidence for and against an ancient attribution for the turtle petroglyph.

Evidence supporting an ancient attribution:	Evidence not supporting an ancient attribution:
	Placement of the petroglyph on a movable boulder and not on an immovable rock surface **
Location of the petroglyph on a major communication route along the Bronx River *	Location of the petroglyph within the busy Bronx River gorge, yet no notice of it until the 1970s **
	Carving consists of narrow lines with no pecking; unlikely to have been created by a stone tool **
Turtle imagery is reminiscent of Lenape myth and religion *	Non-naturalistic rendering, like a caricature **
	Absence of any residual silica glaze buildup within the lines of the carving ***
	Relatively smooth groove sides that suggest recent carving with a sharp chisel compared to the rough exterior surface caused by long exposure to geologically rapid spheroidal weathering ***

*	weak evidence
**	moderately strong evidence
***	strong evidence

gratitude for respecting the cultural heritage of prehistory and displaying it to remind visitors of the earliest human inhabitants of the park.

The Bronx turtle petroglyph is unlikely to be an authentic Native American rock carving, however. It is more likely to be a modern creation with no direct prehistoric connection. Most of the evidence collected here suggests that the petroglyph was produced quite recently and thus is more a reflection of our modern selves than anything else. If a boy scout sought romantic communion with what he took to be a simpler and nobler past by blazing his own trail marker, then his actions demonstrate a widely-shared feeling—an inner desire to participate, vicariously, in an idealized natural life of long ago. Perhaps this desire stemmed from a sense of awe, spiritual connectedness, or a need to follow some "ancestral pathway," though the full cultural package of that pathway was not necessarily understood, and only certain aspects of the whole were likely ever emulated. The turtle petroglyph was probably not intended to fool anyone but instead represents a mid-20th century attempt at emotionally linking across the centuries.

If it wasn't the boy scout, perhaps the Lorillards created the glyph themselves, in which case the turtle carving would have experienced more than a century of weathering before its discovery by Dr. Kazimiroff. The popular Green Turtle brand of plug tobacco[55] may have been conceived by the Lorillards just before production was moved to Jersey City in 1870 (though no traces of green pigmentation have ever been observed on the boulder). Though certainty cannot be claimed on this matter, the carving's freshness implies a much more recent origin within the 20th century; presuming a late 19th century creation still poses the perplexing question of why the glyph was not noticed sooner.

Archaeology, like all exploratory disciplines, aims to uncover the truth, and continuous investigation of remains from the past will eventually fill the gaps in our knowledge about antiquity and resolve our uncertainties about how to interpret the evidence. The apparently modern origin of the petroglyph is sure to elicit much justified disappointment, but without hesitation, archaeology should expose myths and, most likely in this case, false authenticities that obscure the true picture of human progress, regardless which balloons of traditional acceptance or renown may be deflated as a result.

ACKNOWLEDGMENTS

Dr. Tanzhuo Liu, Senior Staff Associate at Columbia University's Lamont-Doherty Earth Observatory examined the turtle and provided valuable advice over several years about the dating of petroglyphs and the interpretation of rock coatings. Appreciation is expressed to Marianne Anderson, Sherene Baugher, Robert Bednarik, Peter Brazaitis, Kimberly Consroe, Ronald Dorn, Kaitilin Griffin, Robert Grumet, Thomas Kavanaugh, Carole Lazio, Ed Lenik, Charles Merguerian, Patricia Nietfield, Daniel Pagano, Marie Sarchiapone, Ralph Solecki, Lou Stancari, Gaynell Stone, Nancy Wallach, Roger Wines, and Elissa Wolfson for research assistance during the preparation of this paper. Daniela Gilbert drew the petroglyph in 2005. Marie Long and Todd Forrest of the NYBG provided invaluable access, respectively, to archival materials and the boulder itself for the detailed microscopic examination described here, but many others at the NYBG helped over the years (Natalie Andersen, Wayne Cahilly, Debra Epstein, and Bruce Riggs, among others). Appreciation is expressed to Prof.

Timothy Bromage (NYU College of Dentistry) for helping to image the petroglyph using his 3D confocal microscope (assisted by Dr. Bin Hu). These images illuminated the deepest parts of the glyph's carved lines, but they could not be reproduced here while still preserving their three-dimensional character.

ENDNOTES

1. David W. Dunlap, "Ancient Bronx turtle finds a home." *The New York Times* (Friday, March 25, 1988): B1,4; John Lewis, "Not turtle soup: 3,000-year Indian carving found." *Daily News* (Friday, March 25, 1988), BXL MBW, p.2. Lewis misunderstood the age estimate of the petroglyph to be 1000 B.C.

2. *Archaeology Magazine*, "The whole world on its back." *Archaeology* 42, no. 1 (1989): 18, 20, 107.

3. Sheila MacGill-Callahan, *And Still the Turtle Watched*. Dial Books for Young Readers, New York, 1991.

4. Edward J. Lenik, "A turtle petroglyph on the Bronx River." *The Bulletin and Journal of the New York State Archeological Association* 97 (Fall, 1988): 17–20; Edward J. Lenik, "Native American rock art in the lower Hudson Valley and coastal New York." In *The Archaeology and Ethnohistory of the Lower Hudson Valley and Neighboring Regions: Essays in Honor of Louis A. Brennan*. Occasional Publications in Northeastern Anthropology 11, pp. 181–183. Archaeological Services, Bethlehem, CT, 1991; Ralph S. Solecki, "A petroglyph found in the New York Botanical Garden, Bronx, New York." *The Bulletin of the Archaeological Society of New Jersey* 43 (1988): 31–33. A later discussion appeared in Edward J. Lenik, *Picture Rocks: American Indian Rock Art in the Northeast Woodlands*. University Press of New England, Hanover & London, 2002, pp. 175–177.

5. In at least two pre-1976 articles (1957 and 1974) from *The New York Times*, reporters relate the highlights of tours through the NYBG conducted by Dr. Kazimiroff. Neither article mentions the petroglyph among all the other historic locations visited along the way. Milton Bracker, "2 experts lead a nature ramble; John Kieran Dr. Kazimiroff conduct informal tour of Botanical Garden." *The New York Times* (May 5, 1957): 74; Paul L. Montgomery, "Justice Douglas, in Bronx Park, gives brief for nature." *The New York Times* (May 10, 1974): 39. Given Kazimiroff's acknowledged enthusiasm for all things archaeological, and especially prehistoric, it seems likely that he would have noted the carving if he had known of its existence at the time. It is also possible, though less likely, that he knew about the glyph but kept silent about its location in an effort to protect it. The best guess would be that Kazimiroff became aware of the petroglyph very shortly before he shared the information with Solecki, his professional archaeologist colleague and dental patient.

6. Solecki, *op. cit.* (note 4).

7. The survey was incorporated within a "Design Through Archaeology" program conducted by the urban archaeologist's office of the New York City Landmarks Preservation Commission in collaboration with the Department of Cultural Affairs. The entire effort was funded by the National Endowment for the Arts and had as its goal the location of archaeological resources within areas under Cultural Affairs jurisdiction in order to provide for their protection and safe incorporation

within future development plans. Sherene Baugher, Edward J. Lenik, and Daniel N. Pagano, "Design Through Archaeology: An Archaeological Assessment of Fifteen City-Owned Cultural Institutions." Prepared for the New York City Dept of Cultural Affairs, on file at the New York City Landmarks Preservation Commission, 1991.

8. Lenik, "A turtle petroglyph on the Bronx River," *op. cit.* (note 4).

9. Dunlap, *op. cit.* (note 1).

10. Sherene Baugher, "Who determines the significance of American Indian sacred sites and burial grounds?" In *Preservation: Of What, For Whom? A Critical Look at Historical Significance*, Michael A. Tomlan, ed., pp. 97–108. National Council for Preservation Education, Ithaca, New York, 1998; Sherene Baugher, "Sacredness, sensitivity, and significance: The controversy over Native American sacred sites." In *Heritage of Value, Archaeology of Renown: Reshaping Archaeological Assessment and Significance*, Clay Mathers, Timothy Darvill, and Barbara J. Little, eds., pp. 248–275. University Press of Florida, Gainesville, 2005.

11. Letter from Bruce K. Riggs, NYBG, to Marie Sarchiapone, Landmarks Preservation Commission, September 17, 1987. Turtle Petroglyph file, LuEsther T. Mertz Library of the New York Botanical Garden.

12. Personal communication, Marie Sarchiapone.

13. *The New York Botanical Garden, Bronx, N.Y., Assessment of Archaeological Resources.* New York City Landmarks Preservation Commission, August 25, 1987, p. 7. Turtle Petroglyph file, LuEsther T. Mertz Library of the New York Botanical Garden.

14. John E. Sanders and Charles Merguerian, "Classification of Pleistocene deposits, New York City and vicinity – Fuller (1914) revived and revised." In Geology of Long Island and Metropolitan New York (18 April 1998, State University of New York at Stony Brook, NY). *Long Island Geologists Program with Abstracts*, 1998, pp. 130–143.

15. Lenik, "A turtle petroglyph on the Bronx River," *op. cit.*, p. 18 (note 4).

16. Charles Merguerian and John E. Sanders, "Bronx River diversion: neotectonic implications." *International Journal of Rock Mechanics and Mineral Science* 34, nos. 3–4, paper no. 198, 1997.

17. Howel Williams, Francis J. Turner, and Charles M. Gilbert, *Petrography; An Introduction to the Study of Rocks in Thin Section.* W.H. Freeman, San Francisco, 1954, pp. 44ff.

18. Solecki, *op. cit.*, p. 31 (note 4).

19. Peter Brazaitis, personal communication, 2007; Brazaitis is retired curator of animals at New York's Central Park Zoo and formerly Superintendent of Herpetology at the Bronx Zoo.

20. Compare the Bronx glyph to the Warner Brothers character of Cecil the Turtle, who first appeared with Bugs Bunny in a 1941 cartoon short entitled "Tortoise Beats Hare" based on the fable by Aesop. Another example might be Dr. Suess's Yertle, initially published in 1958.

21. In September of 2010, The Lorillard Snuff Mill was rededicated as the Lillian and Amy

Goldman Stone Mill after two years of renovation.

22. Harry Dunkak, "The Lorillard family of Westchester County: tobacco, property and nature." *The Westchester Historian* 71, no. 3 (Summer, 1995): 57.

23. Nathaniel Lord Britton, "The mansion." *New York Botanical Garden Journal* XVI, no. 191 (November, 1915): 231–233.

24. Randall Comfort, *History of Bronx Borough, City of New York*. North Side News Press, New York, 1906, p. 46; see also Ruth V. Caviston, *A History of the New York Botanical Garden*. The New York Botanical Garden, New York, 1952, pp. 6–10. The map detail of Figure 13b showing the studio's location is taken from Sheet 6 of New York, Department of Parks, *Topographical map made from surveys by the commissioners of the Department of Public Parks of the City of New York of that part of Westchester County adjacent to the City and County of New York embraced by chapter 534 of laws of 1871 as amended by chapter 878 or laws of 1872*. Department of Public Parks, New York, 1873.

25. New York City, Department of Public Parks. *Report for 1894*. Martin B. Brown, printer, 1895, p. 8; New York City, Department of Parks, *Report of the Department of Parks for the Year Ending December 31, 1901*. Mail and Express Co., New York, 1902, p. 65; New York City, Department of Parks. *Report for the Year 1902*. Martin B. Brown, printer, 1903, p. 83; The New York Times, "Ronalds, of Tally-ho Fame." *The New York Times*, September 3, 1905, p. 7.

26. E.S. Burgess, "Torrey Botanical Club, January 25, 1899." *Science* N.S. IX, no. 223 (April 7, 1899): 520.

27. "A fine new music stand" was designed and built by the Parks Department in 1907 to replace an "old and dilapidated" one that stood on the same site. New York City, Department of Parks, *Annual Report of the Department of Parks of the City of New York for the Year 1907*. Martin B. Brown, printer, New York, 1908, p. 93.

28. New York City, Department of Parks, *Annual Report for the Year Ending December 31, 1900*. Martin B. Brown, printer, New York, 1901, p. 20.

29. A.T.P., "Neglect or inefficiency doing great injury to the taxpayers' property." *Bronx Home News*, vol. 1(26), Friday, July 19, 1907, p. 1.

30. New York City, Department of Parks, *Annual Report for the Year Ending April 30, 1893*. Martin B. Brown, printer, New York, 1894, p. 81.

31. The New York Times, "Raid Shrine to Gambrinus." *The New York Times*, July 3, 1906, p. 9.

32. New York City, Department of Parks, *Annual Report for the Year 1903*. Martin B. Brown, printer, New York, 1904, p. 76.

33. For example, New York City, Department of Parks. *Report for the Year 1904*. Martin B. Brown, printer, 1905, p. 106.

34. Britton, *op. cit.* (note 23).

35. The New York Times, "$144,000 WPA Grant Spurs Work in Botanical Garden." *The New York Times*, August 11, 1935, p. N1.

36. Letter from Arthur J. Corbett, NYBG Superintendent of Buildings and Grounds, to Nathaniel Lord Britton, NYBG Director-in-Chief, April 16, 1923. X319, Box 8, LuEsther T. Mertz Library of the New York Botanical Garden.

37. The New York Times, "Ask City to Rebuild Lorillard Mansion." *The New York Times*, April 1, 1923, p. E7.

38. Resolution of the Executive Committee, May 21, 1924. X319, Box 8, LuEsther T. Mertz Library of the New York Botanical Garden.

39. Charles H. Faulkner, ed., *Rock Art of the Eastern Woodlands: Proceedings from the Eastern States Rock Art Conference (April 10, 1993, Natural Bridge State Park, Kentucky)*. American Rock Art Research Occasional Paper no. 2. San Miguel, California, 1996; Carol Diaz-Granados and James R. Duncan, eds., *The Rock-Art of Eastern North America*. University of Alabama Press, Tuscaloosa, 2004.

40. Fred E. Coy, Jr., "Native American dendroglyphs of the eastern woodlands." In *The Rock-Art of Eastern North America*, Carol Diaz-Granados and James R. Duncan, eds., pp. 3–16. University of Alabama Press, Tuscaloosa, 2004.

41. Christopher Chippindale, "Studying ancient pictures as pictures." In *Handbook of Rock Art Research*, David S. Whitley, ed. AltaMira Press, Walnut Creek, CA, 2001, pp. 262ff.

42. Lenik, "A turtle petroglyph on the Bronx River," *op. cit.*, p. 18 (note 4).

43. Theodore Kazimiroff, "Explore the New York Botanical Garden." *The Garden Journal* 5, no. 2 (March–April 1955): 33; "Nature trail." The New York Botanical Garden, 1983, p. 2.

44. Lenik cites William W. Newcomb, Jr., *The Culture and Acculturation of the Delaware Indians*. Museum of Anthropology, University of Michigan, Anthropological Papers no. 10, Ann Arbor, 1956, p.72.

45. Solecki, *op. cit.*, p. 32 (note 4).

46. Letter from Ralph S. Solecki to Bruce K. Riggs, February 3, 1993. Turtle Petroglyph file, LuEsther T. Mertz Library of the New York Botanical Garden.

47. Letter from Bruce K. Riggs to Ralph S. Solecki, dated February 10, 1993; copy kindly provided by Ralph Solecki.

48. Robert Grumet is a former member of Ranachqua Lodge, the local Bronx Council chapter of the Order of the Arrow, a Boy Scout honor camper organization, and he reports (personal communication) that the Botanical Garden allowed the Delaware Indian-themed organization to hold conclaves and other meetings on its grounds during the 1950s. The lodge was also permitted to use the Lorillard Snuff Mill to store regalia used in its fire-lit outdoor rituals. The lodge totem was an owl, however, a lodge member aware of the importance of the turtle in Delaware Indian belief may have created the petroglyph to mark a site near the dramatic backdrop of the Bronx

River falls. This cannot be proven but represents a possible scenario.

49. James D. Keyser, "Relative dating methods." In *Handbook of Rock Art Research*, David S. Whitley, ed., pp. 116–138. AltaMira Press, Walnut Creek, CA, 2001.

50. Ronald I. Dorn, *Rock Coatings*. Elsevier, Amsterdam, 1998, pp. 279ff.

51. Ronald I. Dorn, "Chronometric techniques: engravings." In *Handbook of Rock Art Research*, David S. Whitley, ed., pp. 167–189. AltaMira Press, Walnut Creek, CA, 2001.

52. Ronald I. Dorn, "Digital processing of back-scatter electron imagery: A microscopic approach to quantifying chemical weathering." *Bulletin, Geological Society of America* 107, no. 6 (June, 1995): 725–741.

53. Robert G. Bednarik, "A new method to date petroglyphs." *Archaeometry* 34 (1992): 279–291; Robert G. Bednarik, "First dating of Pilbara petroglyphs." *Records of the Western Australian Museum* 20 (2002): 414–429.

54. See James Pawley, ed., *Handbook of Biological Confocal Microscopy*, 3rd ed. Springer, New York, 2006, among other texts.

55. Robert K. Heimann, *Tobacco and Americans*. McGraw Hill, New York, 1960, p. 193.

Indians in the Bronx: the ethnohistorical evidence

Robert S. Grumet

Until recently, those interested in the aboriginal history of Bronx County have had to depend upon reconstructions made by local historians. The most enduringly popular of these reconstructions divides the borough, like Gaul, into three parts. These parts are frequently identified as the territories of Siwanoy, Wiechquaeskeck, and Rechgawawanck (often identified as Manhattans) constituents of a Wappinger Confederacy stretching from the east side of the Hudson River to the Connecticut River Valley.

This tripartite division was first set out by Robert Bolton, Jr., in the first edition of his *History of Westchester County* published in 1848. Bolton (1814–1877) was the eldest son of a well-regarded and well-to-do Episcopal churchman in Pelham, New York. Born in Britain, he moved to Westchester with his father in 1836. Comfortably ensconced as a gentleman farmer on a tract of land in present-day Portchester, he had sufficient free time to pursue a burgeoning interest in the history of his new home. Combing the county and its environs for records in public archives and personal collections, his two-volume *History* was among the first studies of its kind to make systematic use of the early first-hand descriptions of Indian life published by Moravian missionary John Heckewelder and pioneering ethnologist Henry Rowe Schoolcraft to broaden understanding of the findings drawn from primary documents dating to the colonial era. Original sources consulted by Bolton included 73 deeds and sale confirmations signed by Indians between 1639 and 1729 to land within the 1848 borders of Westchester County, which then included parts of the towns of Pelham and Eastchester and all the territories of today's Kingsbridge, West Farms, Morrisania, and Westchester itself that now comprise the borough of the Bronx.[1] Other documents identified a neck on Pell's land as a summer planting ground, Spuyten Duyvil as a refuge and fishing place, and land at and around Harlem as a winter village, fishing spot, and place of refuge.

Ten deeds to lands in what is now the Bronx that were signed by Indians survive today. All were executed between 1639 and 1705. Bolton abstracted eight of these in his *History*; the June 27, 1654 Pell deed, was first published in 1941; and a September 21, 1666 payment confirmation for Yonkers land appeared in a compilation of documents associated with the administration of New York Governor Francis Lovelace (1668–1673). Together, these conveyances and the patents, leases, and other legal instruments referring to them, comprise the bulk of the primary data set chronicling the borough's documented indigenous history.[2]

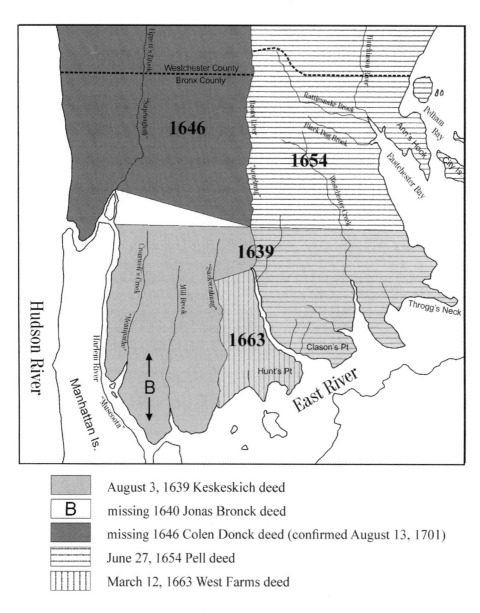

Figure 1. Map of the Bronx showing the locations of deeds bearing Indian signatories executed during the Dutch colonial period (1639–1663). Boundaries are approximate and based on the deeds themselves and coeval maps where available. The white triangular area was a gore, unincorporated and later disputed territory between Colen Donck to the north and Keskeskich to the south.

Figures 1 and 2 are maps showing approximate boundaries of the properties listed in the following inventory, which represents a synopsis of the

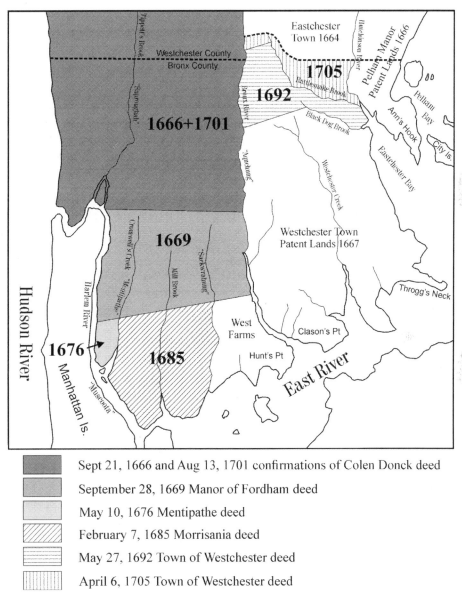

Figure 2. Map of the Bronx showing the locations of deeds bearing Indian signatories executed during the English colonial period (1666–1705). Boundaries are approximate and based on the deeds themselves and coeval maps where available.

data identifying the signing dates, Indian signatories, and areas conveyed through the nine deeds and one payment confirmation.

August 3, 1639: "Tequemeck, Rechgawac, Packamieus, owners of Keskeskich," sell "...a piece of land, located opposite to the flat on the island called Manhattan, called Keskeskich..." to the Dutch West India Company.

June 27, 1654: Shawnarockquot, Anhooke, and others sell land east of Acquaoung comprising the east Bronx to Thomas Pell. Acquaoung is elsewhere noted as Aquehung, the Indian name of today's Bronx River. Pell, however, accepted the interpretation identifying the western boundary of the tract as Aqueanonucke (the present-day Hutchinson River) in his 1666 patent confirming his title.

March 12, 1663: Shonearockite, and others sell present-day West Farms.

September 21, 1666: Tackareek and Claes ye Indian acknowledge payment for "ye Younkers Land" by "Van der Dunck."

September 28, 1669: Indians sell present-day Fordham to John Archer.

May 10, 1676: Indians sell "...a certain piece of land at Mentipathe Kill..." (Tibbetts Brook or an upper branch of Saproughah, the now-filled Cromwell's Creek beneath present-day Jerome Avenue) between University Heights and the "Bronkx River."

February 7, 1685: Taquamarke and Wanacapeen, who claim to have earlier sold land in the southwest corner of the borough to Jonas Bronck, sell the same to Lewis Morris. Morris subsequently patented the tract as his Manor of Morrisania, which in turn became the town of Morrisania in 1855 incorporated into New York County in 1874.

May 27, 1692: Maminepoe, Wampage alias Ann-hook, and others sell land south of Rattlesnake Brook in the Wakefield section of the Bronx claimed by the town of Eastchester to Westchester townsfolk.

August 13, 1701: "Clause Dewilt [Claes the Indian], Karacapacomont, and her son Nemerau," surrender their claim to "Old Younckers," purchased by Adriaen van der Donck in the since-lost 1646 deed.

April 6, 1705: "Patthunck, Sagamore, Hopescoe alias Porrige, Anne Hook, and Elias, Indian proprietors," convey remaining lands along the contested Eastchester-Westchester border to the town of Westchester.

Boundaries of land conveyed by Indians signing these deeds have been subjects of dispute since colonial times. These debates have largely been fueled by the absence of four key documents: the long-lost Bronck and van der Donck deeds, an unfound 1640 conveyance to land comprising the town of Westchester mentioned by Bolton in his *History*, and the June 27, 1654 Pell deed that lay unnoticed in England for nearly three hundred years.

Bronck may not have purchased the land mentioned in the February 7,

1685 confirmation deed from the Indians. A 1640 document leasing land in the area to other colonists affirms that Bronck possessed title to the tract at that time. The absence of an Indian deed registered to him in colony records, however, indicates that he acquired his title from Dutch authorities.

This title may be traced to the August 3, 1639 Keskeskich deed (the more usual Keskeskick is an earlier transcription error rendering the name's terminal "h" as "k"). The land conveyed to the Dutch West India Company by the Indians consisted of "flatlands" located below a line running "mostly east-west" between the "head of the...kill [Dutch for creek]... which runs behind the Island of Manhattan [i.e., the Harlem River] and...the Great Kill." This tract would include most of the present-day borough if the Great Kill is another name for Long Island Sound. The Palisades, which afford a comprehensive overview of the Bronx, may be the high hill opposite the flatlands mentioned in the deed.

The 1639 Keskeskich deed may also be the still-missing 1640 Indian conveyance transferring title to land to settlers at and around Throgg's Neck. Its northern boundary also may have constituted the southern limits of the land purchased from Shawnarockquot, Annhooke, and others by Thomas Pell on June 27, 1654 (see where the Indians recorded their marks in Figure 3). Both Pell and the Throgg's Neck settlers initially claimed all territory east of Bronck's Land. They evidently resolved their differences by the time English authorities required registration of all titles to land within New York shortly after seizing New Netherland from the Dutch in 1664.

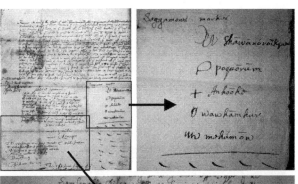

Figure 3. Details of the 1654 Pell deed (upper left), showing marks made by the Indian signatories, including, in the upper right, Anhōōke (+), Shāwānórockquot (scribble), and Poquōrūm (circle with tail), and, at the bottom, Rāmaque (bent line). Images are reproduced here with the permission of the Fort Ticonderoga Museum.

Pell accepted the interpretation identifying Aquaoung, usually regarded as Aquehung, the Bronx River, as "Aqueanonucke, commonly known by the English by the name of Hutchinson's river" as the western boundary of his property in his October 6, 1666 patent. A few months later, the Throgg's Neck settlers patented their town of Westchester in February 13, 1667 between Pell's tract and Bronck's land.[3]

Land above Keskeskich west of the Bronx River was evidently included in the lost van der Donck deed thought to have been finalized in 1646. Other deeds settled disputes on the borders of earlier purchases at places like Wakefield, West Farms, and Fordham.

Data presented within these deeds include names of several people noted as Indian owners, proprietors, or sagamores (chiefs, also called sachems and sakimas). Perhaps the most prominent of these was a leader identified as Shawanarockquot on the June 27, 1654 Pell deed and Shonearockite on the March 12, 1663 West Farms conveyance. These are almost certainly variant spellings of Sauwenaroque, (fl. 1636–1666), a leading Wiechquaeskeck sachem. Many of the other Indians named in these documents as co-signatories or witnesses appear in coeval documents recording other events in nearby places.[4]

The deeds also contain several place names. These include Keskeskich and other locales like Achqueegenom in Fordham, necks of land such as Nausin (Highbridge Point overlooking today's Yankee Stadium) and Quinnahung (Hunt's Point), and streams named Saproughah (beneath today's Jerome Avenue) and Aquehung (today's Bronx River).

Bolton combined data drawn from these and other Westchester County deeds with findings from other sources in a brief introductory chapter titled "Aborigines" placed at the beginning of the first volume of his *History*. Names graphically representing his interpretations of this information were entered onto a map printed as a frontispiece to the chapter (Figure 4). He drew many, but by no means all, of the Indian names from local deeds. A few, like Mosholu and Castle Hill, came from otherwise undocumented local traditions. Others, like Nipnichsen in Riverdale, were transplants relocated from other places.[5]

More than a few of Bolton's Indian map names were originally shown on the widely available Jansson-Visscher map, the Indian data from which were reprinted more or less unchanged in the 31 known versions of the projection published between 1648 and 1779.[6] The three groups with their territories displayed within the approximate environs of today's Bronx included "Manhattans" at the borough's southwestern end, "Siwanoys" along Long Island Sound east of the Bronx River, and "Weecquesqueecks" (standardized today as Wiechquaeskeck) along the east bank of the Hudson River from the borough's northwestern corner up into Westchester County.[7]

Bolton drew *Laaphawachking*, his name for aboriginal Westchester County and its translation, "place of stringing beads," from Heckewelder's

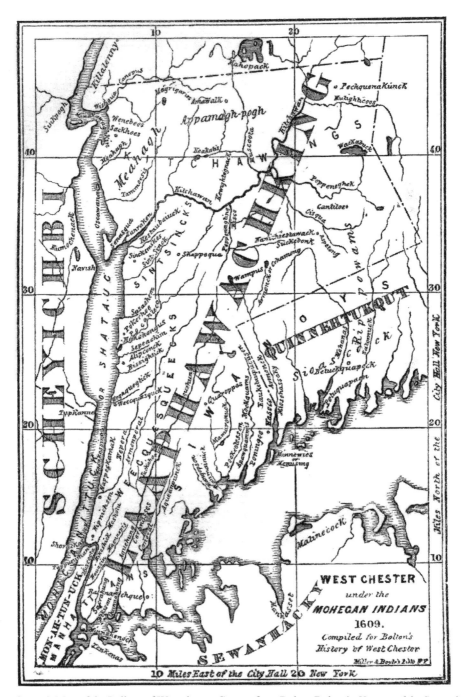

Figure 4. Map of the Indians of Westchester County from Robert Bolton's *History of the Several Towns, Manors, and Patents of the County of Westchester*, Vol. 1, map following p. xxv, 1881.

writings.[8] His use of the spelling *Mon-ah-tun-uck* to identify Manhattan Island, and extension of Manhattan Indian territory into the southwest Bronx, reflect their origins in Schoolcraft's published works.[9]

Bolton's reliance upon derivative sources such as the Jansson-Visscher map and Schoolcraft's studies led him anachronistically to place and employ names of non-existent Indian communities not documented in local colonial records. This is most clearly indicated in his use of Siwanoy. The word itself originally appeared in the form *Sywanois* as the name of a neck of land located to the north of present-day Boston on the 1614 Adriaen Block map. Johan de Laet, a Dutch West India Company director who never visited New Netherland, relocated what he called *Siwanois* along an eight-league-long stretch of shoreline between the Connecticut River and Hell Gate at the western end of Long Island Sound in several editions of his promotional pamphlet for the colony. Heavily drawing upon de Laet's writings, the cartographer who drafted the first edition of the Jansson-Visscher series placed what he called the Siwanoys just inland from the coast between the Hudson and Housatonic rivers. Although all of these are old sources, each is a secondary reference written by someone with no first-hand experience in the region. No known deed or other primary source directly documents a Siwanoy group or individual.[10]

Bolton wrote at a time when Americans tended to regard all old sources as primary records. Like his contemporaries, Bolton was also aware of the fact that European archives contained numbers of primary records far greater than those in local repositories. Bolton and other historians began petitioning politicians to commission diplomatic ministerial staff already in Europe to collect or copy colonial records when interest in early American history began to grow during the second quarter of the 19th century. John Romeyn Brodhead (1814–1873), a scholarly writer fluent in Dutch, was the first such agent assigned the task by the governor and legislature of New York. Arriving in The Hague in 1841 to serve as secretary to the American *chargé d'affaires* to the Netherlands, Brodhead found that he had arrived 20 years too late to consult the records of the Dutch West India Company. This large and extensive paper archive was sold off for recycling a few years after attempts failed in 1800 to revive the defunct Company that had been under control of the Dutch government since 1790. Brodhead nevertheless managed to gather together eighty volumes worth of documents relative to the colonial history of New York from Dutch, French, and British archives by the time he ended his diplomatic career as secretary to the American minister to Great Britain in 1849.

Edmund Bailey O'Callaghan (1797–1880), an Irish-born Canadian immigrant who moved to the United States in 1838 following the collapse of the anti-British insurrection that he supported, oversaw the editing and publication of Brodhead's materials in his capacity as New York State Keeper of Historical Manuscripts. He was appointed to that position in 1849 following publication of his *History of New Netherland*, which emphasized Dutch contributions to New York history. O'Callaghan initially organized a body of important colonial documents into a four-volume set titled *The Documentary History of the State of New York*, published between 1849 and 1851. He subsequently managed to complete work on the first eleven volumes of the *Documents Relating to the Colonial History of the State of New York* by the time he died in 1880.[11]

Further contributions were made during this time by Henry Cruse Murphy (1810–1882), a Dutch-speaking lawyer from Brooklyn who also had a strong interest in early New York history. He published fuller and more accurate translations of such key works as Adriaen van der Donck's *Representation of New Netherland* and David Petersz. de Vries's *Voyages from Holland to America 1633–1644* before sailing to Europe, where he served as the United States Minister to the Netherlands between 1857 and 1861. While at this post, he purchased Jasper Danckaerts's incomparably detailed *Journal of a Voyage to New York in 1679–80* from an Amsterdam bookseller.[12]

The flood of new information made available in these and other publications added considerable context and texture to otherwise fragmentary, disconnected, and terse entries preserved in local records.[13] Writers like Bolton and those who followed him soon used this information to reexamine previous findings and develop new interpretative views of the histories of Indian people, polities, and places in the region.

A historically-minded Newburgh, New York, newspaperman named Edward Manning Ruttenber (1825–1907) used the newly discovered sources to build upon previous findings in his *History of the Indian Tribes of Hudson's River*, published in 1872. Ruttenber constructed his narrative around theoretical ideas then prevalent about social development. He was particularly influenced by "great man" theories emphasizing the importance of powerful political figures. This viewpoint probably accounts for Ruttenber's suggestion that the Rechgawawanck were named after Rechgawac, a chief signatory to the August 3, 1639 deed to the Keskeskich tract.[14]

Bolton's earlier view casting Hudson Valley Indians as members of nomadic bands could not explain how they were able to muster sufficient resources to survive invasion by overwhelmingly more numerous and technologically advanced European intruders. Ruttenber's reclassification of Hudson Valley Indian communities as more complex sedentary chieftaincies organized around, and sometimes named for, prominent leaders like Rechgawac provided a framework that helped him construct a counter narrative. This allowed him to show how leaders able to mobilize people and resources helped followers survive defeat, dispossession, and the loss of their homeland.[15]

Ruttenber specifically identified Westchester County Indians as constituent chieftaincies belonging to a more widespread Mahican-speaking Wappinger tribe. Named for the Wappinger community in present-day Dutchess County, where many descendants of Bronx Indians settled after giving up their lands in the borough, Ruttenber's Wappinger tribe stretched from the east bank of the Hudson River to the Connecticut River Valley.[16] Ruttenber's basic hierarchical structure remained the primary paradigm employed in Hudson Valley Indian studies for more than a century. Working at a time when descriptive concerns dominated discourse in the social sciences, most writers tended to direct much of their energy toward nomenclatural and classificatory issues. Smithsonian Institution ethnologist James C. Mooney's (1861–1921) characterization of the Wappingers as a confederacy was widely adopted following the publication of his entry for the group in the second volume of the influential *Handbook of American Indians* in 1910. Mooney's colleague John Reed Swanton (1873–1958) listed Ruttenber's chieftaincies under the heading "Subdivisions or Sachemships" in his geographically-oriented guide, *The Indians of North America*, published in 1952. Other investigators, like historian Allen W. Trelease (1928–2011) and historical demographer Sherburne Friend Cook (1896–1974), tended to use a wide variety of terms that included band, tribe, sachemdom, and division or sub-division when discussing particular Wappinger Confederacy communities.[17]

Scholars championing Mahican or Delaware linguistic affiliations of the Wappingers tended to exclude findings documenting those speaking the other language. Cook, for example, did not include Delawares on the west bank of the Hudson in findings presented in his monograph. Anthropologist William W. Newcomb, Jr. (1921–2010) and historian-archaeologist Clinton Alfred Weslager (1909–1994) were among many students of Delaware history who excluded what they regarded as Mahican-speaking Wappingers east of the Hudson.

Analyses of archival, linguistic, and archaeological evidence indicating closer linguistic, cultural, and historical connections between the easternmost Delawares and the westernmost Wappingers just across the Hudson made other writers question the importance of documented differences. Swanton, for example, was among those who thought historical and linguistic data showed that what he called "Reckgawawancs" were a Delaware-speaking Unami subdivision.[18] Smithsonian linguist R. H. Ives Goddard has since shown that Indians living on both banks of the lower Hudson River spoke a language most similar to the northernmost Munsee variant or dialect of Delaware.[19]

Pioneering historically-minded archaeologists, such as Alanson Buck Skinner (1886–1925) and Reginald Pelham Bolton (1856–1942) had earlier noted that similarities discerned in artifact type, styles, and assemblages from both sides of the river reflected a similar connection.[20] Other archaeologically-based assertions, however, proved problematic. All archaeologists working before the invention of radiocarbon dating in 1949, for example, could neither accurately date nor culturally affiliate their findings. Globular collared clay pots most frequently encountered farther upstate in historic Iroquois territory tended to be regarded as evidence of sites thought to have been occupied by, or associated with, presumed recent Iroquois immigrants to the Northeast. Cone-shaped collarless wares were seen as relics of earlier "Pre-Iroquoian Algonkian" occupations regarded as simpler and less sedentary than the Iroquois.

Around the turn of the last century, Skinner, Reginald Bolton, and others identified several sites in the Bronx containing globular collared pots as historic occupations. It was then fashionable to give Indian names to these sites. This practice led to some inventions and an increase in the number of toponymic imports from other places. Skinner, for example, gave the name "Snakapins" to a substantial archaeological site that he discovered on Clason's Point in the fall of 1918. The earliest known occurrence of Snakapins as a name of, or on, Cornell's Neck (today's Clason's Point) appears in a list of Westchester County Indian place names published in 1900 by philologist William Wallace Tooker (1848–1917).[21]

Noting the absence of European wares in a site that otherwise contained many broken sherds from globular collared pots, Skinner was led to conclude that the Clason's Point site was occupied from late prehistoric times around 1575 to the early historic period (from 1625 to 1643). Subsequent comparative stylistic analysis of "Clason's Point Focus" pottery undertaken by archaeologist Carlyle Shreeve Smith (1915–1993) indicated that the site was probably most intensively occupied during earlier Late Woodland times between one to two hundred years before colonial contact. Although intact deposits have since been found in Pelham Bay Park, intensive development elsewhere in the borough probably has disturbed or destroyed most other archaeological evidence of Indian occupation in the Bronx.[22]

Investigators continue to use extant archaeological findings to reexamine old ideas and test new hypotheses. Archaeologist Lynn Ceci (1931–1989), for example, superimposed documented archaeological site locations onto soil survey maps showing small patches of arable ground to challenge widely held notions supporting the importance of aboriginal food production in the region. Anthropologist Marshall J. Becker explained away numerous references to Indian plantations and Indian fields as places where corn and other cultigens were produced for trade with colonists. Noting that the environment of the Hudson Valley is far more benign than the tundras, deserts, jungles, and boreal forests inhabited by known hunter-gatherers, most investigators continue to regard numerous documentary references to Indian husbandry as evidence of an already established Late Woodland mixed economy that combined corn, bean, and squash cultivation with the yields from hunting, fishing, and foraging.

No known record directly documents Indian population in or around the Bronx. Noting low population numbers and densities recorded for hunting and gathering foragers elsewhere in the world, anthropologist Becker proposed a population figure of 300 for what he called Siwanoy bands whose numbers included "Kichtawanks, Sinsinks, Wiechquaeskecks, and Rechgawawanks."[23] Most traditional estimates indicate a total Wappinger Confederacy population of from three to four thousand people.[24] More recent studies focusing on high mortality rates caused by epidemic diseases propose aboriginal populations considerably larger than those suggested in earlier estimates.[25] Whatever their population numbers or density, and they were surely higher than Becker's minimal estimates, clearly documented multiple episodes of epidemic disease as well as the twin ravages of all-but-endemic warfare and nearly total land loss acted together to force Indians from their ancestral homeland in the lower Hudson River Valley by the end of the seventeenth century.[26]

Goddard's findings indicating that lower Hudson Valley Munsee languages differed from those spoken in the Housatonic Valley led him to question the existence of a single Wappinger chieftaincy or confederation stretching between the Hudson and Connecticut rivers.[27] Taking a skeptical position towards other undocumented findings in his 1971 paper and his entry on Delaware published in the *Northeast* volume of the *Handbook of North American Indians* in 1978, he also questioned assertions using what he called "early information of a general nature" identifying aboriginal people along Long Island Sound as Siwanois.[28] He further limited identification of Rechgawawanck to two similarly-spelled references numbering the community among those mentioned in documents dated 1643 and 1645.[29]

Goddard's constructively skeptical approach galvanized researchers who questioned the unexamined claims of earlier investigators. New Netherland Project founder Charles T. Gehring generated further excitement through his publication of new translations of Dutch documents thought to have been totally destroyed in the 1911 Albany State Library fire.[30] Inspired by the work of Goddard, Gehring, and other innovators, I began searching for long-neglected primary documents chronicling Indians and Indian relations preserved in state archives, museum collections, and county and town hall records in and around the Hudson Valley. Results from this research replicated Goddard's findings indicating the non-existence of both a Siwanoy band and a Wappinger Confederacy. Failing to find a reference linking the earlier-mentioned sachem Rechgawac with a Rechgawawanck community, I suggested that Sesekemu, noted as a Rechgawawanck or Tappaen sachem (it is uncertain which) in the August 30, 1645 treaty ending Governor Kieft's War, and Ses-Segh-Hout, the "chief of Rewechnongh or Haverstraw" who signed the May 16, 1664 treaty ending the Esopus War, were the same person. I further identified both names as variant renderings of Seyseychkimus, the name of a sachem originally from Brooklyn who moved north up the Hudson River during the late 1630s. These findings joined others used to identify Rechgawawanck as another name for the Haverstraw that centered around the present-day west bank town of Haverstraw in New York's Rockland County.[31]

Very few sources explicitly link any Indians involved in Bronx affairs with named communities. The most direct of these, a statement made by sachems agreeing to sell land in Westchester dated February 14, 1671, identifies "Ramaque, Janorockets Bro: by ye Mothrs. Side" at the head of a list of "Indyans about Wijckerscreeke." English colonists phonetically Anglicized the name Wijckerscreeke as Wicker Creek, the still-used name of the stream that flows into the Hudson River at Dobbs Ferry. Indians called the locale Wiechquaeskeck, and colonists extended use of the term to identify all Indians living in Westchester County. Janorocket is almost certainly another spelling of the name of the Wiechquaeskeck sachem Sauwenaroque.[32] At least two Indians involved in the September 28, 1669 sale of Fordham, Achipor and Minquaes Sachemache, also signed two of the three deeds selling Staten Island.[33] Other deeds to land in the Bronx were signed by Wampage, also known as Ann Hook (fl. 1682–1705), a prominent sachem in Westchester. Claims to lands purchased by Adriaen van der Donck were lodged by Jan Claes, also known as Claes the Indian (fl. 1666–1714). Evidently born on the east bank of the Hudson, Jan Claes became a noted interpreter most closely associated with the Tappan Indian community who served as an interpreter and go-between in negotiations with colonists in the lower Hudson Valley.[34]

Extant documents identify these people as members or leaders of groups identified as Tappans and Wiechquaeskecks. They do not, however, indicate what kind of community these names referred to. Descriptors like band, tribe, and chieftaincy were applied to these names long after the social formations they represented disappeared. The term band best describes highly mobile nomadic groups who travel widely across environmentally challenging terrain.[35] Many anthropologists still regard tribes as adaptive responses to contact with intruders belonging to state systems.[36] Chieftaincies, for their part, went out of style with great man theory. Recent studies of chiefdoms examine stratified social orders little resembling egalitarian societies like those in the lower Hudson Valley.

A more flexible approach that does not pigeon-hole social organization into rigid categories provides a more useful framework for understanding the social organization of the Indians of the Bronx. Verified data documenting identities and connections between individuals associated with communities from particular locales in and beyond borough boundaries suggest the existence of networks of people mostly speaking similar variants of the Munsee languages who were linked by kinship ties extending across successive generations of women. These would allow members to join with others living in more distantly connected communities to form more widely extended networks when needed.[37]

However one chooses to interpret the data, it is time to put to rest unverified identifications of Bronx Indians as Siwanoy or Rechgawawanck constituents of an undocumented Wappinger Confederacy. Long-held notions identifying villages called Nipnichsen in Riverdale and others on Clason's Point and Castle Hill as historic Indian habitations should also be set aside. Pending future discoveries of documents or development of new analytic techniques capable of wringing new data from old evidence, it can most assuredly be said that sachems, most notably the Wiechquaeskeck leader Sauwenaroque, and followers belonging to local groups broadly affiliated with others stretching from the lower Hudson Valley to the shores of New York harbor lived in communities situated in several named locales in the Bronx at one time or another during the first century of direct documented contact with European colonists.

ENDNOTES

1. Primary sources are created by event participants or eyewitnesses. Secondary sources, by contrast, are created by writers at least one step removed from actual events. The Westchester County towns of Kingsbridge, West Farms, and Morrisania initially split off to become what was named the Annexed District attached to the northern end of New York County in 1874. Parts of Pelham, Eastchester, and all of the town of Westchester, including the original county seat at Westchester Square, were absorbed into the District in 1895. The entire Annexed District became the Borough of the Bronx following consolidation of New York City in 1898, adopting a county form of government in 1914.

A brief biography of Robert Bolton originally published in 1878 is reprinted in Pelham historian Blake A. Bell's website, http://www.historicpelham.com. Bolton devoted much time during the latter part of his life to updating his *History* (*A History of the County of Westchester, from its First Settlement to the Present Time*, 2 vols. Alexander S. Gould, New York, 1848), first as director of an academy for young women that he founded in 1859, and later as an ordained Episcopal priest serving as rector of St. John's Church in the Westchester County town of Lewisboro from 1869 until his death in 1877. The second edition of this work was completed in 1881 by his son, the Rev. Cornelius Winter Bolton, and published as *The History of the Several Towns, Manors, and Patents of the County of Westchester, from Its First Settlement to the Present Time* by C. F. Rope, New York.

2. The eight Indian deeds in present-day Bronx County abstracted in Bolton's *History* may be found on p. 211 in the first volume of the 1881 edition and on pp. 290–292, 433–434, 463, 504–505, 517–518, 575–576, and 587–588 in the book's second volume. The September 21, 1666 confirmation of van der Donck's payment to the Indians for "ye Youncker's Land" appears in Paltsits, *Minutes of the Executive Council of the Province of New York: Administration of Francis Lovelace, 1668–1673*. State of New York, Albany, 1910, vol. 1, pp. 234–235. The same Indians reappeared in New York 10 years later on July 25, 1676 complaining that they had not yet been paid for the land; see O'Callaghan and Fernow, vol. 13, 1881, p. 498 (see note 11). The 1654 Pelham deed is published in Pell, 1941 (see note 13).

References to Harlem as a winter village, fishing spot, and place of refuge appear in O'Callaghan and Fernow, vol. 13, 1881, pp. 255, 282, and 303, (see note 11). Pell's land as a planting ground appears on pp. 235–238, and Spuyten Duyvil appears as a refuge on p. 494.

3. Pelham town historian Blake A. Bell recounts his unsuccessful years-long search for the 1640 deed in an August 12, 2015 entry on his Historic Pelham website entitled "Significant research on the first 'Indian deed' reflecting the Dutch purchase of the lands that included today's Pelham," http://www.historicpelham.blogspot.com (last consulted August 12, 2016).

4. For Sauwenaroque, see Robert S. Grumet, *The Munsee Indians: A History*. The University of Oklahoma Press, Norman, 2009, p. 299, note 27.

5. The name Mosholu, first used in the Bronx to identify the small community established along Tibbetts Brook, honored Mushulatubbee, a Creek chief widely lionized for his support of embattled Americans fighting against the British during the War of 1812. Castle Hill was identified by Bolton in a footnote on p. 242 of Vol. 2 of his *History, op. cit.* (note 1) as an otherwise undocumented Indian fort; see Grumet, *Manhattan to Minisink: American Indian Place Names in Greater New York and Vicinity*. University of Oklahoma Press, Norman, 2013, p. 197 for documentation of Castle Hill's origin as an English estate name adopted by the wealthy landowner who purchased the area in 1775. Nipnichsen reflected Bolton's acceptance of Egbert Benson's 1816 relocation of Nip Nickson from New Jersey's Bayonne Peninsula to Riverdale as the name of an otherwise unidentified fort from which Indians sallied forth to attack Hudson's ship, *de Halve Maen* (the Half Moon) in 1609. See Egbert Benson's *Memoir, Read Before the Historical Society of New-York, 31 December 1816*. William A. Mercein, New York, 1817 (also reprinted as "Egbert Benson's Memoir on Names. Read 1816." In *Collections of the New-York Historical Society* series 2, vol. 2, pt 1, pp. 77–148, published in 1849). Further information on Nip Nickson and other Indian names in the borough may be found in Robert S. Grumet, *Native American Place Names in New York City*. Museum of the City of New York, New York, 1981, pp. 39–40. Updated information presenting the result of my 30 year search for the historical source of Mosholu, finally found in the entry for Mashulaville, Mississippi, in William Bright, *Native American Placenames of the United States*. The University of Oklahoma Press, Norman, 2004, p. 270, may be seen in Grumet, *Manhattan to Minisink, op. cit.* (this note), p. 219.

6. See Tony Campbell, *New Light on the Jansson-Visscher Maps of New England*. The Map Collectors' Circle, London, 1965; and Joep M.J. de Koning "From van der Donck to Visscher." *Mercators World: The Magazine of Atlases, Globes, and Charts* 5, no. 4 (2000): 3–10.

7. Spellings of Wiechquaeskeck and other Delaware ethnonyms not specifically drawn from primary documents follow those standardized in R.H. Ives Goddard, "Delaware." In Bruce Trigger, ed., *Handbook of North American Indians, Vol. 15. Northeast*. The Smithsonian Institution Press, Washington, D.C., 1978, pp. 213–239.

8. Heckewelder first noted his formulation of Laaphawachking as the Monsey (i.e., Munsee) name for New York in a letter dated January 26, 1801. He stated in the letter that he collected the word from exiled "Delaware, Monsey, and Mahicanni" (Mahican) elders in Ohio nearly 40 years earlier. Heckewelder's letter subsequently appeared in print in 1819 in the first edition of his *Account of the History, Manners, and Customs of the Indians...*, published as the first volume of the Transactions of the American Philosophical Society. Laaphawachking became more widely known following the publication of Heckewelder's letter in 1841 in "Indian tradition of the first arrival of the Dutch, at Manhattan, now New-York." In *Collections of the New-York Historical Society*, 2nd series, vol. 1, pt. 3, where it appears in a footnote on p. 73.

9. Schoolcraft's belief that Manhattans and other Indians on the east bank of the Hudson spoke what he called Mohegan language (today known to linguists as Mahican) allowed him to accept the statement made by a descendant of New York Indians in Wisconsin identifying *Mon-a-tuns* as the Mohegan word for Manhattan Island translated as "people of the whirlpool" in reference to the swirling waters of the Hell Gate in the East River. Findings made by Bolton also helped him accept Schoolcraft's observation that the Manhattans were closely linked to other Mohegan Indians living at Sin Sinck (today's Ossining) and farther up the east bank of the Hudson. Bolton drew upon many findings made by Schoolcraft in his report, "Comments, Philological and Historical,

on the Aboriginal Names and Geographical Terminology, of the State of New York. Part First: Valley of the Hudson." In *Proceedings of the New-York Historical Society for the Year 1844*, published in 1845, pp. 77–115.

10. For further information, see the entry for *Siwanoy* in Grumet, *Manhattan to Minisink*, *op. cit.* (note 4), pp. 160–161.

11. O'Callaghan's editions of Brodhead's findings primarily appeared in two series published by the State of New York in Albany; the four-volume *Documentary History of the State of New York* (1849–1851), and the 15-volume *Documents Relative to the Colonial History of New York* (1853–1887). Volumes of the latter series published after O'Callaghan's death in 1880 were guided into production by his successor, Berthold Fernow (1837–1908). O'Callaghan's *History of New Netherland* appeared in two volumes in 1846–1848, published by D. Appleton and Company of New York.

12. Murphy had earlier translated and privately published Adriaen van der Donck's 1650 *Representation of New Netherland*. Bartlett and Welford, New York, 1849; and David Petersz. de Vries's *Voyages from Holland to America 1633–1644*. Billin and Bros., New York, 1853. Murphy's edition of Danckaerts's *Journal* was published as the first volume in the Memoirs series produced by the Long Island Historical Society of Brooklyn in 1867.

13. Considerable contributions increasing the number and quality of primary published records documenting Indian affairs in and around the Bronx were made by local historian James Riker in works like *Harlem (City of New York): Its Origin and Early Annals*. Privately published, New York, 1881. Other contributions appear in publications edited by New York State librarian and archivist Arnold Van Laer (1869–1955) and, notably, the two-volume *Minutes of the Executive Council of the Province of New York: Administration of Francis Lovelace, 1668–1673*. State of New York, Albany, 1910, edited by New York State Historian Victor Hugo Paltsits (1909–1952), *op. cit.* (note 2). More recently, S.H.P. Pell, a descendant of Pelham Manor founder Thomas Pell, discovered and published in 1941 as the frontispiece of Vol. 1, no. 6 of *Pelliana*, a copy of the long-lost deed purchasing the manor land on June 27, 1654 from sachems whose number included Shawanarockquot; see Sauwenaroque, below (note 32) and Ann Hook (see here Figure 4).

14. See p. 10 in Charles T. Gehring, transl. and ed., *New York Historical Manuscripts: Dutch. Volume GG, HH, and II: Land Papers*. Genealogical Publishing Company, Baltimore, 1980, for the most accurately translated text of the August 3, 1639 deed to Keskeskich, spelled Keskeskick in earlier translations. Rechgawac was subsequently mentioned as Rechkewacken, one of the signatories to the Indian deed to Rechewanis Point, a neck of land jutting out into the East River just below the mouth of Harlem River opposite the Hell Gate, signed on August 20, 1669 and published on pp. 278–279 of Riker's *Harlem*, *op. cit.* (note 13).

15. For the seminal text on "Great Man Theory," see Thomas Carlyle, *On Heroes, Hero-Worship, and the Heroic in History*. Chapman and Hall, London, 1840. Anthropologist Herbert Spencer subsequently showed that society played a more salient role in social development than individuals in *The Study of Sociology*. D. Appleton and Son, New York, 1896. Ruttenber laid out his general reconstruction of Hudson Valley Indian governance on pp. 47–52 of his *History of the Indian Tribes of Hudson's River*. J. Munsell, Albany, 1872.

16. See pp. 77–85 in Ruttenber's *History*, *op. cit.* (note 15) for his description of the Wappinger tribe and its constituent chieftaincies.

17. See Mooney's "Wappinger" entry on p. 913 in Frederick Webb Hodge, ed., *Handbook of American Indians North of Mexico*, Vol. 2. Bureau of American Ethnology Bulletin 30, Washington, D.C.,1907–1910; see p. 45 under "Wappinger" in John Reed Swanton, *The Indian Tribes of North America*. Bureau of American Ethnology Bulletin 145, Washington, D.C., 1952; see p. 8 in historian Allen W. Trelease (1928–2011), *Indian Affairs in Colonial New York: The Seventeenth Century*. Cornell University Press, Ithaca, New York, 1960 (reprinted in 1997 by the University of Nebraska Press, Lincoln).

18. William W. Newcomb, Jr., *The Culture and Acculturation of the Delaware Indians*. Anthropological Papers of the University of Michigan no. 10, Ann Arbor, 1956; Clinton Alfred Weslager, *The Delaware Indians: A History*. Rutgers University Press, New Brunswick, New Jersey, 1972; for "Reckgawawanc" as a Delaware community, see p. 49 in Swanton, *Indian Tribes*, *op. cit.* (note 17).

19. See R.H. Ives Goddard, "The ethnohistorical implications of Early Delaware linguistic materials." *Man in the Northeast* 1971, no. 1: 14–26 (reprinted on pp. 88–102 in Laurence M. Hauptman and Jack Campisi, eds., *Neighbors and Intruders: An Ethnohistorical Exploration of the Indians of Hudson's River*. National Museum of Man Mercury Series, Canadian Ethnology Service Paper No. 39. National Museums of Canada, Ottawa, 1978.

20. Alanson Buck Skinner, *The Indians of Manhattan Island and Vicinity*. Torch Press, Cedar Rapids, Iowa, 1915; Reginald Pelham Bolton, *New York City in Indian Possession*. Indian Notes and Monographs, Vol. 2, no. 7, pp. 223–395, Museum of the American Indian, Heye Foundation, 1920 (revised 2nd edition published in 1975 by the Museum of the American Indian, Heye Foundation, New York).

21. Reginald Pelham Bolton probably encouraged Skinner to give the name to the site. Bolton simply cites Tooker as the source of the name in his "Historical introduction" to the site area on pp. 75–78 of Skinner's "Snakapins, a Siwanoy site at Clason's Point." In *Exploration of Aboriginal Sites at Throgs Neck and Clason's Point, New York City*. Contributions from the Museum of the American Indian, Heye Foundation, 1919, Vol. 4, No. 4, pt. 2; Tooker's entry for "Snakapins" appears on p. 49 as "Amerindian names in Westchester County," on pp. 45–50, in Frederic Shonnard and W.W. Spooner, eds., *History of Westchester County, New York from its Earliest Settlement to the Year 1900*. New York History Company, New York, 1900.

Examples of Reginald Bolton's attribution of undocumented specific functions to particular place names in the Bronx, including identification of Sackerah as a trail and Cowangongh and Achqueegenom as crossings along the Bronx River, are discussed in Grumet, *Native American Place Names in New York City*, pp. 1, 9–10, and 48, *op. cit.* (note 5). Examples of names appropriated from other places by Reginald Bolton include Asumsowis, first documented as a place near Norwalk, Connecticut, on p. 29 of the second volume of the 1881 edition of Robert Bolton's *History, op. cit.* (note 1), as the Indian name of Rodman's Neck first noted as a locality in Pelham by Tooker on p. 46 in Shonnard and Spooner's *History, op. cit.* (this note). Reginald Bolton also gave the name Maminketesuck, earlier given by Tooker to a stream in Pelham, listed on p. 47 of his article in Shonnard and Spooner's *History*, to an archaeological site that he excavated on its banks within the present-day Split Rock Golf Course.

22. See p. 153 in Carlyle Shreeve Smith, *The Archaeology of Coastal New York*. Anthropological Papers of the American Museum of Natural History Vol. 43, Part 2, 1950, pp. 91–200. Smith also found no evidence directly linking the name Snakapins to the Clason Point site or any other locale.

23. See Lynn Ceci, "Maize cultivation in coastal New York: the archaeological, agronomical, and

documentary evidence." *North American Archaeologist* 1, no. 1 (1979–80): 45–74. A counter argument appears in Annette Silver, "Comments on maize cultivation in coastal New York." *North American Archaeologist* 2, no. 2 (1980–81): 117–130.

Becker's findings are presented in "A summary of Lenape socio-political organization and settlement pattern at the time of European contact: the evidence for collecting bands." *Journal of Middle Atlantic Archaeology* 4 (1988): 79–83. Becker states that documented Indian food cultivation represents native production of foodstuffs primarily traded to colonists for manufactured goods. His low population estimate appears in "The Lenape and other 'Delawarean' peoples at the time of European contact: population estimates derived from archaeological and historical sources." *The Bulletin: Journal of the New York Archaeological Association* 105 (1993): 16–25.

24. See James C. Mooney, "The Aboriginal population of America north of Mexico." *Smithsonian Miscellaneous Collections* 80, no. 7 (1928): 1–40; and Sherburne F. Cook, *The Indian Population of New England in the Seventeenth Century*. University of California Publications in Anthropology 12. University of California Press, Berkeley, 1976, pp. 60–74.

25. The seminal work setting out the framework for higher population numbers is Henry F. Dobyns, "Estimating aboriginal American populations: an appraisal of techniques with a new hemispheric estimate." *Current Anthropology* 7, no. 3 (1966): 395–416. On p. 22 of his 1993 Delawarean population article, *op. cit.* (note 23), Becker regards his low historic estimates as evidence showing that "Delawarean people...suffered no long-term effects from European disease."

26. See Robert S. Grumet, "'Strangely decreast by the hand of God': a documentary appearance-disappearance model for Munsee demography, 1630–1801." *Journal of Middle Atlantic Archaeology* 5 (1989): 129–145 for analysis charting Indian depopulation in the region. Local traditions assert that Indians occasionally appeared in the Bronx during the 18th century. Theodore L. Kazimiroff's popular and engaging book, *The Last Algonquin*. Walker and Company, New York, 1982, tells a "last of his kind" story of an Indian descendant of the borough's original inhabitants living a hidden life on tiny Hunter Island just north of Orchard Beach in the years leading up to the Civil War. Regarded by many readers as a historical document, the presence of a private estate on Hunter Island at this time indicates that the story is more fiction than fact.

27. In R.H. Ives Goddard, "The ethnohistorical implications," *op. cit.* (note 19), pp. 20–21.

28. See R.H. Ives Goddard, "Delaware," *op. cit.* (note 7), p. 214.

29. Rechgawawanc initially appear as one of the communities represented by the Hackensack sachem Oratam noted in the April 22, 1643 truce treaty between the Dutch and the "Achkinckes hacky [Hackensack]... commissioned by the Indians of Tappaen, Rechgawawanc, Kichtawanc, and Sinsinck" in O'Callaghan and Fernow, *New York Colonial Documents*, Vol. 13, p. 14. The Rechgawawanck are subsequently listed with the Tappaens as followers of chiefs named Seskemu and Willem in the final August 30, 1645 treaty ending the hostilities that are today known as Governor Kieft's War on p. 18 of Vol. 13 of the *New York Colonial Documents*.

Seyseychkimus was first noted as a Mareychewikingh (Marechkawick) and Keskaechquerem sachem identified as Heyseys, Seyseys, Sasham, and a place in Brooklyn noted as Sassians Maize Land who sold land on and around western Long Island from 1637 to 1658. He also became an influential leader of Indians living on both banks of the lower Hudson between 1649 and 1677. See pp. 310–311 in Grumet, *Munsee Indians, op. cit.* (note 4) for data documenting his career.

30. Gehring has overseen publication of the New York Historical Manuscript series currently published by Syracuse University Press since the mid-1970s.

31. See Robert S. Grumet, "On the identity of the Rechgawawanck." *The Bulletin: Journal of the New York Archaeological Association* 83 (1982): 1–6. Holding that words like Rewechnongh and Rechgawawanck are too different to be related, Goddard has challenged the validity of such connections in a review of my work: R.H. Ives Goddard, "Review of *First Manhattans: A Brief History of the Munsee Indians* by Robert S. Grumet." *New York History* 92, no. 4 (2011): 290–302. As noted in my response: Robert S. Grumet, "Response to Ives Goddard." *New York History* 93, no. 2 (2012): 233–234, placement within carefully noted chronological and geographical contexts of similar-looking words may reveal connections obscured by orthographic renderings that do not conform to linguistic rules neither understood nor appreciated by colonial scribes unfamiliar with Indian languages.

32. The March 12, 1663 West Farms deed appears on pp. 433–434 in the second edition of Bolton's *History*, *op. cit.* (note 1). Originally from Brooklyn, Sauwenaroque and several of his brothers were prominent leaders who signed at least 18 deeds to land in Westchester and Greenwich, Connecticut, between 1650 and 1666. Also noted as a sachem's son, Romaque signed 12 deeds to land in the Bronx and Westchester between 1660 and 1683. See Figure 4.

33. The text of the Fordham deed first published in 1881 on pp. 504–505 in the second edition of Bolton's *History*, *op. cit.* (note 1) is more accurately transcribed on pp. 212–214, in Vol. 2 of Paltsits, *Executive Council Minutes*, *op. cit.* (note 13). Achipor was a sachem and noted warrior (fl. 1639–1671) associated with several Indian communities around New York harbor. Page 190 in Vol. 3 of O'Callaghan and Fernow, *New York Colonial Documents*, *op. cit.* (note 9), contains a notice of the murder of "King Agapou" above Albany a little more than a year after he signed the Fordham deed. Minquaes Sachemache (fl. 1657–1671) also signed deeds to land along the New Jersey shore of the Hudson River. The text of the July 10, 1657 deed to Staten Island signed by Achipoor and Minquasackingh appears on p. 393 in Vol. 14 of O'Callaghan and Fernow, *New York Colonial Documents*, *op. cit.* (note 11). The April 13, 1670 Staten Island sale identifying signatories as Aquepo and Minqua-Sachemack is transcribed on p. 43 in Vol. 1 of Paltsits, *Executive Council Minutes*, *op. cit.* (note 13).

34. "Claes ye Indyan" first appears in a document dated September 21, 1666 that lists him among Indians claiming compensation for land taken but not paid for in the portion of lower Yonkers that became the present Riverdale section of the Bronx. A transcript of this document is published on p. 234 in the first volume of Paltsits, *Executive Council Minutes*, *op. cit.* (note 13). He reappeared 10 years later as speaker for Wijckerscreeke Indians complaining on July 25 1676 that they had not been paid for the "Youncker's Land" as recorded in O'Callaghan and Fernow, vol. 13, 1881, p. 498, *op. cit.* (note 11). See Grumet, *Munsee Indians*, *op. cit.* (note 4), pp. 345 and 371, for the first and last documented references to Claes.

35. See Eleanor Burke Leacock and Richard B. Lee, eds., *Politics and History in Band Societies*. Cambridge University Press, Cambridge, 1982.

36. See Morton H. Fried, *The Notion of Tribe*. Cummings Modular Program in Anthropology, Menlo Park, California, 1975.

37. For a description detailing the structure and workings of this type of social organization, see Grumet, *Munsee Indians*, *op. cit.* (note 4), pp. 17–23.

An overview of the New York City Archaeological Repository: the Nan A. Rothschild Research Center

Amanda Sutphin

Archaeological excavations can uncover thousands of artifacts per site. These artifacts are important records and are kept primarily so that other scholars may learn more from them about the past. Appropriate curation and storage of archaeological artifacts is a major issue throughout the world.[1]

This need is especially acute in urban settings, where simply acquiring the necessary space, which is generally very expensive, is only the first daunting challenge. It is also very difficult to find sufficient funding to hire knowledgeable and skilled personnel to curate the collections and manage the data. Curation is a pivotal issue for public archaeology projects where the archaeology is conducted in the public's interest and thus should be accessible to the public.

The New York City Archaeological Repository: The Nan A. Rothschild Research Center was officially dedicated by the New York City Landmarks Preservation Commission ("LPC") on October 5, 2016 after many years of effort to make it a reality.[2] Its mission is to curate New York City's archaeological collections and make them accessible to scholars and the public. Located at 114 West 47th Street in Manhattan, the Archaeological Repository is a 1,439 square foot climate-controlled space containing almost a million artifacts that were excavated in all five boroughs, ranging from an 8,000-year-old projectile point used by a hunter in College Point to 19th century ceramics found in Van Cortlandt Park (Figure 1).[3]

New York City is one of a few cities in the United States that possesses an Archaeology Department within its government. The first archaeologist was hired by the City in 1980 largely in response to the passage of environmental review regulations which stipulated that the impacts imposed by certain types of development projects be considered by reviewing agencies.[4] The risk to buried archaeological resources was one of the issues to be considered, after which archaeology must occur if warranted.[5] The Archaeology Department is part of the LPC, which, as the largest municipal preservation agency in the nation, is responsible for protecting New York City sites that are architecturally, historically, and culturally significant.[6]

Intrinsic to this review process, known as archaeological environmental review, is that the information learned through archaeology should be widely shared. The LPC sought to ensure that both the archaeological reports that describe what has been learned as well as the resulting archaeological collec-

Figure 1. Covered vessel, brown transferware, antiquarian pattern, from the excavations at the Van Cortlandt House in the Bronx. Photo Credit: New York City Archaeological Repository: The Nan A. Rothschild Research Center.

tions would become more accessible to both scholars and the public. It developed a multi-step plan to share information that is continually acquired through the city's archaeology. The first step in this plan was to digitize the city's archaeological reports. These reports detail all the archaeology that has been completed as part of the review processes noted above. The digitization was completed in 2009, and the electronically-readable reports were made accessible on the LPC website. Since then, the agency periodically adds new documents to this database, which in 2016 numbers over 1,300 archaeological reports.

The second step was to create an appropriate repository to curate the city's archaeological collections. In 2014, the LPC launched the repository in climate controlled space donated by The Durst Organization. In 2014–2016, the LPC moved the city's archaeological collections into the repository. Previously, they were largely inaccessible because they were stored in over 13 locations throughout the city. Moreover, the quality of the storage spaces varied greatly; for example, two collections were stored in a women's bathroom in Van Cortlandt Park, a location that was clearly unsuitable. During this time, the LPC also partnered with the Museum of the City of New York to create a comprehensive and systematic database for the city's collections. Fourteen collections were integrated into the database by the Museum. After extensive consultation with the archaeological community, the Museum also recommended curation standards for the repository.

The LPC dedicated the repository in 2016 and named it "The New York City Archaeological Repository: The Nan A. Rothschild Research Center." This name was chosen to honor Dr. Nan A. Rothschild (Figure 2), a prominent New York City archaeologist, who greatly advanced the practice of urban archaeology and was instrumental in the creation of the repository itself. As a research center, the repository is dedicated to promoting scholarship as well as curating archaeological collections in an appropriate manner.

One of the primary goals of the mission was to make the collections accessible to the general public, and so the LPC also created a website (www.nyc.gov/archaeology) that provides virtual access to the archaeological collections for multiple audiences, including the public, scholars, and teachers. The website incorporates features such as a map providing overviews of archaeological sites throughout New York City with links to the relevant archaeological reports and archaeological collections.

Figure 2. Dr. Nan A. Rothschild at the Center's dedication on October 5, 2016; photo credit: Kait Ebinger.

It also has online exhibitions designed for the public, quizzes for people to test their archaeological knowledge, and room for teachers to share successful archaeological curricula.[7]

Finally, it should be noted that these efforts were funded creatively. The LPC and the New York City Department of City Planning partnered to ensure that money coming from a construction project in Lower Manhattan, where the developer likely destroyed archaeological resources,[8] was used to benefit the city's archaeology. In addition, the repository received funding and in-kind services from Iron Mountain Incorporated, a storage and information management services company, and from an anonymous donor. The repository continues to seek funding to maintain and expand its services.

These initiatives are creating much greater awareness and appreciation of the city's past, as can be seen in the widespread press coverage that focused on the public launch of these projects. Articles appeared in the *New York Times* and features were published by the Associated Press.[9] Additionally, the website has received visits from thousands of people from all over the world. The LPC continues to build and expand this work to insure that New York City's archaeology is accessible to everyone.

ENDNOTES

1. Neville Agnew and Janet Bridgland, eds., *Of the Past, for the Future: Integrating Archaeology and Conservation. Proceedings of the Conservation Theme at the 5th World Archaeological Congress, Washington, D.C., 22-26 June 2003*. Getty Conservation Institute Symposium Proceedings Series. Getty Conservation Institute, Los Angeles, 2006. Accessed on November 1, 2016: http://www.getty.edu/conservation/publications_resources/pdf_publications/of_past_for_future.html.

2. Sam Roberts, "Objects From New York's Buried Past Find a New Home in Midtown." *New York Times*, October 4, 2016. Accessed October 14, 2016: http://www.nytimes.com/2016/10/05/nyregion/new-york-landmarks-commission-archaeological-collection.html.

3. The collections include those recovered during the Brooklyn College Archaeological Research Center's excavations in Van Cortlandt Park 1990–1992 and the Riverdale Park Archaeological Project conducted by Wave Hill, both of which are discussed in chapters of this volume.

4. See the chapter by Betsy Kearns and Cece Saunders "The business of archaeology: Cultural Resource Management in the Bronx," in this volume for a full explanation of the process.

5. See the history of New York City archaeology in Anne-Marie Cantwell and Diana diZerega Wall, *Unearthing Gotham: The Archaeology of New York City*. Yale University Press, New York, 2001.

6. For more information about the New York City Landmarks Preservation Commission and the Archaeology Department, see: www.nyc.gov/landmarks.

7. See the chapter by Camille Czerkowicz "Opportunities and challenges for Bronx archaeology in the digital age" in this volume for more details about digital access and its importance.

8. The archaeological report about the potential of the 15 Williams Street site, which is the site referred to, is Historical Perspectives, Inc., Stage 1A Documentary Study. "The William," 15 William Street, New York, NY. Prepared for AKRF, Inc., New York, 2005. Accessed on October 14, 2016: http://s-media.nyc.gov/agencies/lpc/arch_reports/978.pdf.

9. Ula Ilnytzky, "NYC launches archaeological repository and digital archive," Associated Press; printed in many national and international outlets including the following. Accessed on November 17, 2016: http://bigstory.ap.org/article/7c43e79f8cb04f689c813a77aafea267/nyc-launches-archaeological-repository-and-digital-archive.

Opportunities and challenges for Bronx archaeology in the digital age

Camille Czerkowicz

INTRODUCTION

The internet has become one of the most versatile and promising platforms supporting archaeological research, analysis, and discovery, and its applications promise to expand in the future. It already allows us to look beyond (or deeply within) our own geographic area, and it lets us explore unfamiliar subjects, easing the difficulties of comparative research by rapidly finding and juxtaposing images of faraway objects and places so they can be viewed side by side. Many archaeological projects in New York City now use the internet and web-based digital tools to pursue and disseminate archaeological research and finds. These projects have the ability to reach a global audience like never before, and the opportunity specifically to bring archaeological collections into the public eye is especially important.

ARCHAEOLOGICAL COLLECTIONS AND THE DIGITAL AGE

Once fieldwork and reporting are finished, finds emerging from an archaeological project are usually placed into storage—archived in boxes and set on shelves to await possible future re-examination. The artifacts are out of sight, and the information associated with their discovery is often hard to find. A digital portal or catalog can give continued life to these collections despite their invisibility, and the recently launched website and search portal for the New York City Archaeological Repository: The Nan A. Rothschild Research Center[1] provides an excellent case study for how archaeology collections and data can become publicly accessible through digital means. Other New York City archaeological collections are digitally accessible in different ways: (1) as online museum collections, (2) as archaeological research online, and (3) as websites dedicated to single excavations. The new NYC Archaeological Repository website represents a hybrid of all three.

Archaeological investigation yields a complicated array of data and objects, often drawing on expertise from specializations ranging from ethnographic research to carbon dating. The combination of these disciplines is an asset to archaeological research as conclusions are derived and confirmed by a myriad of sources and methods. The multi-disciplinary nature of the resulting collections is what makes them significant, but it also renders them potentially difficult to preserve in the long term.

A collection based on a single excavation will likely include research on the site history, survey results from surface and subsurface reconnaissance (Figure 1), extant structures, a large assemblage of artifacts retrieved through excavation, numerous samples of environmental or architectural features, notes, drawings, maps, and photographs. Archaeological evidence is both a collection of objects as well as documents related to the recovery of these objects. From a materials standpoint, a collection may include paper, bricks, shoes, photographs, soil, precious metals, human bones, shells, ceramics, and so on. All together, these make up a discrete collection that can range in size from one to thousands of boxes, depending on the size and scale of the archaeological excavation. This single "collection" could require a number of separate climate controlled environments to prevent it from undergoing rapid deterioration.

The varied nature of these objects can be a challenge for institutions to curate and preserve, and few institutions maintain a sufficiently varied collecting mission to focus on both historical seeds and jewelry, for example. Practically speaking, these two types of object require different storage conditions and long-term care strategies, and they will have different research audiences as well as different experts engaged in their study even though they are both archaeological finds. Within any archaeological collection, conservation and storage "conflicts" between types of objects make it likely that an institution will store one piece of a collection in one place, and another piece somewhere else—if one institution stewards the entire collection, that is. Over time, and as more pieces are separated, it becomes more difficult to track a specific object or type of object and its location; it becomes even more difficult should a researcher wish to compare disparate types of object such as leather, metal, and soils. The multi-disciplinary materials that make archaeological collections important are the very same factors that render the collection vulnerable in the long term.

In addition to conservation concerns, archaeological collections, like those in any institution, are at risk of being lost or forgotten as time passes and technology changes. Objects or records may be misplaced, hardware and software can be updated beyond the readability of older digital files, or a key steward of the collections may retire taking with him or her substantial personal knowledge. Technical reports and publications containing the results of research are often preserved within government institutions, but the physical material associated with the archaeological recovery is most at risk. Such material can benefit greatly from web-based access, which keeps it in the public eye, reducing the chances that it will be forgotten. It also could provide image and information access to all interested persons in the world.

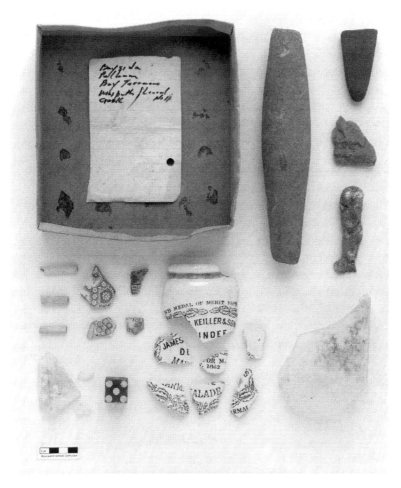

Figure 1. A wide range of objects may be recovered during archaeological research such as this assemblage found by Ralph Solecki and Stanley Wisniewski in the mid-20th century during surface collection in Pelham (Westchester County), and various locations in Queens (Bayside, including Bay Terrace, and Laurel Hill, now West Maspeth). Pictured here are objects typically found at archaeological sites in the Bronx, including a stone pestle, whetstone, scraper, slag (upper right side); decorated tea wares and a smoking pipe stem; a 20th century plastic die (lower left side); a fragment of a "Burnett's Cocaine" medicine bottle (lower right); and several fragments of a James Keiller & Son's Dundee Marmalade jar (center). Objects in this photo provide a window into the lives of 19th century city residents. Burnett's Cocaine was a popular late 19th century treatment to sooth scalp irritation and stimulate hair growth. Keiller's marmalade was produced in the United Kingdom and was the first company to distribute that product commercially. The marmalade would have been served on dishes with patterns similar to those pictured here. More information about these objects can be found by searching for the Schurz site on the New York City Archaeological Repository: Nan A. Rothschild Research Center website. Wisniewski-Solecki collection, box 2. Image courtesy of the NYC Landmarks Preservation Commission, Nan A. Rothschild Research Center.

The subfield of "digital archaeology" encompasses everything from using interactive maps to data analysis to "excavating" content from the depths of the internet. Journals, conferences, and research institutes have been established to incorporate new technologies into archaeological work, and in practical terms, archaeologists have access to more tools than ever before. Mapping, recording, analysis, and publishing are now possible through digital means, and disseminating information about a specific site can be as easy as creating a blog. This 'digital turn' is as varied and imaginative as archaeologists themselves, and some argue that the use of digital technology is still in its infancy.[2] For archaeological collections, simply posting a series of objects online can help bring them out of the shadows of long-term storage and make them digitally available to a wider audience.

Digital access to archaeological collections can disseminate images and information in a way that far surpasses the traditional paper publications and exhibitions that represented the only approaches for earlier generations of researchers. It can also help resolve issues of access discussed above, as online catalogs or excavation websites can keep researchers and the public aware of institutional holdings or recent discoveries.

A digital presence can also allow researchers to make connections between excavations down to the level of the individual object. When an unusual object is excavated, we ask: is this one-of-a-kind? How did this get here? What does it mean? Making archaeological collections accessible online allows these researchers to look for similar objects outside the context of the specific site. Perhaps a certain china pattern has never been excavated in New York City, but was common in Philadelphia. The brown transferware vessel from the Van Cortlandt House site illustrated on p. 202 in this volume demonstrates how images of specific objects can be transmitted digitally to other interested persons who might have found examples of identical or similar wares in distant locations. Bronx collections are particularly significant in this respect, as excavations present a wide range of Native American ceramic patterns, but in very small pieces. These patterns are typical of peoples throughout the region, indicating that the Bronx was part of a central trade route during a time without any written records (Figure 2). Making these objects accessible online can help Bronx researchers identify these wares and showcase how historically (and prehistorically) significant the Bronx is.

The current growing interest in "public archaeology" among archaeologists prioritizes increased accessibility to archaeological discoveries and enfranchisement in archaeological projects by non-archaeologists. It has already led to substantial benefits to the archaeological community.[3] Press and other media coverage can shine a light on issues of site and collection preservation, and internet accessibility through a search engine and can create sufficient public

Figure 2. Photograph of Native American ceramic fragments from the Schurz site in the southern Bronx, recovered by Ralph Solecki and Stanley Wisniewski in the mid-twentieth century. Excavations at this site uncovered several varieties of Native American earthenware fragments identified as Throgs Neck Corded, Clearview Stamped, North Beach Plain, North Beach Cordmarked, Wickham Punctate and other stamped and incised fragments. This image shows a group of incised fragments likely dating to the early contact period. Digital access to high resolution images such as these can allow researchers to compare sherds from other sites in the Bronx and elsewhere to trace out geographic patterns of prehistoric pottery decoration and, by extension, cultural movements and lifeways. More information about these objects can be found by searching for the Schurz site on the New York City Archaeological Repository: Nan A. Rothschild Research Center website. Wisniewski-Solecki collection, box 12. Image courtesy of the NYC Landmarks Preservation Commission, Nan A. Rothschild Research Center.

recognition that might help rescue at-risk materials. Within New York City, several digital projects have been created in response to public enthusiasm for archaeological research, and their existence further encourages that enthusiasm and participation. The harmonious cycle created when public enthusiasm leads to additional archaeological research, leading to more enthusiasm, leading to more research can protect archaeological work in an environment of funding cuts, museum closures, or heavy pressure from developers to avoid what to them would be costly excavations.

TYPES OF DIGITAL PRESENTATION

The specifics of digital accessibility can vary, as different modes are appropriate for different archaeological projects and different audiences. Four main models of digital interfacing are common in New York City. These are "museum collections online," "archaeological research online," "individual excavation websites," or a combination of these. The online presentation may include features such as a searchable database, zoomable object images, links to historical content, and interactive site maps. These allow users to create and save their own assemblages or slide shows ("lightboxes") to develop their own content, compare objects across sites, and download reports and/or 3-D images of objects or sites.

An online museum collection is one of the most common access points to view archaeological material. A museum or other institution may create a simple list of objects in their holdings and make it accessible on the internet. More advanced versions may include a searchable online database where individual objects are described and accompanied by images or additional information about their history and discovery. Museums such as the American Museum of Natural History (AMNH) and the New-York Historical Society have archaeological finds from the Bronx and other parts of New York City listed in their online collections databases. The Tenement Museum also has a small group of artifacts excavated from nearby 97 Orchard Street available to search online.[4] Collections Manager Paul Beelitz from the AMNH has noted that putting material online led to additional research requests rather than fewer.[5]

Whereas online museum collections are focused on individual objects, online archaeological research tends to be driven by field analysis of object assemblages and samples. Although the Digital Archaeological Record (tDAR; www.tdar.org) is not local to New York City, it has become a standard access point for professionals to share information. The site allows archaeologists to post tables, reports, links, or photographs, and it has become one of the main sharing tools for archaeological data. Unlike a museum-style database, tDAR is aimed at professionals, with content that is searchable at the excavation-site level, and information about archaeological projects in the Bronx is readily available.

A third type of digital archaeology featuring New York City collections is represented by individual websites devoted to a specific project or excavation. Within New York City, websites have been created for the Five Points, Seneca Village, South Ferry, and Hunt's Point projects.[6] These websites provide an easily accessed way of sharing the research and conclusions of excavators, and they can be as complex or as simple as needed. Such a model can be aimed at professionals or the public, and it can feature collections, research, and site information that can be updated as excavations are underway.

The Hunt's Point Slave Burial Ground project is the most recently created website from this group. During 2014, students at P.S. 48 began to conduct neighborhood historical research, and in the process, they discovered an image digitized by the Museum of the City of New York of their local park (Joseph Rodman Drake Park) dating to 1905. The image indicated that the land had previously been used as a slave burial ground. After researching the locality, they began working with archaeologists and the New York City Department of Parks and Recreation to learn more about it. Their website, created at the very beginning of the project, details the history of the site and documents their ongoing research.

The Landmarks Preservation Commission (LPC) has recently created a publicly accessible website representing a hybrid of these three models. It is a cloud-based database containing New York City sites, collections, and archaeological research using materials in the New York City Archaeological Repository. The process that led to the creation of this portal illustrates many of the opportunities and challenges associated with developing such tools. Aiming to be forward looking, the LPC worked with the Museum of the City of New York, the New York City Department of Education, and stakeholders in the archaeological community to create a publicly accessible database that show-cased the complexity of archaeological data while also being friendly to those who are unfamiliar with the material.

Work began in 2014 to develop a digital artifact catalog and build the new database for the LPC collections. The artifacts in the LPC's holdings reflected excavation work conducted over the past 60 years, and each excavation had a separate artifact catalog with different information and structure unique to that project. One challenge was for the Museum of the City of New York project team to transfer these catalogs into one database. Since many collections in the LPC's holdings did not possess digital catalogs, significant time was also taken up recreating catalogs that had been paper-only or that had been lost. Catalogers worked to preserve the original data while making modifications to merge many datasets into one new database: updated terminology was added alongside the original terminology so as to allow cross-searching between archaeological collections excavated at different times. Archaeological reports and site information were connected with object records, and over 9,000 images depicting objects and object assemblages were included. Unlike older databases, the new one was designed to be accessible online, making a public website a simple transition.

The challenges in creating this database involved staff time and the degree to which the original archaeological data were available. Older projects were more likely to be missing datasets, analytical reports, or artifacts. The cost and effort associated with recataloging older archaeological collections is a major hurdle that can delay or even prevent site information from becoming accessible. Even the most well-funded institutions may balk at the cost of hiring specialists to unearth and decode old collections, the time alone needed to remove 100,000 objects from their storage boxes may already be prohibitive.

The final database is a hybrid of the three models of digital accessibility used by New York City collections. By combining all three methods, the LPC was able to reach the widest range of potential audiences. Similar to a museum collection database, the LPC database features images, dates, and descriptions of each object within an archaeological collection. Similar to individual excavation-based websites, the LPC database contains information about individual sites, and online exhibitions feature site-level research and images. To illustrate, objects from the Van Cortlandt House excavations are featured; the site is described, and users are invited to browse site information as well as individual finds.

Similar to other websites that post archaeological information online, the LPC database links all grey literature (contract archaeology reports) to excavation sites and artifacts. Further, archaeological context information was attached to each artifact the way it would be in a standard field database. Users are able to search for significant sections of archaeological sites as well as call up all artifacts associated with a particular category, such as "Chinese export porcelain."

One of the most innovative aspects of the database allows users to connect sites and artifacts through common markers, events, or themes. This "Z-axis" allows users to connect any items relating, for example, to the great fire of 1835, all objects relating to water pipes, or other entities sharing a key similarity. A significant artifact from one site may relate to an assemblage from another site, and these items can be linked within the LPC database (Figure 3).

In addition to the LPC, London and other municipalities have launched crowdsourced archaeological documentation projects to encourage the public's participation in watching out for cultural resources and, in the process, educating

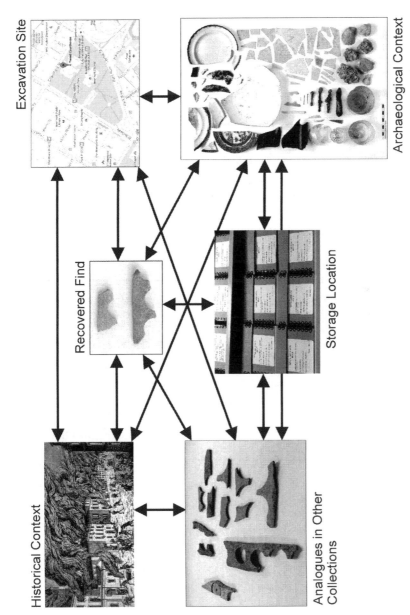

Figure 3. The LPC database allows users to connect individual recovered objects to sites, historical events, assemblages of similar objects found elsewhere, archaeological context (other artifacts from the same site), and storage locations. Importantly, these relationships all link to one another, providing users with multiple points of access to the collections.

themselves about the importance of archaeological remains. For instance, the Thames Discovery Programme in London was initiated to inform about the archaeology of the Thames foreshore, as well as provide a record of the river as it has changed, and will continue to change, over time. Trained members of the public are asked to document their findings in a "wiki" called the Riverpedia. Such projects suggest possible directions in which the LPC database and website might expand in the future.

FUTURE CHALLENGES

We are poised at the start of a new era for archaeology and archaeological collections in New York. Online tools have the potential to make Bronx collections accessible to everyone with an internet connection. This is a powerful and exciting prospect, though not without challenges.

For existing websites and other digital tools, long-term maintenance and software/code upgrading is critical to keeping users and information current. Such maintenance is often technical, requiring updated archaeological as well as IT (information technology) abilities. As new web browsers are created, existing websites will need to be updated to keep them compatible; likewise, as software is upgraded, databases need to be checked and modified to assure that they can still be accessed. This baseline technical upkeep is often difficult for archaeologists to sustain, as they do not usually receive this training, and funding for professional assistance may not be in place years after a project has ended, when only the website remains to be managed.

Another challenge is to expand the number of collections and content available online (Figure 4). The re-cataloguing and organizational process required to create metadata and make a collection accessible can be significant and often requires specialized staff possessing the expertise to identify and systematize artifacts. Significant investment in time and money are often required to bring it up to modern cataloguing standards. Recreating a dataset for a collection after 50 years in storage often involves revisiting field and lab notes, original curatorial decisions, and often rehousing and photographing the objects.

This problem can be exacerbated by the scale of some collections—as one can imagine the resources needed when the number of artifacts rises into the millions. Once a large collection has languished in storage for several years, it can be especially challenging to raise sufficient funds to organize and make it accessible. Once a collection becomes invisible to researchers, students, and the public, its importance—no matter how great—is also often forgotten. Sustaining funding for continued collections management is a major obstacle for all such archaeological digitizing projects.

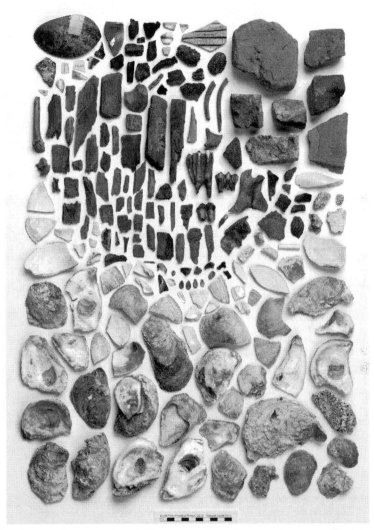

Figure 4. A large-scale excavation yields many artifacts incorporating a complicated range of materials—the very situation that makes such collections significant yet difficult to curate over the long term. This photograph documents some of the materials excavated from the South Ferry Terminal Project in lower Manhattan during 2005–2006. This small subset of the total collection was excavated together as part of one archaeological context. Across the top of this image are man-made household objects such as bottle glass, ceramics, and smoking pipe stems. The striped fragments at the top center are English slipware from the 18th century. At the upper right are architectural objects such as brick, mortar, roofing tile, and an iron nail. Below those are wood fragments and bone—some of which have been cut and carved. The lower half of the image contains shell and coral including oyster, conch, clam, and mussel. The tiny objects at the center are seeds: cherry, squash, walnut, pecan, and peach. Image courtesy of the NYC Landmarks Preservation Commission: Nan A. Rothschild Research Center. South Ferry Terminal Project, context 16196.160.

Still, the opportunities afforded by having information available online far outweigh the difficulties associated with them. Websites can provide long term preservation for archaeological site information and research. They can create a baseline for future analysis and make information accessible for cross-site comparison. Making information accessible to the public democratizes access to information, and it can inspire new generations of archaeologists as well as respect for the archaeological record.

Existing digital access points to New York City archaeological collections whether through museum-type databases, archaeological data online, archaeological sites online, or a hybrid of these three as seen in the NYC Archaeological Repository website have already made Bronx archaeological sites accessible to anyone with an internet connection. As we look ahead to the future, the advantages of digitizing will make the internet a growing platform to facilitate both archaeological research and public accessibility.

ENDNOTES

1. See the chapter by Amanda Sutphin on the New York City Archaeological Repository in this volume.

2. Katy Meyers, "Defining Digital Archaeology," *Cultural Heritage Informatics Initiative.* Department of Anthropology, Michigan State University (blog), October 6, 2011. http://chi.anthropology.msu.edu/2011/10/defining-digital-archaeology/.

3. Background on 'public archaeology' can be found in Tim Schadla-Hall, "Editorial: public archaeology." *European Journal of Archaeology* 2, no. 2 (1999): 147–158; Nick Merriman, ed., *Public Archaeology.* Routledge, London, 2004. See also the chapter by Valerie Hauser on public archaeology in Riverdale Park in this volume.

4. The online database for the American Museum of Natural History can be found here: https://anthro.amnh.org/collections. Additional access is granted for researchers upon request.
    The online collection for the New-York Historical Society can be found here:
http://nyhistory.org/exhibits/category/about/56/table/paged/title
    The online gallery for the Tenement Museum can be found here:
http://www.tenement.org/collections.html

5. Paul Beelitz, personal communication, August 20, 2013.

6. Individual websites for the projects are as follows:
    Five Points: http://r2.gsa.gov/fivept/fphome.htm;
    Seneca Village: http://www.mcah.columbia.edu/seneca_village/index.html;
    South Ferry: http://web.mta.info/capconstr/sft/archaeology.htm;
    Hunt's Point: http://hpsbg.weebly.com/

Archaeological ecology:
Conserving New York's past for the future

Allan S. Gilbert

The unprecedented growth in industry and world population during the 20th century has made it increasingly evident in the 21st that the earth's natural resources have limits and that our extravagant use of those resources can have complex ecological consequences. As the demands of technological change, population increase, and development escalate, we seem far more adept at intensifying production than cooperatively trying to find solutions that will control exploitation and avoid resource depletion. Fortunately, environmental awareness is spreading and bringing with it a concern for preserving the earth's varied ecosystems for the future. We also know now that what we do environmentally within our own community can have far-reaching implications regionally and even globally.

Less well known in the current ecological awakening is the plight of archaeological resources, especially those located in densely settled, urban areas like New York City. They face the same risks of depletion that natural resources do, yet a similar awareness of their predicament is not nearly as widespread.

Public fascination with archaeology runs deep, but it can nonetheless appear arcane and trivial compared to other, "more pressing," social needs. Not surprisingly, dusty ruins and the trash of ages do not possess universal appeal, but their historical usefulness is undeniable. In reality, archaeology is an unrivaled means of establishing many of the facts of our past. Its focus upon the discarded remains of former times provides a window on events that were poorly if at all documented by historical observers, and more critically, gives access to prehistoric cultures that left no written testimony whatever. By helping us understand where we came from and how we came to be who we are, archaeology enriches our lives no less than the raw materials, fertile soils, species diversity, clean air and water, and scenic landscapes that have received more attention.

Like many natural resources, buried remains are non-renewable in that any form of excavation disturbs their internal structure and permanently disassembles their clues. The act of digging up a site cannot be repeated, so archaeologists must carefully observe and document what they find the first time. Unfortunately, archaeologists have also been observing with mounting dismay the rising rates of site destruction. Bulldozers erase virtually all significant information that might be obtained from the layers of an untouched archaeological deposit, and if no records are made of the evidence before the march of progress obliterates it, we remain almost completely ignorant of even the most basic details about prior occupation by our predecessors on the spot. Artifact hunters inflict further damage. Their pitting and backfilling in search of curiosities remove important specimens and displace those they leave behind, thereby severely reducing the prospects for successful scientific study.

When viewed from an ecological perspective, therefore, archaeological resources are subject to long-term impacts and risks of destruction similar to those upon which conservationists have long expounded in the course of their own efforts. Furthermore, the same concerned public involvement and community activism characteristic of the environmental movement can and should be harnessed by preservationists to safeguard the buried archaeological record so that the cultural heritage it contains can be shared by all.[1]

WHY WE NEED ARCHAEOLOGICAL CONSERVATION IN NEW YORK CITY

Environmental crises have forced us to take compensatory actions, and equally important choices will have to be made in dealing with archaeological resource conservation in New York. If we abdicate our responsibility to confront the complex issues of protection and enlightened management of the city's buried sites, we will be allowing affairs to be settled by the competition of other forces (economic, social, and political) that normally do not reserve a high priority for the concerns of preserving evidence of the past.

Ecologists have suggested that bringing about positive social changes frequently necessitates a transformation in people's attitude—that is, their world view. The popular phrase "think globally, act locally"[2] that has spearheaded some of these changes embodies the premise that small-scale decisions about environmental stewardship must be motivated by their overall contribution to the big picture. But before there is any shift in outlook regarding the need for archaeological conservation, communities must first come to realize that buried remains contain a significant historical record with direct relevance for them as well as for society in general.

The social significance of archaeology

Social attitudes influence how much value we assign to the past compared to our present endeavors or future aspirations. Interest in archaeology can honor a broad range of heritages. As Americans, we view discoveries at Plimoth Plantation, Jamestown, Williamsburg, and other places of national prominence with some awe because of their pre-eminent role and symbolic meaning in U.S. history. Many of us are fascinated by classical antiquities, perhaps because they reflect in part the philosophical, esthetic, and political mainsprings of western civilization. Others delve more deeply into the fossil remains of our earliest human ancestors, lured by the mysteries surrounding the origin of our species. Yet others become attached to places they have seen in books or travels, acknowledging the accomplishments of people who lived intriguing lives different from our own.

Notwithstanding these exotic attractions, the archaeological resources with the most direct relevance to New Yorkers are those that lie within the city. Such sites contain our own historic roots. They might epitomize the struggles of an ethnic group or an immigrant experience from which we arose. They might explain celebrated events or landmarks with which we closely identify. They might provide information missing from the historical record that reflects upon life in the neighborhoods of long ago. Archaeological studies can illuminate the details of daily life in the past and cast its players in more familiar light, and when the finds are properly curated and displayed in local museums and restorations, or posted digitally to the internet, they can serve as educational mileposts on the long road of social change. But the success of efforts at conserving sites and the remains recovered from them depends ultimately upon how well a community recognizes the value of its own neighborhood history. One might ask, "How could archaeological discoveries in my small corner of our immense city be significant?"

Environmental issues are analogous in this regard and readily demonstrate the significance of local events. The "global thinking" espoused by many environmentalists reflects their understanding that the earth behaves as a complex system, and that modifications to parts of this system may have wide-ranging repercussions. Global warming provides a good illustration.[3] Rising atmospheric levels of certain gases—principally carbon dioxide caused by the cumulative effects of many point source emissions from factories and automobiles as well as the shrinking area of the world's forests—create a blanketing effect that absorbs the earth's heat, preventing it from escaping into space. This blanket of carbon dioxide acts as a greenhouse, raising average temperatures everywhere on the planet. This example and others teach us that every small part of the systemic whole plays a contributory role that is interrelated with other small parts elsewhere. We learn not only about the detailed local processes that affect us directly but also about the broader planetary relationships in which our local ecosystem participates.

Just as small, localized ecological changes can be influential on a broader horizon, isolated and seemingly inconspicuous archaeological finds can be critical to the solution of historical problems. In archaeological terms, research within the individual communities of New York offers small increments to our knowledge about each neighborhood's past. The results of every study become valuable, and sometimes crucial, pieces to a much larger puzzle when they are combined with information obtained from other sources and communities. The steadily mounting archive of archaeological data from increasingly greater numbers of "point sources" eventually maps out a panorama of material evidence that can replace the testimony of written documents where they are non-existent, augment it in places where that testimony is thin, corroborate it in places where confirmation is needed, and rectify it in places where we appear to have unknowingly based our conclusions upon errors or biases in the original texts. Every carefully explored archaeological site in the city makes a precious contribution to a rich historical tapestry in which the threads of cultural tradition from Native American and Old World origins interweave to form textures and patterns that illuminate prehistoric adaptations as well as the evolution of early New York society. Being an immense place with a complex history, New York City will eventually weave a long and intricate tapestry, reflecting in often minute detail the events and people of its various eras and neighborhoods.

Destroying archaeological sites has the same effect as losing a puzzle piece or, more aptly, tearing pages from a rare book. The lost words from such discarded pages obscure parts of the book's message in much the same way that the lost archaeological remains eliminate potentially important information, leaving elements of the archaeological record mute and historically impoverished. If damage is minimal, the tapestry emerges with only threadbare patches. But if the loss is greater, critical narrative strands end at the frayed edges of large gaps which obscure our view of the cultures we are exploring as well as our understanding of their pathway through the fabric of time.

The importance of world view

Conflicts of interest sometimes arise during the design of urban development projects when preserving the past costs money or causes delay. Planners or developers may assign greater significance to lucrative ventures or politically mandated projects than to the cultural resources that could be placed in harm's way. As it relates to questions of ecology, this conflict has been ascribed fundamentally to a clash of values. The value systems, in turn, emanate from opposing perspectives that may be contrasted as "mechanistic" and "organismic" world views.

Mechanistic thinking

Those possessing a mechanistic world view assume that the earth's resources are there to be exploited to their economic ends, often for immediate, short-term gain. An emphasis on control is frequently the basis for highly competitive actions driven by a focus on achieving specific goals.

In its extreme, such behavior is epitomized by biologist Garrett Hardin as a "tragedy of the commons."[4] He compares the self-interested use of the resources we share on earth to the motivation of herders in early English farming towns who would graze as many of their own cattle as they could on the public commons. In so doing, all gains in livestock improvement would accrue to them alone while the attendant deterioration of pasture from overgrazing would result not in any private loss but rather an overall depreciation of common property that would be absorbed by all members of the community.

Applications of extreme mechanistic thinking as it relates to the archaeological record include two inauspicious practices: antiquities trafficking and unmitigated development.

Antiquities trafficking. Acquisition of rare artifacts as collectibles or objects for trade is all too common. To the trained eye of an archaeologist, such artifacts convey decisive clues when careful excavation uncovers them in their undisturbed state, and with all their spatial associations to other artifacts and ruined structures recorded in the process of discovery. Tearing up the ground in search of curiosities disrupts these relationships, often beyond the point of salvage. Ultimately, objects abducted from their earthen matrix provide personal enjoyment to their finders, and some may bring a high price on the antiquities market, however, they are truly little more than historical orphans that offer few indications as to who brought them into the world, how they were used, and why. They add little to our knowledge of the past because, lacking context, they cannot be associated with other evidence. The buried record of human experience that is left behind is diminished, perhaps critically, by the loss.

Lamentably, archaeological sites are ransacked all the time. The sad fate of the Slack Farm site near Uniontown, Kentucky, is among the most pitiful North American examples.[5] The Slacks protected the aboriginal remains on their property—apparently a large late Mississippian settlement and cemetery in use from about A.D. 1450 to 1650—but when the farm was sold in the late 1980s, the new owner peddled rights to pot hunters who wanted to dig for Indian artifacts. The onslaught, which took place after fall harvest in 1987, left the site cratered like a lunar landscape, incurred enormous loss of scientific information, and demonstrated appalling disregard for the sanctity of a Native American burial ground as well as the Kentucky statutes that prohibit violation of sepulcher. The looting of ancient sites in the Sumerian area of southern Iraq in the aftermath of the Gulf War is yet another unfortunate example. Here, clandestine digging provided meager income to chronically impoverished Iraqis. Their theft of evidence from the large mound sites, or tells, has permanently obscured rare glimpses of the pathways taken by the world's first civilization while it has proffered rare artifacts and afforded high profits to global art dealers.[6]

Evidence of looting constantly turns up in antiquities trade fairs, though sellers will invariably claim that their goods were purchased from someone else, not dug illicitly from a protected site. Decades ago, a man from Virginia earned the dubious distinction of being the first person charged with a major interstate violation of the 1990 federal legislation entitled NAGPRA (Native American Graves Protection and Repatriation Act). In attempting to sell a leg bone from an Indian burial to an undercover agent of the U.S. Bureau of Land Management, he unwittingly admitted to an act of both theft and desecration.[7] The original findspot of the bone was not established with certainty, but presumably to increase its value, it was offered as having come from the Little Bighorn Battlefield National Monument where General George A. Custer's detachment of the U.S. Seventh Cavalry met its end in the famous 1876 encounter with Sitting Bull. In this case as in many others, money was the prime motivator for grave robbing, and neither historical truth nor respect for the dead seemed to matter. As a small part of his penalty, the accused had to pay the costs of returning the bone to the Northern Cheyenne for reburial.

The amount of damage to archaeological resources through illicit digging is staggering, and the constant pillaging of public lands has forced those charged with conservation to withhold the locations of sites in order to protect them. Looters are quite active in their search for places to dig, however, and when they encounter a site, they also keep its whereabouts a secret—not to preserve it but, like leopards with their kill, to consume their prey in peace. Archaeologists often find evidence of their former presence during the course of excavations. For example, the discovery of a 19th century well by archaeologists at a site located within a Bronx park led to the further discovery of a styrofoam McDonald's cup 12 feet down within the debris that filled the hole.[8] Covertly it would seem, these raiders of the lost well burrowed headlong into the deposit in their quest for the trash used a century or more ago to fill the well up. They likely took every historic object they found and left a fast food memento as witness to their coffee break. See also Valerie Hauser's account on page 119 of this volume relating how her own archaeological explorations in Riverdale Park were ransacked by looters after she halted her excavations for the day.

Amateurs interested in participatory archaeology should instead lend their energies and support to the many surveys and excavations carried out each year by professionals who have the proper training, equipment, conservation backup for recovered materials, and official permission to conduct an effective scientific project. Archaeologists frequently need the public's help in the field, and the number of volunteers flocking to well-organized projects has soared.[9] The *Archaeological Fieldwork Opportunities Bulletin*, an extensive listing of expeditions in search of assistance, has been published annually by the Archaeological Institute of America at Boston University expressly for those seeking to contribute in this way to our knowledge of the past.[10]

Unmitigated development. A second unfortunate tendency is for land owners to ignore sites on their property because the development value of the land appears to them far greater than its archaeological significance. Whether buried remains are annihilated, left unexamined, or even concealed in order to avoid the nominal expenses of recovery and study, these archaeological resources do not contribute to the puzzle, and their history becomes just so much landfill. In New York City, archaeological excavation is not required by law in every instance of ground breaking for construction, but episodes of illegal site destruction have nevertheless occurred even when only a limited investigation would have sufficed to record the information and sample the remains for the benefit of all.

During the 1980s, the building of a large office tower in southern Manhattan ruined an important block of old New Amsterdam for just this reason. The developer requested a variance to construct a skyscraper on a plot that was not zoned for tall buildings. The project thereby became subject to the City Environmental Quality Review, or CEQR.[11] CEQR (see chapter by Kearns and Saunders, this volume) assesses the impact on city resources of proposals that would violate existing zoning regulations, and in this case, it required prior archaeological exploration of what promised to be 17th century Dutch colonial remains in the path of destruction. Despite the vigilance of CEQR, the Buildings Department issued an "as of right" permit to proceed without the necessary scientific exploration because the developer's application to that agency guaranteed no deviation from zoning guidelines. Before preventive action could be taken, the damage had been done. In a decision handed down by the Board of Standards and Appeals, the developer's restitution to the people of the city consisted of underwriting the establishment of a small archaeology exhibit and conservation laboratory called "New York Unearthed" (Figure 1) for the South Street Seaport Museum. The ruling provided a facility for the treatment and preservation of objects from New York's past. The case establishes a clear incentive for developers to work with rather than against the laws that protect the city's archaeological resources.[12]

Most of the time, developers follow CEQR guidelines, and professional archaeologists are able to explore their work sites, determine the presence of buried cultural resources, and mitigate destruction to any archaeological remains at risk. In addition to the three examples provided by Kearns and Saunders in their chapter of this book, another example is the major City Hall Rehabilitation Archaeology Project of 2010–2011, for which there is a report in digital form that the Landmarks Preservation Commission has made available.[13]

These examples demonstrate how mechanistic thinking can place greater value on short-term uses of non-renewable archaeological resources than on the acknowledgment of their cultural significance and protection of their substance or memory into the future.

Figure 1. The columns of 17 State Street are reflected in the windows of "New York Unearthed,"
the former exhibit space and conservation lab for the South Street Seaport Museum, New York
City. Photograph by A.S. Gilbert.

Organismic thinking

    The organismic world view in ecology acknowledges the complexity and
diversity of life, recognizes the importance of symbiotic relationships in which
the needs of all are interconnected, and resists competition in favor of cooperation as the mode by which accommodation is sought. Instead of the calculated
motivations that guide mechanistic initiatives, the organismic approach seeks
simplicity and spontaneity, inspired by qualitative, humanistic values.

    Applied to archaeological conservation, the organismic approach
similarly acknowledges the existence of competing interests. The multiple view-
points that characterize most preservation issues can be resolved by considering
all sides of an argument and distributing the impact of actions taken as justly as
possible. The goal is consensus among the diverse attitudes and imperatives held
by different groups on the importance of endangered archaeological sites and the
appropriate arrangements to be made concerning them.

    This challenge to reconcile divergent views is also based upon a moral
issue. Given that archaeological sites are finite and non-renewable, reckless and
destructive treatment inflicts irreparable damage upon them. Archaeologists and
historians are denied a fair chance at recovering data and fitting the findings to

established knowledge, while the community at large loses a piece of the grand puzzle that chronicles its past. And for some, whose ancestry is directly reflected in the remains, objects and information of very personal significance are forfeited and, perhaps, desecrated. In the seemingly intractable problem of equitable disposition of archaeological resources according to the varied interests that deserve a share in the decision-making, thinking organismically is a matter of ethics.

ETHICS IN ARCHAEOLOGY

Laws are enacted in the U.S. to promote justice and the protection of personal liberties, and we legitimize them as an ethical foundation for social behavior when we uphold and obey them. Professional archaeologists deem it necessary to observe additional rules of conduct contained in ethical codes drafted by a number of prominent organizations.

Professional archaeologists undergo years of graduate training to equip themselves with special expertise in uncovering and interpreting the buried record and its wealth of artifacts. Committed to becoming caretakers of the past, they are morally obligated to a measure of public accountability because they recognize archaeological remains as a public resource whether the sites are on public or private land. In addition, most archaeologists will candidly acknowledge that their excavation and research costs are often borne by grants from public funds.

Agreeing to be held accountable, however, frequently creates complicated situations in which a professional must carry out complex scientific procedures while remaining responsive to concerned citizens who wish to learn about and participate in the exploration. The burden of leadership for archaeologists is therefore to demonstrate, simultaneously, responsible action in the performance of their duties, sensitivity and open-mindedness toward public requests to become involved, and impeccable honesty and impartiality in relating the nature and possible significance of the finds. Ethical codes provide ready reminders of the depth and breadth of dedication necessary to conduct research and mediate a way toward effective stewardship over archaeological resources.

In addition, ethical codes promulgate at least minimum standards for those bound to comply with them. There is always the danger that persons claiming professional credentials will prove to be incompetent, irresponsible, or corrupt and, in their foul-ups, incur substantial loss of historical information, a deep breach of trust, and a waste of money. Though enforcement has been weak under many of the presently published codes, the threat of censure holds potentially adverse consequences in matters of reputation and job prospects.

Existing codes contain many provisions in common. Virtually all assert that archaeological resources belong collectively to the public, and all condemn the destruction of sites and sale or possession of looted goods, but differences are worthy of note because of the various constituencies represented. Three codes—from the Register of Professional Archaeologists (RPA), the Society for American Archaeology (SAA), and the Archaeological Institute of America (AIA)—are here compared to explore the dimensions of ethical practice.

Register of Professional Archaeologists

The Register of Professional Archaeologists (RPA) has perhaps the most exacting code. The Register originated in 1998 as a reorganized successor to the national Society of Professional Archaeologists (SOPA). SOPA was founded in 1976 to serve foremost as a certifying body to evaluate the education and experience of archaeologists, especially those working within the then emerging field of *cultural resource management*, or CRM. CRM firms bid on government or private contracts to conduct archaeological investigations in locations due to be impacted by development (see chapter by Kearns and Saunders in this volume). Such investigations must be done in order to comply with historic preservation and environmental impact laws,[14] yet, until the birth of SOPA, no boards could certify that those making bids met at least minimum standards.

SOPA's limited membership (about 730 nationwide) meant that relatively few American archaeologists had committed themselves to its standards. For this reason, initiatives were taken in the mid 1990s to replace SOPA with a more general Registry that would attract wider participation through the cooperation of other major archaeological organizations, which would provide partial support as well as representatives to sit on the RPA's board of directors.[15] Listees in the new Registry would still be bound by rigorous ethical provisions as well as grievance and censure procedures that could address malpractice-type complaints. By 2013, the number of RPA archaeologists reached 2,600.

The RPA guidelines[16] contain two sets of provisions: a Code of Conduct and Standards of Research Performance. The Code of Conduct covers three areas of responsibility: (1) to the public, (2) to colleagues, students, and other co-workers in the scholarly pursuit of the past, and (3) to business associates—such as employers and clients—with whom the immediate task of recovering and mitigating the destruction of archaeological remains must be discharged.

Responsibilities to the public include protection and conservation of archaeological resources and acting in a responsible manner that is sensitive to the reasonable concerns of interested parties. To archaeological colleagues, responsibilities involve sharing of credit for work accomplished, issues of quality of scholarship, legal compliance, prompt reporting, and providing access to data and finds so that others might engage in further studies.

Responsibilities to business associates in CRM are covered by contractual agreements that should be approved only when the archaeological
professional judges the arrangements to be consistent with the best interests of
the public and compatible with RPA standards. The pressures of time and
budget, however, often raise conflicts, especially when there is competition
between differing world views. Clients usually desire to pay for only the
minimum amount of work that still complies with the law. Because the profit
motive keeps CRM firms in business, they must make fiscally attractive bids that
still cover expenses, meet deadlines, and avoid compromises in ethical standards
when identifying sites, and excavating, registering, treating, and evaluating their
archaeological contents. Substandard proposals are usually halted by various
governmental agencies authorized to review the contract process. Invaluable
service in this regard is performed by the Advisory Council on Historic
Preservation for projects on federal land, the office of the State Historic
Preservation Officer for state jurisdictions, and, for local communities, an agency
similar to New York City's Landmarks Preservation Commission. Cases of
unethical conduct in the field are sometimes detected by members of independent
groups, such as the New York Archaeological Council (NYAC), the New York
State Archaeological Association (NYSAA), and the Professional Archaeologists
of New York City (PANYC), whose commitment to archaeological conservation
prompts them to play a watchdog role in addition to their avocational or
professional activities.

The Standards of Research Performance reflect RPA's expectations of
adequate preparation, satisfactory research design and procedure, competent
fieldwork, proper curation and organization of finds together with field notes and
context data, safe storage of recovered materials in accessible repositories, and
dissemination of results as quickly and efficiently as possible.

Society for American Archaeology

Founded in 1934 and backed presently by more than 7,000 members, the
Society for American Archaeology (SAA) has been the leading organization
dedicated to the archaeology of the Americas. It has maintained a mostly
scholarly orientation and a traditionally academic membership. In 1996, eight
newly formulated Principles of Archaeological Ethics of the SAA replaced the
ethical guidelines originally issued in 1961.[17]

The principles deal with eight areas of responsibility that combine old
concerns with relatively recent problems. The first principle emphasizes
stewardship, insisting that the archaeological record—including intact sites,
collections, records, and reports of previous research—is a public trust and must
be preserved for the benefit of all people. The second principle demands
accountability and counsels archaeologists to establish sound working relation-

ships with persons affected by their research. The third principle urges archaeologists to *avoid commercialization* by not engaging in activities that increase the
monetary value of archaeological materials and thereby encourage looting. The
fourth recommends *public education and outreach* to demonstrate the
importance of archaeology and promote respect for sites and artifacts. The fifth
deals with the question of *intellectual property*, asserting that the privilege of
investigators to exclusive control over their finds, data, and unpublished writings
is not unlimited. After an interval of study, the materials must be made available
to others and the information released in appropriate ways. The sixth principle
requires *publication* of the results of archaeological investigation within a
reasonable time for the benefit of the public. Principle seven deals with the
preservation of collections and records as well as their storage in repositories
offering continued access. The eighth and final principle insists that those who
investigate the buried past have the appropriate *training and resources* to carry
out their research according to the other principles.

Archaeological Institute of America

Amateur archaeologists, collectors, and property owners receive
relatively little attention by RPA and SAA, though the latter annually awards a
prize to an individual for avocational contributions to the discipline. The
Archaeological Institute of America (AIA) is the oldest archaeological
organization in North America, having been founded in 1879. A substantial
percentage of its more than 210,000 members worldwide are amateurs and
collectors, and thus its Code of Ethics[18] expresses for the general membership
provisions that relate to the behavior of non-professionals.

To discourage buffs or casual dabblers from undertaking their own
excavations independently and in private, the code calls for the highest standards
of archaeological exploration conducted "under the direct supervision of qualified personnel" and that "the results of such research be made public." For
private collectors, who might be attracted to rare and exceptional artifacts for
their investment potential, it cautions against participation in illegal antiquities
trade or engaging in "activities that enhance the commercial value of such
objects." To encourage a vigilant public, it also calls for members to report im-
proper and illicit conduct with regard to archaeological sites and their contents.

Adopted in 1994, the AIA's Code of Professional Standards[19] advocated
additional guidelines intended for persons engaged in archaeology for a living.
Responsibilities are accorded to the archaeological record, to the public, and to
colleagues, and although the provisions incorporate the AIA Code of Ethics as
well as other standards common to RPA and SAA, some are worthy of mention.
With regard to archaeological sites, for example, the code requests that excavation be minimal and entertained only after other, less damaging forms of

study—such as surveying the ground surface—are implemented. Like the SAA's fourth principle, the code encourages involvement in outreach, including lecturing, popular writing, and school visits, and it discourages archaeological projects "whose primary goal is private gain." With organismic sensitivity, the code cautions that the "legitimate concerns of people who claim descent from, or some other connection with, cultures of the past must be balanced against the scholarly integrity of the discipline," with a "mutually acceptable accommodation" being sought.

Why are ethical standards important?

Archaeologists adhere to the provisions of their various codes because, in the absence of licensing for the profession as a whole, the boundaries of appropriate conduct must be drawn so that the public can determine when the borders of responsible behavior have been crossed. The standards are intended to edify by furnishing ethical guidelines for the practice of the discipline.

Persons who hold divergent views on the uses of the archaeological record and refuse to be edified demonstrate by their actions that they do not identify the buried evidence of our common heritage as a public trust and do not feel that any accountability for their actions is owed to society. In taking their own mechanistic initiative, they reveal an ethical deficit that can result in destruction of sites and irretrievable loss of history that belongs to us all.[20]

CONCLUSION

The design inherent in nature is at once complex and marvelous, but the urban design of our built environment is our own creation, and it is often taken for granted if successful, cursed more likely if not. Designing a plan for archaeological conservation in the city confronts the same difficulties as urban planning in that it ideally must strive to meet all expectations. The result must adequately protect the city's heritage while satisfying a public with diverse connections to the buried remains and varied attitudes toward preservation.

A crucial precondition to any progress in formulating an effective policy is education by the public about the importance of the buried archaeological record. Environmental conservation provides a parallel in that the loss of cultural resources can be viewed in a manner similar to ecosystem damage. There is, however, one important difference. Ecosystems can recover from destruction after cessation of deleterious activities and with restoration efforts and the passage of time to allow for regeneration. In contrast, archaeological sites will never regrow themselves, and stolen artifacts will never inform about their original contexts.

At present, laws are the major protectors of the archaeological record, but only in situations where the legal provisions apply. In circumstances where they don't, such as excavations on private property and construction projects that are not subject to mandated environmental review, only public education and respect for the recovery of historical evidence using best practices stand in the way of information loss. Archaeologists affiliated with the major archaeological organizations, whether or not they are themselves professional, are expected to adhere to ethical guidelines that encourage the preservation of sites and their contextual information, and sustain other recommendations that reduce the threat of loss and contribute to the steady accumulation of details from our past. With public vigilance and cooperation, there will be fewer gaps in the rich urban history of New York and more intriguing discoveries that show us what life was like centuries ago.

The ideas expressed here are not original, nor are conservation efforts aimed at protecting and recording the buried remains of history unique to New York. Archaeological ecology is a global phenomenon, and therefore similar dialogues and struggles are being played out elsewhere within America and in other countries. Appreciation is expressed not only to those who generously contributed information to this essay but also to those committed to the cause of archaeological resource conservation who continue to seek the most ethical means possible of balancing the concerns of preserving the past with the need to prepare for the future.

ENDNOTES

1. Appreciation is expressed to Daniel Pagano for many of the ideas that form the core of this discussion of archaeological ecology.

2. The concept of working at a local level while considering the impact at a regional or global level originated in urban planning during the early 20th century, but the phrase "think local, act global" was coined in the late 1960s to early 1970s in connection with environmental conservation. Its first appearance in print may be: Truman Temple, "Think locally, act globally: An interview with Dr. Rene Dubos." *EPA Journal* 4, no. 4 (1978): 4–11.

3. For example, David E. Newton, *Global Warming: A Reference Handbook*. ABC-CLIO, Santa Barbara, California, 1993; Spencer R. Weart, *The Discovery of Global Warming*. Harvard University Press, Cambridge, 2003; Susan Solomon, *Climate Change 2007:The Physical Science Basis*. Published for the Intergovernmental Panel on Climate Change by Cambridge University Press, New York, 2007.

4. Garrett Hardin, "The tragedy of the commons." *Science* 162 (1968): 1243–1248.

5. Brian M. Fagan, "Black day at Slack Farm." *Archaeology* 41, no. 4 (1988): 15–16,73; Harvey

Arden, "Who owns our past?" *National Geographic Magazine* 175, no. 3 (1989): 376–393.

6. John Russell, "Art loss in Iraq: An overview of the losses." *IFAR Journal* 7, no. 2, (2004): 54–63; Susan Breitkopf, "Lost: The looting of Iraq's antiquities." *Museum News* 85, no. 4 (January/February 2007): 43–51; Micah Garen, "Iraq: must cultural heritage be a casualty of war?" *The UNESCO Courier* (December 2006): 4–5; Neela Banerjee and Micah Garen, "Saving Iraq's archaeological past from thieves remains an uphill battle." *The New York Times* (Sunday, April 4, 2004): sec. 1, p. 16; Milbry Polk and Angela M.H. Schuster, *The Looting of the Iraq Museum, Baghdad: The Lost Legacy of Ancient Mesopotamia.* Harry N. Abrams, New York, 2005; Matthew Bogdanos and William Patrick, *Thieves of Baghdad.* Bloomsbury, New York, 2005; see also the story of the kidnapped photojournalist who was documenting the looting: Micah Garen and Marie-Hélène Carleton, *American Hostage: A Memoir of a Journalist Kidnapped in Iraq and the Remarkable Battle to Win His Release.* Simon and Schuster, New York, 2005.

7. "The struggle to protect Indian graves." *The New York Times* (Sunday, March 26, 1995): sec. 1, p. 16.

8. H. Arthur Bankoff, personal communication, 1995.

9. Richard A. Wertime, "The boom in volunteer archaeology." *Archaeology* 48, no. 1 (1995): 66–73.

10. The *Archaeological Fieldwork Opportunities Bulletin* was published in print by the Archaeological Institute of America from 1981 to 2008, when it became entirely digital and available at https://www.archaeological.org/fieldwork/afob.

11. City of New York, *City Environmental Quality Review Technical Manual.* The Department of City Planning, New York, 2014 (with revisions added on April 27, 2016). It is available on line at http://www1.nyc.gov/site/oec/environmental-quality-review/technical-manual.page.

12. The continued existence of the "New York Unearthed" facility under the management of the South Street Seaport was made possible by the generous sponsorship of the Teachers Insurance and Annuity Association-College Retirement Equities Fund, now TIAA, which carried the costs of maintenance for ten years until it sold the building at 17 State Street in 2000. The building's current owner, RFR Realty, is obligated to maintain the space under the original mitigation agreement, but visitation ceased and in 2007, nearly all the artifacts housed in the museum were returned to their owners. The lower level was flooded by Hurricane Sandy in the fall of 2012, and presently, the upper level contains empty display cases that continue to await renewed financial support for a return of the archaeological exhibit. See Alexander Nazaryan, "City history, locked away: The short, unhappy life of New York Unearthed." *The New York Daily News* Sunday, December 18 (2011).

13. The City Hall Rehabilitation Archaeology Project of 2010–2011 is accessible at: http://s-media.nyc.gov/agencies/lpc/arch_reports/1555.pdf.

14. See also Thomas F. King, Patricia Parker Hickman, and Gary Berg, *Anthropology in Historic Preservation: Caring for Culture's Clutter.* Academic Press, New York, 1977; George S. Smith and John E. Ehrenhard, *Protecting the Past.* CRC Press, Boca Raton, FL, 1991; Thomas F. King, *Cultural Resource Laws and Practice.* AltaMira Press, Walnut Creek, California, 1998; Francis P. McManamon and Alf Hatton, eds., *Cultural Resource Management in Contemporary Society:*

Perspectives on Managing and Presenting the Past. Routledge, London, 2000.

15. Bill Lipe and Keith Kintigh, "ROPA proposal moves toward membership vote in the fall." *Bulletin, Society for American Archaeology* 15, no. 3 (1997): 6–9; Charles R. McGimsey, III, Bill Lipe, and Donna Seifert, "SAA, SHA, SOPA, and AIA discuss register of professional archaeologists." *Bulletin, Society for American Archaeology* 13, no. 3 (1995): 6–9, 14–15. Eventually, the RPA was endorsed by four major archaeological organizations: the Society for American Archaeology, the Society for Historical Archaeology, the Archaeological Institute of America, and the American Anthropological Association.

16. The ethical code is published on the RPA website (http://www.rpanet.org).

17. A detailed discussion appears in Mark J. Lynott and Alison Wylie, eds., *Ethics in American Archaeology*, 2nd revised edition. Society for American Archaeology, Washington, D.C., 2002. The Principles of Archaeological Ethics are published on the SAA website: http://www.saa.org/AbouttheSociety/PrinciplesofArchaeologicalEthics/tabid/203/Default.aspx.

18. The Code of Ethics was approved on December 29, 1990 and last amended on January 8, 2016. It can be accessed from the website of the Archaeological Institute of America at: https://www.archaeological.org/sites/default/files/files/Code%20of%20Ethics%20(2016).pdf.

19. The Code of Professional Standards was approved on December 29, 1994 and last amended on January 8, 2016. It can be accessed from the Archaeological Institute of America website at: https://www.archaeological.org/sites/default/files/files/Code%20of%20Professional%20Standards%20(2016).pdf. Grievance procedures were approved in December, 1996.

20. See Larry J. Zimmerman, Karen D. Vitelli, and Julie Hollowell-Zimmer, eds., *Ethical Issues in Archaeology*. AltaMira Press, Walnut Creek, California, 2003; Karen D. Vitelli and Chip Colwell-Chanthaphonh, eds., *Archaeological Ethics*, 2nd edition. AltaMira Press, Walnut Creek, California, 2006; Christopher Scarre and Geoffrey Scarre, *The Ethics of Archaeology: Philosophical Perspectives on Archaeological Practice*. Cambridge University Press, Cambridge, 2006.

Cumulative References[1]

A map of the survey made by Peter Berrien, June 13, 1717
1717   Archives of the Collegiate Church of the City of New York. [Ch. 3]

A map of the country adjacent to Kingsbridge, surveyed by order of His Excellency Sir Henry Clinton, K.B. Commander in Chief of His Majesty's forces &c &c &c
1781   Clinton Papers ms. map no. 152. William M. Clements Library, University of Michigan, Ann Arbor. [Ch. 3]

A.T.P.
1907   "Neglect or inefficiency doing great injury to the taxpayers' property." *Bronx Home News* vol. 1, no. 26 (Friday, July 19), p. 1. [Ch. 6]

Agnew, Neville, and Janet Bridgland, eds.
2006   *Of the Past, for the Future: Integrating Archaeology and Conservation. Proceedings of the Conservation Theme at the 5th World Archaeological Congress, Washington, D.C., 22-26 June 2003*. Getty Conservation Institute Symposium Proceedings Series. Getty Conservation Institute, Los Angeles.
        http://www.getty.edu/conservation/publications_resources/pdf_publications/of_past_for_future.html. [Ch. 8]

Alexandria Urban Archaeology Program
1983   *Approaches to Preserving a City's Past*. Alexandria Urban Archaeology Program, Alexandria, Virginia. [Ch. 4]

Anonymous
1989   "The whole world on its back." *Archaeology* 42(1): 18, 20, 107. [Ch. 6]

Anonymous [Rev. Michael Nash, S.J.]
1891   "Fordham College and the way from New York City to it in the year 1846," *The Fordham Monthly* IX, no. 4 (January/February): 70. [Ch. 3]

Apuzzo, Robert
1989   "The Indians of Clason Point." *The Bronx County Historical Society Journal* 26, no. 1: 9–11. [Preface, Ch. 1]
2008   *The Endless Search for the HMS Hussar*. R & L Press, New York. [Ch. 1]

Archaeological Institute of America, *Archaeological Fieldwork Opportunities Bulletin*.
2017   https://www.archaeological.org/fieldwork/afob. [Ch. 10]

Archer, John, to Roger Barton, November 20, 1678
1678   Westchester County Clerk Deeds, Liber C, p. 68. [Ch. 3]

---

1. Chapter(s) in which reference is cited appear in square brackets after each source.

Arden, Harvey
1989 "Who owns our past?" *National Geographic Magazine* 175, no. 3: 376–393. [Ch. 10]

Bailey, Rosalie Fellows
1968 *Pre-Revolutionary Dutch Houses and Families in Northern New Jersey and Southern New York.* Dover Publications, New York [orig. publ. 1936]. [Ch. 3]

Banerjee, Neela, and Micah Garen
2004 "Saving Iraq's archaeological past from thieves remains an uphill battle." *The New York Times* (Sunday, April 4): sec. 1, p. 16. [Ch. 10]

Bankoff, H. Arthur, and Frederick A. Winter
1992 "Van Cortlandt House Excavations." Typescript on file, Department of Anthropology, Brooklyn College, Brooklyn, New York. [Ch. 2]

Barton, Roger, and Bridget Barton to Reyer Michielsen, June 9, 1694
1694 Westchester Town Records, Liber 56, p. 206. [Ch. 3]

Barton, Roger, and Bridget Barton to William Davenport, Sr., February 26, 1704–05
1704–05 Westchester County Clerk Deeds, Liber D, pp. 27–29. [Ch. 3]

Baugher, Sherene
1998 "Who determines the significance of American Indian sacred sites and burial grounds?" In *Preservation: Of What, For Whom? A Critical Look at Historical Significance,* Michael A. Tomlan, ed., pp. 97–108. National Council for Preservation Education, Ithaca, New York. [Ch. 6]
2005 "Sacredness, sensitivity, and significance: The controversy over Native American sacred sites." In *Heritage of Value, Archaeology of Renown: Reshaping Archaeological Assessment and Significance,* Clay Mathers, Timothy Darvill, and Barbara J. Little, eds., pp. 248–275. University Press of Florida, Gainesville. [Ch. 6]

Baugher, Sherene, Edward J. Lenik, and Daniel N. Pagano
1991 "Design Through Archaeology: An Archaeological Assessment of Fifteen City-Owned Cultural Institutions." Prepared for the New York City Dept of Cultural Affairs, on file at the New York City Landmarks Preservation Commission. [Chs. 5, 6]

Becker, Marshall J.
1988 "A summary of Lenape socio-political organization and settlement pattern at the time of European contact: the evidence for collecting bands." *Journal of Middle Atlantic Archaeology* 4: 79–83. [Ch. 7]
1993 "The Lenape and other 'Delawarean' peoples at the time of European contact: population estimates derived from archaeological and historical sources." *The Bulletin: Journal of the New York Archaeological Association* 105: 16–25. [Ch. 7]

Bednarik, Robert G.
1992 "A new method to date petroglyphs." *Archaeometry* 34: 279–291. [Ch. 6]
2002 "First dating of Pilbara petroglyphs." *Records of the Western Australian Museum* 20: 414–429. [Ch. 6]

Beers, F.W.
1868 *Atlas of N.Y. and Vicinity,* F.W. Beers, A.D. Ellis, and G.G. Soule, New York. [Ch. 5]

Bell, Blake A.
n.d.   Historic Pelham website, http://www.historicpelham.com. [Ch. 7]

Benson, Egbert
1817   *Memoir, Read Before the Historical Society of New-York, 31 December 1816.* William
            A. Mercein, New York. [Ch. 7]
1849   "Egbert Benson's Memoir on Names. Read 1816." In *Collections of the New-York
            Historical Society*, series 2, vol. 2, pt 1., pp. 77–148. [Ch. 7]

Boesch, Eugene J.
1996   Archaeological Evaluation and Sensitivity Assessment of the Prehistoric and Contact
            Period Aboriginal History of the Bronx, New York. Prepared for the New York City
            Landmarks Preservation Commission, July 19, 1996. On file at the New York City
            Landmarks Preservation Commission. [Ch. 1]

Boesch, Eugene J., and Philip Perazio
1990   Cultural Resources Report for Chapel Farm II, Riverdale. Prepared for Robert Kahn,
            Hastings, New York. On file at the New York City Landrnarks Preservation
            Commission. [Ch. 1]

Bogdanos, Matthew, and William Patrick
2005   *Thieves of Baghdad.* Bloomsbury, New York. [Ch. 10]

Bolton, Robert, Jr.
1848   *A History of the County of Westchester, from its First Settlement to the Present Time*,
            2 vols. Alexander S. Gould, New York. [Ch. 7]
1881   *The History of the Several Towns, Manors, and Patents of the County of Westchester,
            from its First Settlement to the Present Time*, Vol. II. C. F. Roper, New York. [Chs. 2,
            3, 7]

Bolton, Reginald Pelham
1915   "Military camp life on upper Manhattan Island and adjacent mainland during the
            American Revolution: disclosed by recent archaeological excavations." *Annual Report
            of the American Scenic and Historic Preservation Society* 20: 347–502. J.B. Lyon,
            Albany. [Ch. 1]
1916   *Relics of the Revolution; the Story of the Discovery of the Buried Remains of Military
            Life in Forts and Camps on Manhattan Island.* Privately published, New York. [Ch. 1]
1919   "Historical introduction." In Alanson B. Skinner, "Snakapins, a Siwanoy Site at Clason's
            Point." *Exploration of Aboriginal Sites at Throgs Neck and Clason's Point, New York
            City.* Contributions from the Museum of the American Indian, Heye Foundation, Vol.
            4, no. 4, pt. 2, pp. 75–78. [Ch. 7]
1920   *New York City in Indian Possession.* Indian Notes and Monographs, Vol. 2, no. 7, pp.
            223–395. Museum of the American Indian, Heye Foundation, New York (revised 2nd
            edition published in 1975 by the Museum of the American Indian, Heye Foundation,
            New York). [Chs. 1, 7]

1934   *Early History and Indian Remains on Throg's Neck, Borough of the Bronx, City of New York*. Bronx Society of Arts and Sciences, Document 6 (Reprinted in Indian Notes XI, Museum of the American Indian, Heye Foundation 1976). [Ch. 1]
1972   *Indian Life of Long Ago in the City of New York*. Harmony Books, New York. [Chs. 2, 6]

Bracker, Milton
1957   "2 experts lead a nature ramble; John Kieran Dr. Kazimiroff conduct informal tour of Botanical Garden." *The New York Times* (May 5): 74. [Ch. 6]

Brawer, Catherine Coleman, ed.
1983   *Many Trails: Indians of the Lower Hudson Valley*. The Katonah Gallery, Katonah, New York. [Ch. 6]

Breitkopf, Susan
2007   "Lost: The looting of Iraq's antiquities." *Museum News* 85, no. 4 (January/February): 43–51. [Ch. 10]

Bright, William
2004   *Native American Placenames of the United States*. The University of Oklahoma Press, Norman. [Ch. 7]

Britton, Nathaniel Lord
1915   "The Mansion." *New York Botanical Garden Journal* XVI, no. 191 (November): 231–233. [Ch. 6]

Brodhead , John Romeyn, Berthold Fernow, and E.B. O'Callaghan
1853–87 *Documents Relative to the Colonial History of the State of New-York: Procured in Holland, England, and France*, 15 vols. Weed, Parsons & Co., Albany. [Ch. 1]

Burgess, E.S.
1899   "Torrey Botanical Club, January 25, 1899." *Science* N.S. IX, no. 223 (April 7): 520. [Ch. 6]

Butler, Joseph T.
1978   *Van Cortlandt Manor*. Sleepy Hollow Restorations, Tarrytown, New York. [Ch. 2]

Calver, William Louis, and Reginald Pelham Bolton
1950   *History Written with Pick and Shovel; Military Buttons, Belt-plates, Badges and Other Relics Excavated from Colonial, Revolutionary, and War of 1812 Camp Sites by the Field Exploration Committee of the New-York Historical Society*. New-York Historical Society, New York. [Ch. 1]

Campbell, Tony
1965   *New Light on the Jansson-Visscher Maps of New England*. The Map Collectors' Circle, London. [Ch. 7]

Cantwell, Anne-Marie, and Diana diZerega Wall
2001   *Unearthing Gotham: The Archaeology of New York City*. Yale University Press, New Haven. [Preface, Introduction, Chs. 1, 8]

2010   "New Amsterdam: The subordination of native space." In *Soldiers, Cities, and Landscapes: Papers in Honor of Charles L. Fisher*, P.B. Drooker and J. Hart, eds., *New York State Museum Bulletin* 513: 199–212. [Introduction]

Carlyle, Thomas
1840   *On Heroes, Hero-Worship, and the Heroic in History*. Chapman and Hall, London. [Ch. 7]

Caviston, Ruth V.
1952   *A History of the New York Botanical Garden*. The New York Botanical Garden, New York. [Ch. 6]

Ceci, Lynn
1979–80   "Maize cultivation in coastal New York: the archaeological, agronomical, and documentary evidence." *North American Archaeologist* 1, no. 1: 45–74. [Ch. 7]
1984   "Shell midden deposits as coastal resources." *World Archaeology* 16, no. 1: 62–74. [Ch. 4]
1990   *The Effect of European Contact and Trade on the Settlement Pattern of Indians in Coastal New York, 1524–1665*. Garland, New York. [Ch. 4]

Chippindale, Christopher
2001   "Studying ancient pictures as pictures." In *Handbook of Rock Art Research*, David S. Whitley, ed., pp. 247–272. AltaMira Press, Walnut Creek, California. [Ch. 6]

City of New York
2014   *City Environmental Quality Review Technical Manual*. The Department of City Planning, New York, 2014 (with revisions added on April 27, 2016). http://www.nyc.gov/html/oec/html/ceqr/technical_manual_2014.shtml. [Chs. 5, 10]

Cleere, H., ed.
1984   *Approaches to the Archaeological Heritage: A Comparative Study of World Cultural Resource Management Systems*. Cambridge University Press, Cambridge. [Ch. 5]

Cohen, David S.
1992   *The Dutch-American Farm*. New York University Press, New York and London. [Ch. 3]

Cohn, Michael
1962   The fortifications of New York City during the Revolutionary War. NY Archaeological Group (later partly reprinted in the *Bulletin of the New York State Archaeological Association* 28 (July, 1963): 19–26, and 29 (November, 1963): 19–23. [Ch. 1]

Cohn, Michael, and Robert Apuzzo
1988   "The Pugsley Avenue site." *The Bulletin. Journal of the New York State Archeological Association* 96 (Spring): 5–7. [Preface, Chs. 1, 5]

Comfort, Randall
1906   *History of Bronx Borough, City of New York*. North Side News Press, New York. [Ch. 6]

Continental Army
1776   "Mss Orderly Book of the Continental Army." Records for Kingsbridge, NY, August
        22, 1776. Yale University Library, New Haven, Misc. Mss. 40, GP no. 352, Series XIV,
        Box 68, Folder 1488, p. 10. [Ch. 3]

Cook, Sherburne F.
1976   *The Indian Population of New England in the Seventeenth Century.* University of
        California Publications in Anthropology 12. University of California Press, Berkeley.
        [Ch. 7]

Corbett, Arthur J. (NYBG Superintendent of Buildings and Grounds) to Nathaniel Lord Britton
(NYBG Director-in-Chief)
1923   letter of April 16. X319, Box 8, LuEsther T. Mertz Library of the New York Botanical
        Garden. [Ch. 6]

Cormican, Patrick J., S.J.
1904   "A Sketch of St. John's College, Fordham, N. Y." Unpublished typescript, Walsh
        Library Archives and Special Collections, Fordham University, Bronx, New York. [Ch.
        3]

Corsa, Benjamin, borrows £155 from Robert Watts of New York City on November 8, 1766
1786   New York State Archives, Albany, Mss. Chancery Court Records, J0065–W62 (back
        of p. 62), June 4, 1786. [Ch. 3]

Corsa, Benjamin, of New York married Jannetje Reyers of the Manor of Fordham in the Dutch
Reformed Church, April 17, 1718
1884   *New York Genealogical and Biographical Record* XII: 194. [Ch. 3]

Corsa, Benjamin, exchanged his common rights in Fordham Manor for land adjacent to his farm
1902   Acts of the Consistory of the Reformed Dutch Church in *Ecclesiastical Records of the
        State of New York* IV: 2793–2797. [Ch. 3]

Corsa, Isaac, indictment, August 23, 1783
1783   New York Court of Oyer and Terminer, Mss. Records of the Supreme Court of the State
        of New York, New York City Hall of Records. [Ch. 3]

Corsa, Isaac, Statement, September 3, 1783
1783   "Loyalist Transcripts–Royal Institution Transcripts," mss., VI, no. 21, 1783, New York
        Public Library'. [Ch. 3]

Corsa, Isaac, of Annapolis, Nova Scotia, Loyalist Claims, April 4, 1786, rejected for
nonappearance, May 27, 1786
1786   "New Claims at Halifax," Public Archives of Nova Scotia, Halifax, N.S., A/0 13,
        Halifax Loyalist Claims no. 162. [Ch. 3]

Corson, Gale (Corson/Colson Family Association) [Ch. 3]
2007a   "Jan Corszon." *Corson Cousins* 27, no. 1 (January).
2007b   "Jan Corszon." *Corson Cousins* 27, no. 2 (April). Republished article by Henry Hoff.
2008a   "Isaac Corsa." *Corson Cousins* 28, no. 1 (January).
2008b   "Isaac Corsa and John Courser." *Corson Cousins* 28, no. 2 (April). Republished article

by Marian Elder.

2008c   "Benjamin Corsa." *Corson Cousins* 28, no. 3 (July).

2008d   "Andrew Corsa." *Corson Cousins* 28, no. 4 (October).

Coy, Fred E., Jr.

2004   "Native American dendroglyphs of the eastern woodlands." In *The Rock-Art of Eastern North America*, Carol Diaz-Granados and James R. Duncan, eds., pp. 3–16. University of Alabama Press, Tuscaloosa. [Ch. 6]

Coysh, A.W., and R.K. Henrywood

1982   *The Dictionary of Blue and White Printed Pottery, 1780–1880*, Volume I. Antique Collectors' Club, Woodbridge, Suffolk, England. [Ch. 2]

1989   *The Dictionary of Blue and White Printed Pottery, 1780–1880*, Volume II. Antique Collectors' Club, Woodbridge, Suffolk, England. [Ch. 2]

Cronon, William

1983   *Changes in the Land: Indians, Colonists, and the Ecology of New England*. Hill and Wang, New York. [Introduction]

Curran, Francis X., S.J.

1968   "Archbishop Hughes and the Jesuits." *Woodstock Letters* XCVII: 5–56 [reprinted in Thomas C. Hennessy, S.J., ed., *Fordham, The Early Years*, pp. 177–221, Something More Publications, distributed by Fordham University Press]. [Ch. 3]

Daily News

1990   "Dirt on Donck." *The Daily News, Bronx Edition* (Friday, June 22): 31. [Ch. 2]

Danckaerts, Jasper

1867   *Journal of a Voyage to New York: And a Tour in Several of the American Colonies in 1679–80*, transl. by Henry Cruse Murphy. Long Island Historical Society Memoir 1. Long Island Historical Society, Brooklyn. [Ch. 7]

de Koning, Joep M. J.

2000   "From Van der Donck to Visscher." *Mercators World: The Magazine of Atlases, Globes, and Charts* 5, no. 4: 3–10. [Ch. 7]

de Vries, David Petersz.

1853   *Voyages from Holland to America, A.D. 1633 to 1644*, transl. by Henry Cruse Murphy. Billin and Bros., New York. [Ch. 7]

DeCarlo, Valerie G.

1996   "Public archaeology in Riverdale Park." *The Bronx County Historical Society Journal* 33, no. 1: 13–20. [Preface, Ch. 4]

deNoyelles, Daniel, IV

1982   *Within These Gates*. Privately published, Thiells, New York. [Ch. 3]

[DePeyster, John Watts]
1881   *Local Memorials Relating to the DePeyster and Watts and Associated Families Connected with Red Hook Township, Dutchess, NY.* Charles H. Ludwig, New York. [Ch. 3]

Department of Parks, New York City
1873   *Topographical map made from surveys by the Commissioners of the Department of Public Parks of the City of New York of that part of Westchester County adjacent to the City and County of New York embraced by chapter 534 of laws of 1871 as amended by chapter 878 or laws of 1872.* Department of Public Parks, New York. [Chs. 3, 6]
1890   *Minutes and Documents of the Board of Commissioners of the Department of Public Parks for the Year Ending April 30th, 1890.* Martin B. Brown, printer, New York. [Ch. 5]
1894   *Annual Report for the Year Ending April 30, 1893.* Martin B. Brown, printer, New York. [Ch. 6]
1895   *Report for 1894.* Martin B. Brown, printer, New York. [Ch. 6]
1901   *Annual Report for the Year Ending December 31, 1900.* Martin B. Brown, printer, New York. [Ch. 6]
1902   *Report of the Department of Parks for the Year Ending December 31, 1901.* Mail and Express Co., New York. [Ch. 6]
1903   *Report for the Year 1902.* Martin B. Brown, printer, New York. [Ch. 6]
1904   *Annual Report for the Year 1903.* Martin B. Brown, printer, New York. [Ch. 6]
1904   *Minutes and Documents of the Board of Commissioners of the Department of Parks for the Year Ending December 31, 1903.* Mail and Express Co., New York. [Ch. 6]
1905   *Report for the Year 1904.* Martin B. Brown, printer, New York. [Ch. 6]
1908   *Annual Report of the Department of Parks of the City of New York for the Year 1907.* Martin B. Brown, printer, New York. [Ch. 6]

Diaz-Granados, Carol, and James R. Duncan, eds.
2004   *The Rock-Art of Eastern North America.* University of Alabama Press, Tuscaloosa. [Ch. 6]

Dierickx, Mary B.
1983   "Decorative metal roofing in the United States." In *The Technology of Historic American Buildings; Studies of the Materials, Craft Processes, and the Mechanization of Building Construction*, H. Ward Jandl, ed., pp. 153–187. Association for Preservation Technology, Washington, D.C. [Ch. 3]

Dobyns, Henry F.
1966   "Estimating aboriginal American populations: an appraisal of techniques with a new hemispheric estimate." *Current Anthropology* 7, no. 3: 395–416. [Ch. 7]

Dorn, Ronald I.
1995   "Digital processing of back-scatter electron imagery: A microscopic approach to quantifying chemical weathering." *Bulletin, Geological Society of America* 107, no. 6 (June): 725–741. [Ch. 6]
1998   *Rock Coatings.* Elsevier, Amsterdam. [Ch. 6]
2001   "Chronometric techniques: engravings." In *Handbook of Rock Art Research*, David S. Whitley, ed., pp. 167–189. AltaMira Press, Walnut Creek, California. [Ch. 6]

Dunkak, Harry
1995   "The Lorillard family of Westchester County: tobacco, property and nature." *The Westchester Historian* 71, no. 3 (Summer): 51–58. [Ch. 6]

Dunlap, David W.
1988   "Ancient Bronx turtle finds a home." *The New York Times* (Friday, March 25): B1,4. [Ch. 6]

Dutch Reformed Church to Benjamin Corsa, July 18, 1764, for the sum of £157 7d 4½p
1905   *Ecclesiastical Records of the State of New York* VI: 3941–3942. [Ch. 3]

F., '93
1897   "Recollection! The old infirmary." *The Fordham Monthly* XV, no. 9 (April): 128–129. [Ch. 3]

Fagan, Brian M.
1988   "Black day at Slack Farm." *Archaeology* 41, no. 4: 15–16, 73. [Ch. 10]

Falco, Nicholas
1971   "The old cemetery in Fordham University." *The Bronx County Historical Society Journal* 8, no. 1: 20–25. [Ch. 5]

Faulkner, Charles H., ed.
1996   *Rock Art of the Eastern Woodlands: Proceedings from the Eastern States Rock Art Conference (April 10, 1993, Natural Bridge State Park, Kentucky).* American Rock Art Research Occasional Paper no. 2. San Miguel, California. [Ch. 6]

Ferris, Mrs. Morris Patterson
1897   *Van Cortlandt Mansion.* DeVinne Press, New York. [Ch. 2]

French, Alvah P.
1925   *History of Westchester County, New York*, Vol. V. Lewis Historical Publishing Co., New York. [Ch. 3]

Fried, Morton H.
1975   *The Notion of Tribe.* Cummings Modular Program in Anthropology, Menlo Park, California. [Ch. 7]

Gallo, Daniel R., and Frederick A. Kramer
1981   *The Putnam Division: New York Central's Bygone Route through Westchester County.* Quadrant Press, New York. [Ch. 2]

Gannon, Robert I., S.J.
1967   *Up to the Present: The Story of Fordham.* Doubleday, Garden City, New York. [Ch. 3]

Garen, Micah, and Marie-Hélène Carleton
2005   *American Hostage: A Memoir of a Journalist Kidnapped in Iraq and the Remarkable Battle to Win His Release.* Simon and Schuster, New York. [Ch. 10]

Garen, Micah
2006   "Iraq: must cultural heritage be a casualty of war?" *The UNESCO Courier* (December): 4–5. http://unesdoc.unesco.org/images/0019/001915/191575e.pdf. [Ch. 10]

Gehring, Charles T. (transl. and ed.)
1980   *New York Historical Manuscripts: Dutch. Volume GG, HH, and II: Land Papers.* Genealogical Publishing Company, Baltimore. [Ch. 7]

Geismar, Joan H.
1989   "History and Archaeology of the Greenwich Mews Site, Greenwich Village, New York." Submitted to Greenwich Mews Associates. Copy on file, New York City Archives. [Ch. 2]

Gilbert, Allan S.
1988   "Fordham archaeologists reach new depths." *The Ram* 70, no. 26 (November 10): 9, 16, 18. [Ch. 3]
1990   "The hole story." *the paper* 19, no. 2 (February 13): 10, 26. [Ch. 3]

Gilbert, Allan S., ed.
2017   *Encyclopedia of Geoarchaeology.* Springer, Dordrecht. [Ch. 5]

Gilbert, Allan S., and Roger Wines
1998   "From earliest to latest Fordham: background history and ongoing archaeology," in Thomas C. Hennessy, S.J., ed., *Fordham, The Early Years*, pp. 139–176. Something More Publications, distributed by Fordham University Press, Bronx, New York. [Ch. 3]

Gilbert, Allan S., Garman Harbottle, and Daniel deNoyelles
1993   "A ceramic chemistry archive for New Netherland/New York." *Historical Archaeology* 27, no. 3: 17–56. [Chs. 1, 3]

Gilbert, Allan S., Richard B. Marrin, Jr., Roger A. Wines, and Garman Harbottle
1992   "The New Netherland/New York brick archive at Fordham University." *The Bronx County Historical Society Journal* 29, no. 2: 51–67. [Preface, Chs. 1, 3]

Glazier, Ira A., ed.
1983   *The Famine Immigrants: Lists of Irish Immigrants Arriving at the Port of New York, 1846–1851*, Vol IV. Genealogical Publishing Co., Baltimore. [Ch. 3]

Goddard, R. H. Ives
1971   "The ethnohistorical implications of Early Delaware linguistic materials." *Man in the Northeast* 1971, no. 1, pp. 14–26 (reprinted on pp. 88–102 in Laurence M. Hauptman and Jack Campisi, eds., 1978. *Neighbors and Intruders: An Ethnohistorical Exploration of the Indians of Hudson's River.* National Museum of Man Mercury Series, Canadian Ethnology Service Paper No. 39. National Museums of Canada, Ottawa). [Ch. 7]
1978   "Delaware." In *Handbook of North American Indians, Vol. 15. Northeast*, Bruce Trigger, ed., pp. 213–239. Washington, D.C.: The Smithsonian Institution Press. [Ch. 7]
2011   "Review of *First Manhattans: A Brief History of the Munsee Indians* by Robert S. Grumet." *New York History* 92, no. 4: 290–302. [Ch. 7]

Godden, Geoffrey A.
1991   *Encyclopaedia of British Pottery and Porcelain Marks.* Barrie and Jenkins, London. [Ch. 3]
1992   *An Illustrated Encyclopedia of British Pottery and Porcelain.* Magna Books, Wigston, Leicester, England. [Ch. 2]

Goldberg, Paul, and Richard I. Macphail
2006   *Practical and Theoretical Geoarchaeology.* Blackwell, Malden, Massachusetts. [Ch. 5]

Grumet, Robert S.
1981   *Native American Place Names in New York City.* Museum of the City of New York, New York. [Ch. 7]
1982   "On the identity of the Rechgawawanck." *The Bulletin: Journal of the New York Archaeological Association* 83: 1–6. [Ch. 7]
1989   "'Strangely decrease by the hand of God': a documentary appearance-disappearance model for Munsee demography, 1630–1801." *Journal of Middle Atlantic Archaeology* 5: 129–145. [Ch. 7]
2009   *The Munsee Indians: A History.* The University of Oklahoma Press, Norman. [Ch. 7]
2012   "Response to Ives Goddard." *New York History* 93, no. 2: 233–234. [Ch. 7]
2013   *Manhattan to Minisink: American Indian Place Names in Greater New York and Vicinity.* University of Oklahoma Press, Norman. [Ch. 7]

Hardin, Garrett
1968   "The tragedy of the commons." *Science* 162: 1243–1248. [Ch. 10]

Harper's Weekly
1884   "Van Cortlandt mansion." *Harper's Weekly* XXVIII, no. 1451 (October 11), p. 665. [Ch. 2]

Harrington, Marie
1985   *On The Trail of Forgotten People: A Personal Account of the Life and Career of Mark Raymond Harrington.* Great Basin Press, Reno. [Ch. 1]

Harrington, M.R.
1909   "Ancient shell heaps near New York City." In *Indians of Greater New York and the Lower Hudson*, Clark Wissler, ed., pp. 167–179. Anthropological Papers of the American Museum of Natural History Vol. 3. [Ch. 1]
1926   "Alanson Skinner." *American Anthropologist* 28 N.S.: 275–280. [Ch. 1]

Hauptmann, Laurence M., and Jack Campisi, eds.
1978   *Neighbors and Intruders: An Ethnohistorical Exploration of the Indians of Hudson's River.* National Museum of Man Mercury Series, Canadian Ethnology Service Paper No. 39. National Museums of Canada, Ottawa. [Ch. 7]

Heckewelder, John Gottlieb Ernestus
1819   *An Account of the History, Manners, and Customs, of the Indian Nations: Who Once Inhabited Pennsylvania and the Neighbouring States.* Transactions of the Historical and Literary Committee of the American Philosophical Society 1. American Philosophical Society: Philadelphia. [Ch. 7]
1841   "Indian tradition of the first arrival of the Dutch, at Manhattan, now New-York." In

Collections of the New-York Historical Society, 2nd series, vol. 1, pt. 3, pp. 69–74. [Ch. 7]

Heimann, Robert K.
1960   *Tobacco and Americans*. McGraw Hill, New York. [Ch. 6]

Hermalyn, Gary, and Reginald Pelham Bolton
1976   "Historical perspectives on the site of the Indian village at Throg's Neck in the Bronx." *Indian Notes, Museum of the American Indian, Heye Foundation* 11 (3–4): 98–127. [Ch. 1]

Herman, Bernard L.
1994   "Van Cortlandt House Museum: Architectural Inspection, February 10, 1994." Typescript on file, New York City Parks Historic Houses Division. [Ch. 2]

Herrick, Pamela
1992   "Van Cortlandt Tour Manual." Typescript on file, New York City Parks Historic Houses Division. [Ch. 2]

Historical Perspectives, Inc.
1987a   "Phase IA Archaeological Assessment Report on the Shorehaven Project, The Bronx, New York." Prepared for Soundview Associates. Copy on file, New York City Landmarks Preservation Commission, 1987. [Ch. 5]
1987b   "Phase 1A Archaeological Assessment Report for the Tibbett Gardens Project, Bronx, New York." Prepared for Allee King Rosen & Fleming, Inc. Copy on file, New York City Landmarks Preservation Commission. [Ch. 5]
1988   "Shorehaven Project, Phase IB Archaeological Fieldwork Report, Fall 1987." Prepared for Soundview Associates. Copy on file, New York City Landmarks Preservation Commission. [Ch. 5]
1993a   "Stage IA Archaeological Assessment for the New York Botanical Garden, Bronx, New York." Prepared for Vollmer Associates and the City of New York Department of Cultural Affairs. [Ch. 5]
1993b   "Stage IB Topic-Intensive Research: Jesuit Cemetery on the Grounds of the New York Botanical Garden." Prepared for Vollmer Associates and the City of New York Department of Cultural Affairs. [Ch. 5]
2005   Stage 1A Documentary Study. "The William," 15 William Street, New York, NY. Prepared for AKRF, Inc., New York, 2005. http://s-media.nyc.gov/agencies/lpc/arch_reports/978.pdf. [Ch. 8]

Hoff, Henry B.
1993   "The identity of Eva (Philipse) Van Cortlandt." *The New York Genealogical and Biographical Record* 124, no. 3 (July): 153–155. [Ch. 2]

Hopkins, A.D., and K.J. Evans
1999   "Raymond of the Caves: Mark Harrington (1882–1971)." In *The First 100: Portraits of the Men and Women Who Shaped Las Vegas*, pp. 48–50. Huntington Press, Las Vegas. [Ch. 1]

Howard, David S.
1984   *New York and the China Trade*. The New-York Historical Society, New York. [Ch. 2]

Howson, Jean E.
1992–93 "The archaeology of nineteenth-century health and hygiene at the Sullivan Street Site, New York City." *Northeast Historical Archaeology* 21–22: 137–160. [Ch. 2]

Hunt, S., E. W. Jones, and M. E. McAllister, eds.,
1992   *Archaeological Resource Protection*. National Trust for Historic Preservation, Washington, D.C. [Ch. 5]

Ilnytzky, Ula
2016   "NYC launches archaeological repository and digital archive," Associated Press. [Ch. 8]

Jacobs, Jaap
2005   *New Netherland: A Dutch Colony in Seventeenth-Century America*. Brill, Leiden. [Introduction]

Jameson, J. Franklin, ed.
1909   *Narratives of New Netherland, 1609–1664*. Charles Scribner's Sons, New York. [Introduction]

Jerome, Pamela S., Norman R. Weiss, Allan S. Gilbert, and John A. Scott
1998   "Ethyl silicate as a treatment for marble: conservation of St. John's Hall, Fordham University." *Bulletin, Association for Preservation Technology* XXIX, no. 1: 19–26. [Ch. 3]

Jesuit Consultors
1895   "Minutes of April 30." Walsh Library Archives and Special Collections, Fordham University, Bronx, New York. [Ch. 3]

Jones, Thomas
1879   *History of New York During the Revolutionary War*, 2 Vols. Printed for the New-York Historical Society, New York. [Ch. 3]

Jones, Olive R., and Catherine Sullivan
1985   *The Parks Canada Glass Glossary*. Canada Parks Service, Ottawa, Ontario. [Ch. 2]

Judd, Jacob
1976   *The Revolutionary War Memoir and Selected Correspondence of Philip Van Cortlandt*. Sleepy Hollow Restorations, Tarrytown, New York. [Ch. 2]

Kaeser, Edward J.
1962   "The Archery Range Site: A preliminary report." *Bulletin of the New York State Archaeological Association* 24 (March): 4–7. (Reprinted in Long Island Archaeology and Ethnology, Vol II, Suffolk County Archaeological Association). [Ch. 1]
1963   "The Morris Estate Club site." *Bulletin of the New York State Archaeological Association* 27 (March): 13–21. [Preface, Ch. 1]
1970   "The Archery Range Site ossuary, Pelham Bay Park, Bronx, New York." *Pennsylvania Archaeologist* 40 (1–2): 9–34. [Ch. 1]

Kazimiroff, Theodore
1954   "Millstones from the Lorillard Snuff Mill." *The Garden Journal of the New York Botanical Garden* 4(Jan.-Feb.): 25–26. [Ch. 1]
1955a   "A Bronx Forest 1000 B.C." *The Garden Journal of the New York Botanical Garden* (Jan.–Feb.): 22–23, 26. [Ch. 1]
1955b   "Explore the New York Botanical Garden." *The Garden Journal* 5, no. 2 (March–April): 33–34, 58. [Chs. 1, 6]
1983   "Nature trail." The New York Botanical Garden, Bronx, New York. [Chs. 1, 6]

Kazimiroff, Theodore L.
1982   *The Last Algonquin*. Walker and Company, New York. [Ch. 7]

Kent, Bretton W.
1992   *Making Dead Oysters Talk: Techniques for Analyzing Oysters from Archaeological Sites*, rev. ed. Maryland Historical and Cultural Publications for Maryland Historical Trust, Historic St. Mary's City, and Jefferson Patterson Park and Museum, Crownsville, Maryland. [Ch. 4]

Kerber, Jordan E., ed.
1994   *Cultural Resource Management: Archaeological Research, Preservation Planning, and Public Education in the Northeastern United States*. Bergin and Garvey, Westport, Connecticut. [Ch. 5]

Ketchum, William C., Jr.
1987   *American Country Pottery*. Alfred A. Knopf, New York. [Ch. 2]
1991   *American Redware*. Henry Holt & Company, New York. [Ch. 2]

Keyser, James D.
2001   "Relative dating methods." In *Handbook of Rock Art Research*, David S. Whitley, ed., pp. 116–138. AltaMira Press, Walnut Creek, California. [Ch. 6]

King, Thomas F.
1998   *Cultural Resource Laws and Practice*. AltaMira Press, Walnut Creek, California. [Ch. 10]
2002   *Thinking About Cultural Resource Management: Essays from the Edge*. AltaMira Press, Walnut Creek, California. [Ch. 5]
2004   *Cultural Resource Laws and Practice: An Introductory Guide*, 2nd edition. AltaMira Press, Walnut Creek, California. [Ch. 5]
2005   *Doing Archaeology: A Cultural Resource Management Perspective*. Left Coast Press, Walnut Creek, California. [Ch. 5]

King, Thomas F., Patricia Parker Hickman, and Gary Berg
1977   *Anthropology in Historic Preservation: Caring for Culture's Clutter*. Academic Press, New York. [Ch. 10]

Klein, Christa R.
1976   *The Jesuits and Catholic Boyhood in Nineteenth-Century New York City: A Study of St. John's College and the College of St. Francis Xavier, 1846–1912*. Unpublished Ph.D. dissertation, University of Pennsylvania, Philadelphia. [Ch. 3]

Krause, Richard A.
1994   "Obituary of Carlyle Shreeve Smith, 1915–1993." *Plains Anthropologist* 39 (148):
          221–227. [Ch. 1]

Landmarks Preservation Commission, New York City
1987   *The New York Botanical Garden, Bronx, N.Y., Assessment of Archaeological Resources.*
          New York City Landmarks Preservation Commission, August 25. Turtle Petroglyph file,
          LuEsther T. Mertz Library of the New York Botanical Garden. [Ch. 6]

Leacock, Eleanor Burke, and Richard B. Lee, eds.
1982   *Politics and History in Band Societies.* Cambridge University Press, Cambridge. [Ch.
          7]
Lee, Jean Gordon
1984   *Philadelphians and the China Trade, 1784–1844.* Philadelphia Museum of Art,
          Philadelphia. [Ch. 2]

Lenik, Edward J.
1988   "A turtle petroglyph on the Bronx River." *The Bulletin and Journal of the New York
          State Archeological Association* 97 (Fall): 17–20. [Ch. 6]
1991   "Native American rock art in the lower Hudson Valley and coastal New York." In *The
          Archaeology and Ethnohistory of the Lower Hudson Valley and Neighboring Regions:
          Essays in Honor of Louis A. Brennan.* Occasional Publications in Northeastern
          Anthropology 11, pp. 177–191. Archaeological Services, Bethlehem, Connecticut. [Ch.
          6]
1992   "Native American archaeological resources in urban America: a view from New York."
          Bulletin and Journal of the New York State Archaeological Association 103: 20–30. [Ch.
          5]
2002   *Picture Rocks: American Indian Rock Art in the Northeast Woodlands.* University Press
          of New England, Hanover and London. [Ch. 6]

Lenik, Edward J., and Nancy L. Gibbs (Sheffield Archaeological Consultants)
1994   An Evaluation of Prehistoric Cultural Resources at the Chapel Farm Estate Property,
          Bronx, New York. Prepared for Tim Miller Associates. Copy on file at the New York
          City Landmarks Preservation Commission. [Ch. 1]

Lewis, John
1988   "Not turtle soup: 3,000-year Indian carving found." *Daily News* (Friday, March 25),
          BXL MBW, p. 2. [Ch. 6]

Lipe, Bill, and Keith Kintigh
1997   "ROPA proposal moves toward membership vote in the fall." *Bulletin, Society for
          American Archaeology* 15, no. 3: 6–9. [Ch. 10]

Lopez, Julius
1955   "Preliminary report on the Schurz site, Throggs Neck, Bronx County, New York."
          Nassau Archaeological Society Bulletin 1, no. 1: 6–21. (Reprinted in *The Second
          Coastal Archaeology Reader: 1900 to the Present*, James E. Truex, ed., Readings in
          Long Island Archaeology and Ethnology Vol. V, Suffolk County Archaeological
          Society [1982]). [Ch. 1]

1978   "The history and archeology of Fort Independence on Tetard's Hill, Bronx County,
        N.Y." *Bulletin, New York State Archaeological Association* 73 (July): 1–28. (Edited
        posthumously by Stanley Wisniewski.). [Preface, Chs. 1, 5]
1983   "Ft. Independence regimental data." *Bulletin and Journal of the New York State
        Archaeological Association* 87 (Summer): 40–44. (Edited posthumously by Stanley
        Wisniewski.). [Ch. 1]

Lynott, Mark J., and Alison Wylie, eds.
2002   *Ethics in American Archaeology*, 2nd revised edition. Society for American
        Archaeology, Washington, D.C. [Ch. 10]

MacGill-Callahan, Sheila
1991   *And Still the Turtle Watched.* Dial Books for Young Readers, New York. [Ch. 6]

Markman, Charles
1991   *Chicago Before History: The Prehistoric Archaeology of a Modern Metropolitan Area.*
        Illinois Historic Preservation, Springfield, Illinois. [Introduction]

McCracken, George E.
1952–53 "Roger Barton of Westchester Co., NY and some of his earlier descendants." *New
        England Historic Genealogical Register* 106: 168–180, 290–304, 107:49–58, 111–122,
        202–213, 292–303. Also http://www.rootsweb.ancestry.com/~genepool/bartonrog.htm.
        [Ch. 3]

McDonald, John McLean
1844   "The McDonald Interviews, mss.," "Interview with Dennis Valentine and Andrew Corsa
        on August 26, 1844," p. 103. Thomas Paine Historical Society Library, New Rochelle,
        New York. [Ch. 3]
1847   "Interview with Frederick Valentine on August 24, 1847," pp. 482–83. Thomas Paine
        Historical Society Library, New Rochelle, New York. [Ch. 3]
1851   "The McDonald Interviews, mss., Interview with Andrew Corsa on October 27, 1851,"
        p. 8. Thomas Paine Historical Society Library, New Rochelle, New York. [Ch. 3]
1926–27 *The McDonald Papers*, William S. Hadaway, ed., 2 vols. Westchester County Historical
        Society, White Plains, New York. [Ch. 3]

McGimsey, Charles
1972   *Public Archaeology.* Seminar Press, New York. [Ch. 4]

McGimsey, Charles R., III, Bill Lipe, and Donna Seifert
1995   "SAA, SHA, SOPA, and AIA discuss register of professional archaeologists." *Bulletin,
        Society for American Archaeology* 13, no. 3: 6–9, 14–15. [Ch. 10]

McManamon, Francis P., and Alf Hatton, eds.
2000   *Cultural Resource Management in Contemporary Society: Perspectives on Managing
        and Presenting the Past.* Routledge, London. [Ch. 10]

Meeske, Harrison F.
1998   *The Hudson Valley Dutch and Their Houses.* Purple Mountain Press, Fleischmanns,
        New York. [Ch. 3]

Melick, Harry C.W.
1950   *The Manor of Fordham and Its Founder.* Fordham University Press, New York. [Ch. 3]
1952   "The Fordham ryott of July 16, 1688." *New York Historical Society Quarterly* XXXVI
        (April): 210–220. [Ch. 3]

Merguerian, Charles, and John E. Sanders
1997   "Bronx River diversion: neotectonic implications." *International Journal of Rock
        Mechanics and Mineral Science* 34, nos. 3–4, paper no. 198. [Ch. 3]

Merriman, Nick, ed.
2004   *Public Archaeology.* Routledge, London. [Ch. 9]

Merwick, Donna
2005   "Extortion." *De Halve Maen* 78, no. 3: 43–48. [Introduction]

Meyers, Katy
2011   "Defining Digital Archaeology." *Cultural Heritage Informatics Initiative.* Department
        of Anthropology, Michigan State University (blog), October 6, 2011.
        http://chi.anthropology.msu.edu/2011/10/defining-digital-archaeology. [Ch. 9]

Miller, George
1980   "Classification and economic scaling of 19th century ceramics." *Historical Archaeology*
        14: 1–40. [Ch. 2]
1994   "Nineteenth century lists of cups from jobber's invoices." Unpublished listing table.
        [Ch. 2]

Miller, Donald L., and Richard E. Sharpless
1985   *The Kingdom of Coal.* University of Pennsylvania Press, Philadelphia. [Ch. 3]

Montgomery, Paul L.
1974   "Justice Douglas, in Bronx Park, gives brief for nature." *The New York Times* (May 10):
        39. [Ch. 6]

Mooney, James C.
1910   "Wappinger." In *Handbook of American Indians North of Mexico*, Vol. 2, Frederick
        Webb Hodge, ed., p. 913. Bureau of American Ethnology Bulletin 30, Washington, D.C.
        [Ch. 7]
1928   "The Aboriginal population of America north of Mexico." *Smithsonian Miscellaneous
        Collections* 80, no. 7, 1928: 1–40. [Ch. 7]

Mudge, Jean McClure
1986   *Chinese Export Porcelain in North America.* Clarkson N. Potter, Inc., New York. [Ch.
        2]

Mursberger, Julie
1990a   "Van Cortlandt family history." Typescript on file, New York City Parks Historic
        Houses Division. [Ch. 2]
1990b   "Van Cortlandt House—Official Tour Manual." Typescript on file, New York City
        Parks Historic Houses Division. [Ch. 2]

Nazaryan, Alexander
2011   "City history, locked away: The short, unhappy life of New York Unearthed." *The New York Daily News* Sunday, December 18. [Ch. 10]

Nelson, Sarah M.K., Lynn Berry, Richard F. Carrillo, Bonnie J. Clark, Lorie Rhodes, and Dean Saitta
2001   *Denver. An Archaeological History.* University of Pennsylvania Press, Philadelphia. [Introduction]

Neumann, Thomas W., and Robert M. Sanford
2001   *Cultural Resources Archaeology.* AltaMira Press, Walnut Creek, California. [Ch. 5]

New York Archaeological Council
1994   *Standards for Cultural Resource Investigations and the Curation of Archaeological Collections.* New York Archaeological Council, Rochester, New York. [Ch. 5]
2000   *Cultural Resource Standards Handbook.* New York Archaeological Council. [Ch. 5]

New York Botanical Garden, Executive Committee
1924   Resolution of the Executive Committee, May 21. X319, Box 8, LuEsther T. Mertz Library of the New York Botanical Garden. [Ch. 6]

New York State Office of Parks, Recreation and Historic Preservation
2005   "State Historic Preservation Office Phase I Archaeological Report Format Requirements." Peebles Island, Waterford, New York. [Ch. 5]

New York Times
1883   "Above the Harlem River; the progress in improving the annexed district." April 29, 1883, p. 14. [Ch. 3]
1890   "Winter weather at last." *The New York Times* (Thursday, January 23): 8, col. 1. [Ch. 5]
1905   "Ronalds, of Tally-ho Fame." *The New York Times* (September 3), p. 7. [Ch. 6]
1906   "Raid Shrine to Gambrinus." *The New York Times* (July 3), p. 9. [Ch. 6]
1923   "Ask City to Rebuild Lorillard Mansion." *The New York Times* April 1, p. E7. [Ch. 6]
1935   "$144,000 WPA Grant Spurs Work in Botanical Garden." *The New York Times*, August 11, p. N1. [Ch. 6]
1995   "The struggle to protect Indian graves." *The New York Times* (Sunday, March 26): sec. 1, p. 16. [Ch. 10]

Newcomb, William W., Jr.
1956   *The Culture and Acculturation of the Delaware Indians.* Anthropological Papers of the University of Michigan no. 10. University of Michigan, Ann Arbor. [Chs. 6, 7]

Newton, David E.
1993   *Global Warming: A Reference Handbook.* ABC-CLIO, Santa Barbara, California. [Ch. 10]

Noël Hume, Ivor
1969   *A Guide to Artifacts of Colonial America.* Alfred A. Knopf, New York. [Ch. 2]

O'Callaghan, E.B.
1846–48   *History of New Netherland, or, New York under the Dutch*, 2 vols. D. Appleton and Co., New York. [Ch. 7].
1849–51   *The Documentary History of the State of New-York; Arranged under Direction of the Hon. Christopher Morgan, Secretary of State*, 4 vols. Weed, Parsons & Co., Albany. [Ch. 7]

O'Callaghan, E.B., John Romeyn Brodhead, and Berthold Fernow
1853–87   *Documents Relative to the Colonial History of the State of New-York: Procured in Holland, England, and France*, 15 vols. Weed, Parsons & Co., Albany. [Ch. 7]

Omwake, H. Geiger
1958   "Kaolin pipes from the Schurz site." *Bulletin of the Archaeological Society of Connecticut* 29: 2–13. [Ch. 1]

One of the Old Boys
1899   "More about the good old days." *The Fordham Monthly* XVIII, no. 3 (December): 153. [Ch. 3]

Paltsits, Victor Hugo (ed.)
1910   *Minutes of the Executive Council of the Province of New York: Administration of Francis Lovelace, 1668–1673*. State of New York, Albany. [Ch. 7]

Pawley, James, ed.
2006   *Handbook of Biological Confocal Microscopy*, 3rd ed. Springer, New York. [Ch. 6]

Pell, S.H.P.
1941   Pell of Pelham. *Pelliana* 1(6): frontispiece. [Ch. 7]

Pelletreau, William Smith
1898   *Early Wills of Westchester County, New York, from 1664–1784*. F.P. Harper, New York. [Ch. 3]

Polk, Milbry, and Angela M.H. Schuster
2005   *The Looting of the Iraq Museum, Baghdad: The Lost Legacy of Ancient Mesopotamia*. Harry N. Abrams, New York. [Ch. 10]

Potter, Parker B.
1994   *Public Archaeology in Annapolis: A Critical Approach to History in Maryland's Ancient City*. Smithsonian Institution Press, Washington, D.C. [Ch. 4]

Ramirez, Jan Seidler
2005   "A history of the New-York Historical Society." *The Magazine Antiques* (January): 138–145. [Ch. 1]

Rapp, George, Jr, and Christopher L. Hill
2006   *Geoarchaeology: the Earth-Science Approach to Archaeological Interpretation*, 2nd edition. Yale University Press, New Haven. [Ch. 5]

Reynolds, Helen Wilkinson
1965   *Dutch Houses in the Hudson Valley Before 1776*. Dover Publications, New York [orig. publ. 1929]. [Ch. 3]

Rickard, Jonathan
1993   "Mocha ware: Slip-decorated refined earthenware." *The Magazine Antiques* CXLIV, no. 2 (August): 182–190. [Ch. 2]

Riggs, Bruce K. (NYBG) to Marie Sarchiapone (Landmarks Preservation Commission)
1987   letter of September 17, 1987. Turtle Petroglyph file, LuEsther T. Mertz Library of the New York Botanical Garden. [Ch. 6]

Riggs, Bruce K. to Ralph S. Solecki
1993   letter of February 10, 1993. Copy kindly provided by Ralph Solecki. [Ch. 6]

Riker, James
1881   *Harlem (City of New York): Its Origin and Early Annals*. Privately published, New York. [Ch. 7]

Ritchie, William A.
1961   *A Typology and Nomenclature for New York Projectile Points*. New York State Museum and Science Service Bulletin 384, Albany, New York. [Ch. 1]
1965   *Archaeology of New York State*. Natural History Press, Garden City, New York. [Ch. 1]

Roberts, Sam
2016   "Objects From New York's Buried Past Find a New Home in Midtown." *New York Times*, October 4, 2016.
        http://www.nytimes.com/2016/10/05/nyregion/new-york-landmarks-commission-archaeological-collection.html?rref=collection%2Fbyline%2Fsam-roberts&action=click&contentCollection=undefined&region=stream&module=stream_unit&version=latest&contentPlacement=9&pgtype=collection&_r=0. [Ch. 8]

Rothschild, Nan A., and Diana diZerega Wall
2014   *The Archaeology of American Cities*. University Press of Florida, Gainesville. [Introduction]

Rothschild, Nan A., and Lucianne Lavin
1977   "The Kaeser site: A stratified shell midden in the Bronx, New York." *The Bulletin of the New York State Archaeological Association* 70: 1–27. [Ch. 1]

Russell, John
2004   "Art loss in Iraq: An overview of the losses." *IFAR Journal* 7, no. 2: 54–63. [Ch. 10]

Ruttenber, Edward Manning
1872   *History of the Indian Tribes of Hudson's River: Their Origin, Manners and Customs, Tribal and Sub-tribal Organizations, Wars, Treaties, etc.* J. Munsell, Albany. [Ch. 7]

Salwen, Bert, and Rebecca Yamin
1990   "The Archaeology and History of Six 19th Century Lots: Sullivan Street, Greenwich Village, New York City." Typescript on file, New York City Archives. [Ch. 2]

Salwen, Bert
1973   "Archeology in megalopolis." In *Research and Theory in Current Archeology*, Charles
          L. Redman, ed., pp. 151–163. John Wiley & Sons, New York. [Ch. 5]

Sanborn-Perris Map Co., Ltd
1896   *Insurance Maps of the City of New York.* New York, New York. [Ch. 3]

Sanders, John E., and Charles Merguerian
1998   "Classification of Pleistocene deposits, New York City and vicinity – Fuller (1914)
          revived and revised." In Geology of Long Island and Metropolitan New York (18 April
          1998, State University of New York at Stony Brook, NY), *Long Island Geologists
          Program with Abstracts*, pp. 130–143. [Ch. 6]

Scarre, Christopher, and Geoffrey Scarre
2006   *The Ethics of Archaeology: Philosophical Perspectives on Archaeological Practice.*
          Cambridge University Press, Cambridge. [Ch. 10]

Schadla-Hall, Tim
1999   "Editorial: public archaeology." *European Journal of Archaeology* 2, no. 2: 147–158.
          [Ch. 9]

Scharf, J. Thomas
1886   *History of Westchester County, New York*, Vol. I. L.E. Preston & Co., Philadelphia. [Ch.
          2]

Schneiderman-Fox, Faline, and A. Michael Pappalardo
1996   "A paperless approach toward field data collection: an example from the Bronx."
          Bulletin, Society for American Archaeology 14, no. 1: 1,18–20. [Ch. 5]

Schoolcraft, Henry Rowe
1845   "Comments, philological and historical, on the aboriginal names and geographical
          terminology, of the State of New York. Part First: Valley of the Hudson." *Proceedings
          of the New-York Historical Society for the Year 1844*. New-York Historical Society,
          New York, pp. 77–115 . [Ch. 7]

Schuberth, Christopher J.
1968   *The Geology of New York City and Environs.* Natural History Press, Garden City, New
          York. [Ch. 3]

Schuldenrein, Joseph, Curtis Larsen, Michael Aiuvaslatsit, Mark A. Smith, and Susan Malin-
Boyce
2007   *Geomorphology/Archeological Borings and GIS Model of the Submerged
          Paleoenvironment in the New York/New Jersey Harbor and Bight in Connection with the
          New York and New Jersey Harbor Naviagation Project, Port of New York and New
          Jersey, Draft Report.* Prepared for NEA, Portland, Maine under contract to U.S. Army
          Corps of Engineers, New York District, under subcontract to Hunter Research, Inc.,
          Trenton, New Jersey. Contract No. DACW 51-01-D-00184, NEA Delivery Order 0065,
          Hunter Research, Inc. Project 06017. [Introduction]

Schumach, Murray
1958   "5 amateur archaeologists find Revolutionary fort in the Bronx." *The New York Times*,
         July 18, p. 23. [Ch. 1]

Scott, Kenneth, compiler
1973   *Rivington's New York Newspaper: Excerpts from a Loyalist Press 1773–1783.*
         New-York Historical Society, New York. [Ch. 3]

Sebastian, Lynne, and William D. Lipe, eds.
2009   *Archaeology and Cultural Resource Management: Visions for the Future.* School for
         Advanced Research Press, Santa Fe. [Ch. 5]

Seymann, Jerrold
1939   *Colonial Charters, Patents, and Grants to the Communities Comprising the City of New
         York.* Board of Statutory Consolidation of the City of New York, New York. [Ch. 3]

Shackel, Paul A.
1993   *Personal Discipline and Material Culture—An Archaeology of Annapolis, Maryland,
         1695–1870.* University of Tennessee Press, Knoxville. [Ch. 2]

Silver, Annette
1980–81 "Comments on maize cultivation in coastal New York." *North American Archaeologist*
         2, no. 2: 117–130. [Ch. 7]

Skinner, Alanson Buck
1909   "The Indians of Manhattan Island and vicinity: a guide to the special exhibition at the
         American Museum of Natural History." In *Indians of Greater New York and the Lower
         Hudson,* Clark Wissler, ed., pp. 113–121. Anthropological Papers of the American
         Museum of Natural History 3. [Ch. 1]
1915   *The Indians of Manhattan Island and Vicinity.* Torch Press, Cedar Rapids, Iowa. [Ch.
         7]
1919   "Exploration of Aboriginal Sites at Throg's Neck and Clason's Point, New York City;
         Part I: The Throgs Neck Schley Avenue Shellheap. Part II: Snakapins, a Siwanoy Site
         at Clason's Point." *Contributions from the Museum of the American Indian, Heye
         Foundation* 5, no. 4, New York. [Introduction, Chs. 1, 5]
1925   "Notes on Mahikan Ethnology." *Bulletin of the Public Museum of the City of Milwaukee*
         2, no. 3 (January 20): 87–116. [Ch. 1]

Smith, Carlyle Shreeve
1950   *The Archaeology of Coastal New York.* Anthropological Papers of the American
         Museum of Natural History 43, Part 2, pp. 91–200. [Chs. 1, 4, 7]

Smith, George S., and John E. Ehrenhard
1991   *Protecting the Past.* CRC Press, Boca Raton, Florida. [Ch. 10]

Smith, James Reuel
1938   *Springs and Wells of Manhattan and the Bronx, New York City, at the End of the
         Nineteenth Century.* The New-York Historical Society, New York. [Chs. 1, 2]

Solecki, Ralph S.
1988   "A petroglyph found in the New York Botanical Garden, Bronx, New York." *The Bulletin of the Archaeological Society of New Jersey* 43: 31–33. [Ch. 6]

Solecki, Ralph S. to Bruce K. Riggs
1993   letter of February 3, 1993. Turtle Petroglyph file, LuEsther T. Mertz Library of the New York Botanical Garden. [Ch. 6]

Solomon, Susan
2007   *Climate Change 2007:The Physical Science Basis.* Published for the Intergovernmental Panel on Climate Change by Cambridge University Press, New York. [Ch. 10]

Sons of Reyer Michielsen to Benjamin Corsa, April 26, 1736
1736   Westchester County Clerk Deeds, Liber G, pp. 204–205. [Ch. 3]

Speck, Frank G.
1909   "Notes on the Mohegan and Niantic Indians." In *Indians of Greater New York and the Lower Hudson*, Clark Wissler, ed., pp. 183–210. Anthropological Papers of the American Museum of Natural History Vol. 3. [Ch. 1]

Spencer, Herbert
1896   *The Study of Sociology.* D. Appleton and Son, New York. [Ch. 7]

St. John's College
1872   Entry in the Treasurer's records for October 10, 1872, indicating purchase of fire clay for the infirmary's furnace, "Cash Book, October 1, 1871 to February 28, 1873." Walsh Library Archives and Special Collections, Fordham University, Bronx, New York. [Ch. 3]

St. John's College
1890   *Catalogue, St. John's College, Fordham, N. Y. City, 1889-90.* The Bedell Press, New York. [Ch. 3]

Stein, Julie K., ed.
1992   *Deciphering a Shell Midden.* Academic Press, San Diego. [Ch. 4]

Stryker-Rodda, Harriet Mott
1975   *Watts; Ancestry and Descendants of Ridley Watts.* Polyanthos, New Orleans. [Ch. 3]

Swanton, John Reed
1952   *The Indian Tribes of North America.* Bureau of American Ethnology Bulletin 145. Smithsonian Institution, Washington, D.C. [Ch. 7]

Taaffe, Thomas Gaffney
1891   *A History of St. John's College, Fordham, N. Y.* The Catholic Publication Society Co., New York. [Ch. 3]
1896   "The old manor house." *The Fordham Monthly* XV, no. 1 (October): 11. [Ch. 3]

Taylor, Clifton James
1981   *John Watts in Colonial and Revolutionary New York.* Unpublished Ph.D. dissertation,

University of Tennessee, Knoxville, and University Microfilms/Bell and Howell. [Ch. 3]

Temple, Truman
1978   "Think locally, act globally: An interview with Dr. Rene Dubos." *EPA Journal* 4, no. 4: 4–11. [Ch. 10]

The 1939 Commencement
1939   "The 1939 Commencement." *The Fordham Alumni Magazine* VII, no. 3 (October): 3. [Ch. 3]

The Ram
1934   "Taaffe on Fordham." *The Ram* 15, no. 25 (May 11): 2, col. 3. [Ch. 3]

Thébaud, Augustus J., S.J.
1904   *Forty Years in the United States of America.* Catholic Historical Society, New York. [Ch. 3]

Tieck, William A.
1968   *Riverdale, Kingsbridge, Spuyten Duyvil: New York City: a Historical Epitome of the Northwest Bronx.* F.H. Revell, Old Tappan, New Jersey. [Ch. 1]

Tooker, William Wallace
1900   "Amerindian names in Westchester County." In Frederic Shonnard and W. W. Spooner, eds., *History of Westchester County, New York From its Earliest Settlement to the Year 1900.* New York History Company, New York, pp. 45–50. [Ch. 7]

Trelease, Allen W.
1960   *Indian Affairs in Colonial New York: The Seventeenth Century.* Cornell University Press, Ithaca, New York (reprinted in 1997 by the University of Nebraska Press, Lincoln). [Ch. 7]

Town of Westchester to Roger Barton, July 4, 1682
1682   Westchester Town Records, Vol. 53, p. 105. [Ch. 3]

Trigger, Bruce G., ed.
1978   *Handbook of North American Indians: Vol 15. Northeast.* Smithsonian Institution Press, Washington, D.C. [Ch. 7]

Turnbaugh, Sarah Peabody, ed.
1985   *Domestic Pottery of the Northeastern United States, 1625–1850.* Academic Press, Orlando, Florida. [Ch. 2]

U.S. Geological Survey
1924   New York–New Jersey: Harlem Quadrangle. Surveyed 1888–89 and 1897; partially revised shoreline 1924 by polyclinic projection. Washington, D.C. [Ch. 1]

Ultan, Lloyd
1983a   "A History of Van Cortlandt Park—Borough of The Bronx, New York, New York." Storch Associates, New York. Typescript on file, New York City Parks Historic Houses

Division. [Ch. 2]

1983b *Legacy of the Revolution: the Valentine-Valerian House.* Bronx County Historical Society, Bronx, New York. [Ch. 1]

1993 *The Bronx in the Frontier Era: From the Beginning to 1696.* Written in collaboration with the Bronx County Historical Society. Kendall/Hunt, Dubuque, Iowa. [Ch. 3]

2002 "The Grand Reconnaissance." *The Bronx County Historical Society Journal* 39, no. 1: 14–37. [Ch. 3]

Valentine, Alan

1969 *Lord Stirling.* Oxford University Press, New York. [Ch. 3]

Van der Donck, Adriaen

1655 *Beschrijvinge van Nieuw Nederlant.* Evert Nieuwenhof, T'Aemsteldam (English transl. *A Description of New Netherlands.* Collections of the New-York Historical Society, New York, 1841). [Ch. 2]

1849 *Representation of New Netherland,* transl. by Henry Cruse Murphy. Bartlett and Welford, New York. [Ch. 7]

Van Laer, A.J.F., translator and editor

1974 *New York Historical Manuscripts, Dutch, Vol. 4. Council Minutes, 1638–1649,* Genealogical Publishing Company, Baltimore. [Introduction]

Vitelli, Karen D., and Chip Colwell-Chanthaphonh, eds.

2006 *Archaeological Ethics,* 2nd edition. AltaMira Press, Walnut Creek, California. [Ch. 10]

von Krafft, Lt. John Charles Philip

1883 Journal of Lieutenant John Charles Philip von Krafft, of the Regiment von Bose, 1776–1784. *Collections of the New-York Historical Society for the Year 1882, Publication Fund XV,* pp. 1–202. The New-York Historical Society. [Ch. 1]

Wall, Diana diZerega

1994 *The Archaeology of Gender.* Plenum Press, New York. [Ch. 2]

Wall, Diana diZerega, and Anne-Marie Cantwell

2004 *Touring Gotham's Archaeological Past.* Yale University Press, New Haven. [Introduction]

Weart, Spencer R.

2003 *The Discovery of Global Warming.* Harvard University Press, Cambridge. [Ch. 10]

Weiss, Dennis

1987 "Paleo-Environmental Interpretation of the Tibbett Gardens Project Site, Bronx, New York." Submitted to Historical Perspectives, Inc. and Allee King Rosen and Fleming, Inc. Copy on file, New York City Landmarks Preservation Commission, August 26. [Ch. 5]

Wertime, Richard A.

1995 "The boom in volunteer archaeology." *Archaeology* 48, no. 1: 66–73. [Chs. 4, 10]

Weslager, Clinton Alfred
1972   *The Delaware Indians: A History*. Rutgers University Press, New Brunswick, New Jersey. [Ch. 7]

Westchester Historical Society
1932   "Andrew Corsa." *Quarterly Bulletin of the Westchester County Historical Society* 8, no. 2 (April): 55–58. [Ch. 3]

Wetherbee, Jean
1996   *White Ironstone: A Collector's Guide*. Antique Trader Books, Dubuque, Iowa. [Ch. 3]

Williams, Howel, Francis J. Turner, and Charles M. Gilbert
1954   *Petrography; An Introduction to the Study of Rocks in Thin Section*. W.H. Freeman, San Francisco. [Ch. 6]

Wilson, James G.
1893   *The Memorial History of the City of New-York from Its First Settlement to the Year 1892*, Volumes I–II. New York History Company, New York. [Ch. 2]

Wilson, James Homer
1995   "Great doggs and mischievous cattle: Domesticated animals and Indian-European relations in New Netherland and New York." *New York History Quarterly Journal of the New York State Historical Society* 76: 245–264. [Introduction]

Wines, Roger, and Allan S. Gilbert
2014   "St. John's College at Fordham and its pioneering electrification in the Bronx." *Bronx County Historical Society Journal* 51, nos. 1–2: 28–46. [Ch. 3]

Wisniewski, Stanley
1962   "Julius Lopez, 1918–1961." *American Antiquity* 28, no. 1: 82. [Ch. 1]

Wrightson, Karolyn
1997   "Tracking down the history of the Spy House." *New Rochelle Standard Star* (September 27): Lifestyles, p. 1. [Ch. 3]

Yamin, Rebecca
2008   *Digging the City of Brotherly Love*. Yale University Press, New Haven. [Introduction]

Zaboly, Gary
1977   "The Indian Field massacre." *The Bronx County Historical Society Journal* 14, no. 2: 63–68. [Ch. 2]

Zimmerman, Larry J., Karen D. Vitelli, and Julie Hollowell-Zimmer, eds.
2003   *Ethical Issues in Archaeology*. AltaMira Press, Walnut Creek, California. [Ch. 10]

Zwinge, Joseph, S.J.
1889   "Father Minister's diary, entry for September 19, 1889." Walsh Library Archives and Special Collections, Fordham University, Bronx, New York. [Ch. 3]
1891   "Father Minister's diary, entry for November 11, 1891." Walsh Library Archives and Special Collections, Fordham University, Bronx, New York. [Ch. 3]

1892   "Father Minister's diary, entry for August 24, 1892." Walsh Library Archives and Special Collections, Fordham University, Bronx, New York. [Ch. 3]

1893   "Father Minister's diary, entry for August 7, 1893." Walsh Library Archives and Special Collections, Fordham University, Bronx, New York. [Ch. 3]

1893–94 "Maps of Property of St. John's College since the beginning by Father Minister." Walsh Library Archives and Special Collections, Fordham University, Bronx, New York. [Chs. 3, 5]

Index

Index

THE BRONX COUNTY HISTORICAL SOCIETY
Chartered in 1955
Main Office: 3309 Bainbridge Avenue, The Bronx, NY 10467

The Bronx County Historical Society was founded for the purpose of promoting knowledge, interest and research in The Bronx and New York City. The Society administers The Museum of Bronx History, Edgar Allan Poe Cottage, a Research Library, and The Bronx County Archives; the founder of a new Bronx High School, The Bronx Latino History Project and The Bronx African-American History Project. The Society publishes books, journals, catalogues, bibliographies, and newsletters; conducts school programs, historical tours, lectures, courses, archaeological digs and commemorations; designs exhibitions, sponsors various expeditions, and produces the Bronx History Radio and cable television programs. The Society is active in furthering the arts, in preserving the natural resources of The Bronx, and in creating a sense of pride in the Bronx community.

MEMBERSHIP
Persons interested in historic studies, whether professionally or otherwise, are invited to membership.

Members of The Bronx County Historical Society receive:

Free admission to MUSEUM OF BRONX HISTORY
3266 Bainbridge Avenue at East 208th Street, The Bronx, New York

and

EDGAR ALLAN POE COTTAGE
East Kingsbridge Road and Grand Concourse, The Bronx, New York

Invitation to

The Society's Annual High School Valedictorians Awards Program, Bronx Authors' Night, Historical Tours, Lectures, Exhibitions, and other Educational Projects

PUBLICATIONS AND SERVICES
The Bronx *County Historical Society Journal* is published yearly and sent to all members. It is available by subscription to institutions.

The Society also publishes *The* Bronx *Historian* and *Library News*, mailed to all members.

The Society produces a wide variety of books, pamphlets, catalogues, bibliographies, illustrated lectures and documentaries on historical subjects. To promote history and assist historians, The Society offers many other educational services, including an Institutional Services Program.

VALENTINE-VARIAN HOUSE

c. 1758

MUSEUM OF BRONX HISTORY

*The Valentine-Varian House is owned and administered by
The Bronx County Historical Society and is a member of the
Historic House Trust of New York City.*

Open

Saturday 10:00 A.M.-4:00 P.M., Sunday 1:00 P.M.-5:00 P.M.

Monday to Friday 9:00 A.M.-5:00 P.M.
for Guided Tours by appointment

3266 Bainbridge Avenue at East 208th Street
The Bronx, New York 10467
Telephone: (718) 881-8900
www.bronxhistoricalsociety.org

Mr. William F. Beller purchased the Valentine-Varian House in 1905. His son, Mr. William C. Beller, donated the landmark structure to The Bronx County Historical Society in 1965. In recognition of this, the trustees in 1974 established The Society's most prestigious annual award, the William Beller Award of Excellence and Achievement.

EDGAR ALLAN POE COTTAGE

c. 1812

Edgar Allan Poe Cottage is owned by the City of New York Department of Parks and Recreation, operated by The Bronx County Historical Society, and is a member of the Historic House Trust.

The Poe Cottage is open for guided tours:

Thursday & Friday	10 A.M.-3 P.M.
Saturday	10 A.M.-4 P.M.
Sunday	1 P.M.-5 P.M.

Group tours during week by appointment.

POE PARK
Grand Concourse & East Kingsbridge Road
The Bronx, New York
Telephone: (718) 881-8900
www.bronxhistoricalsociety.org

PUBLICATIONS
OF
THE BRONX COUNTY HISTORICAL SOCIETY PRESS

Life in The Bronx Series

The Birth of The Bronx: 1609-1900 (Lloyd Ultan & Gary Hermalyn)
The Bronx in the Innocent Years: 1890-1925 (Lloyd Ultan & Gary Hermalyn)
The Beautiful Bronx: 1920-1950 (Lloyd Ultan)
The Bronx It Was Only Yesterday: 1935-1965 (Lloyd Ultan & Gary Hermalyn)

The History of The Bronx Project

The Bronx in the Frontier Era: From The Beginning to 1696 (Lloyd Ultan)
Legacy of the Revolution: The Valentine-Varian House (Lloyd Ultan)
The Northern Borough: A History of The Bronx (Lloyd Ultan)
The Bronx: Then and Now (Kathleen A. McAuley & Gary Hermalyn)
Theatres of The Bronx (Michael Miller)
Westchester Town: Bronx Beginnings (Kathleen A. McAuley)
Digging The Bronx: Recent Archaeology in the Borough (Allan S. Gilbert, editor)
A Historical Sketch of The Bronx (G. Hermalyn & L. Ultan)

New York City Series

**Morris High School and the Creation of the New York City Public High School
        System** (Gary Hermalyn)
The Greater New York Centennial (Elizabeth Beirne)
New York City at the Turn of the Century (Elizabeth Beirne)
Tunneling To The Future (Peter Derrick)
The Centennial of The Bronx; Commemorative Issue (Peter Derrick & Gary Hermalyn)
New York City: A Short History (George Lankevich)
A History of The Riverdale Yacht Club (Ruben P. Mendez)
By the El: Third Avenue and Its El at Mid-Century (Lawrence Stelter)
Yankee Stadium: 1923-2008 Images of Baseball (Gary Hermalyn & Anthony Greene)

New York State Series

The Hudson River (Elizabeth Beirne)
Re-inspired: The Erie Canal, America's First Great Work of Civil Engineering
        (Douglas Lazarus, Gary Hermalyn, & G. Koeppel)

Roots of the Republic Series

Presidents of the United States (Lloyd Ultan)
The First House of Representatives and The Bill of Rights (George Lankevich)
The First Senate of The Unite States (Richard Streb)
Chief Justices of The U.S. Supreme Court (George Lankevich)
The Signers of the Constitution of the United States (Bro. C. Edward Quinn)
The Signers of the Declaration of Independence (Bro. Edward Quinn)

Edgar Allan Poe Series

Poems and Tales of Edgar Allan Poe at Fordham (Elizabeth Beirne)
Edgar Allan Poe Workbook (Kathleen A. McAuley & Anthony C. Greene)

Streets of the City Series

History in Asphalt: The Origin of Bronx Street & Place Names Encyclopedia
(John McNamara)
McNamara's Old Bronx (John McNamara)
History of Morris Park Racecourse (Nicholas DiBrino)
Landmarks of The Bronx (Gary Hermalyn & Robert Kornfeld)
Bronx Views: Post Cards of The Bronx (Gary Hermalyn & Thomas X. Casey)
The New Parks Beyond The Harlem (John Mullaly)

Of Special Interest

The Bronx Cookbook (Peter Derrick & Gary Hermalyn, Editors)

Research Library & Archives

The Bronx in Print (Gary Hermalyn, Laura Tosi & Narciso Rodriguez)
Elected Public Officials of The Bronx Since 1898 (Laura Tosi & Gary Hermalyn)
Genealogy of The Bronx (Gary Hermalyn & Laura Tosi)
Publications of the Bronx County Historical Society Since 1955 (Gary Hermalyn)
Guide to The Bronx County Historical Society Media Collection
(Laura Tosi & Gary Hermalyn)
Guide to The Bronx County Historical Society Audio Collection
(Gary Hermalyn & Laura Tosi)
Index to the Atlas Collection of The Bronx County Historical Society 1868-1969
(Laura Tosi & Gary Hermalyn)
**Guide to Microfilm/Microfiche Collection of The Bronx County Historical
Society** (Laura Tosi & Gary Hermalyn)
A Guide to Collections of the Bronx County Archives (Dorthea Sartain & Peter
Derrick, First Edition; Kathleen A. McAuley & Elizabeth Nico, Second
Edition)
Newspaper Titles of The Bronx (Dominick Caldiero, Mark Sgambettera, Laura
Tosi, & Gary Hermalyn)
Index to the Sheet Map Collection of The Bronx County Historical Society
(Laura Tosi, Mark Sgambettera, & Gary Hermalyn)
Ethnic Groups in The Bronx: a Selected Bibliography (Elizabeth Nico, Laura Tosi
& Gary Hermalyn)
Education and Culture in The Bronx: A Research Guide (Elizabeth Nico,
Catherine Pellicano, Laura Tosi & Gary Hermalyn)

THE BRONX AFGHAN

Depicts attractive scenes of beloved Bronx institutions:
Valentine-Varian House/Museum of Bronx History,
Edgar Allan Poe Cottage, The Bronx Zoo, Van Cortlandt
House, Wave Hill, Lehman Center for the Performing Arts,
Bronx Museum of the Arts, Orchard Beach,
Hall of Fame for Great Americans, Bartow-Pell Mansion,
New York Botanical Garden and old Yankee Stadium.

50" x 65"   100% washable cotton

$50.00

Endowed Funds

THE BRONX COUNTY HISTORICAL SOCIETY encourages the establishment of named endowment funds.

Funds may be created to support many different programs of The Society or may be established for restricted use.

The funds appear permanently on the financial records of The Historical Society in recognition of their ongoing support of its work. Named endowment funds are established for a gift of $5,000 or more, and once begun additional contributions may be made at any time.

The following funds currently support The Society's work:

Astor Fund, Bingham Fund,
Fernandez Fund, General Board Fund,
Gordon Fund, Gouverneur Morris Fund,
Halpern Memorial Fund,
Hermalyn Institute, Isabelle Fund,
Khan Fund, Lampell Fund, Library Fund,
Parisse Fund, and Sander Fund.

For further details contact:

Mr. Joel Podgor, C.P.A.
Treasurer, Emeritus
718-881-8900

94145971R00173

Made in the USA
Lexington, KY
26 July 2018